To Jason & Kirsty

Best Wishes

Elgin

© 2024 Michael O'Rourke.

MO Publishing.

Working Class Millionaires

by Michael O'Rourke

All rights reserved. No part of this publication may be reproduced, distributed, or transmitted in any form or by any means, including photocopying, recording, or other electronic or mechanical methods, without the prior written permission of the publisher, except in the case of brief quotations embodied in critical reviews and certain other noncommercial uses permitted by copyright law.

Cover, graphics and layout by **2cheeseburgers**

©2cheeseburgers 2024

* * * *

About the author

Michael O'Rourke was born in Staffordshire. He has many eclectic hobbies and interests. His writing style is unusual as he takes serious subjects and gives them a lighter, more comedic touch without losing the underlying serious essence of the story.

His first book **BLACK EYES AND BLUE BLOOD** was a top seller in its genre (True Crime) and is now selling for more than its original published price over a decade ago. This true story of Norman Johnson is now regarded as a 'British gangster classic'. With no vainglorious violence, it was painstakingly put together with eyewitness accuracy, and depicts the halcyon days of the underworld in Britain and the United States when mobsters ruled the roost.

Next was **LIFE IN THE FAZ LANE;** the amazing, true life account of notorious, international con man and fraudster Faisal Madani, whose illegal activities prompted changes in the statute laws in Britain. He was an international smuggler, worked with the British secret service, had a stable of premier league footballers working for him and faced a daily battle fending off the 'Old Bill'. The book contains a healthy dose of serious anecdotes, but with laughs a-plenty and a plethora of tales of his many court appearances, the book is great entertainment.

In 2019, Michael collaborated with his friend and legendary bookie and gambler GARY WILTSHIRE for his third offering. A roller coaster ride from Britain's most famous TV bookmaker. Big Gary bares his soul in **ANGELS, TEARS AND SINNERS.** From the famous occasion he lost over a million pounds in a single day, right through to the present. Both hilarious and heart-rending, this is a fascinating insight into the mind of the peoples' favourite bookie. The captivating, bitter-sweet tale of a genial, but occasionally troubled man.

Book number four, **CHEF ON THE RUN,** concerned international celebrity chef, Sidney Sharratt. Whatever country he turned up in, mayhem broke out, culminating into all out war, a bloody coup or political and religious revolution. He was twice assigned to partake in covert missions for the American FBI as you do. Sid was shot two times, stabbed which resulted in losing a lung and poisoned at various times. He has seen more death and destruction than most serving soldiers, but this was regularly interwoven with hilarious fun and frolics in many escapades. Still today, only the second British guy with Salman Rushdie to have a Fatwa hanging over his head, Sid resolved to defend his honour worldwide - armed only with a cheese grater, wooden spoon and egg whisk!

* * * *

WORKING CLASS MILLIONAIRES

Contents

	Chapter	Page
	Introduction	9
1	Beginning of the end	29
2	Big house blues	38
3	Napoleon So Low	50
4	Dumped!	59
5	The Lost Years	74
6	Into The Damp Game	81
7	For Better, For Worse	92
8	Continental - We've All Gone Mental	106
9	Spaniard in the Works	118
10	Need for Wheels, Before Deals	127
11	Derby Delight... and Doldrums	143
12	Done Up Like a Kipper	157
13	Breaking Bad	167
14	Horses and Damp Courses	180
15	You Can Go Your Own Way	201
16	Bouncebackability	213

Bonus section:

Elgin and Micky's 10 Golden Rules of Selling — 226

* * * *

WORKING CLASS MILLIONAIRES
The Saga of The Staffordshire Two

by Michael O'Rourke

A gold mine is a hole in the ground with a liar at the top.

Mark Twain
(1835-1910)

WORKING CLASS MILLIONAIRES

Introduction

I first bumped into Mr Elgin Hounds at the teen disco in Stafford in the very early 1970s; a time of the Vietnam War, flower power, peace and love, *man*. It couldn't have reached the Midlands at that juncture, as I knew no hippies and even fewer Vietcong snipers. At that particular moment he was surrounded by three or four rather lovely young ladies, each seemingly holding on to his every last word. This was very impressive in my eyes as I would struggle to get a grunt or even a roll of the eyes from the opposite sex at that age. I made it my mission to get to know this debonair young man around town. Maybe I could even get an introduction to some of his cast-offs? *Nil desperandum*... These were tough growing up times. When you didn't know whether to stick or twist.

"Hiya mate, I'm Micky, how's it hanging?"

"Couldn't be better pal, I'm Elgin."

Smoke on the Water by Deep Purple was being played very loudly by the resident DJ at that precise moment. I thought he said 'Elgar'.

"What sort of a redneck name is that? Do you mean *Land of Hope and Glory*?"

He shook his head. "Not bloody Elgar! My dad christened me 'Elgin' because he was a champion marbles player at school."

I saw the light and quick as a flash I retorted, "Good job he wasn't a chess prodigy, you would have been called 'Checkmate'."

He burst out laughing and that has been the constant state of affairs ever since.

Our paths had never crossed previously; he had attended Corporation Street Church of England School and for me it was the Catholic School of Saint Patrick's. We were like ships in the night, but after that we stuck around together, I made him laugh and he was never short of female attention. As we were always together, girls used to approach me to get an introduction to Elgin. I never took umbrage, I was interacting with young ladies and my confidence grew daily and it did me a power of good.

Working Class Millionaires is about two young men from Stafford who came from nothing; no silver spoons or gentrification. We weren't exactly born on the wrong side of the tracks, but every penny we earned in our own unique way was first to keep the bailiffs from the door. Elgin is the main protagonist of this tale - I merely weave in and out of the escapades, spreading levity and sometimes becoming a bad influence. But when we were together, the magic happened. We were very similar in so many ways and lightyears apart in others and, really, that was the catalyst for numerous scrapes, dilemmas, comedic classics, triumphs, wealth and empire-building - plus the odd disaster and the strength to carry on when most would have 'cried uncle' and retreated back to normality. We were made from a different clay - tough, resolute and malleable, prepared to be shaped into the finest porcelain that money could buy. When the doubters, haters, naysayers and flat-earthers said, *it's impossible, it can't be achieved*, that was like an ordained ultimatum for us to go out and just make it happen.

The narrative chronicles Elgin's early life and his quest to leave behind a string of dead-end jobs, much like myself, so here's a quick account of *Michael o' Rourke* growing up. Born on the 21st of April 1955 - that was the Queens birthday as well - the first day of Taurus, on the cusp with Aries. The astrological characteristics are loyalty, stubborness and a great sense of humour. That was me to a 'T'. My beloved blue Chelsea were winning the football league for the first time that month. I was an eleven-pound baby elephant, a tiddler compared to my gran Lily who came out at a staggering thirteen pounds. She lived to be 94. I know nothing about gynaecology, but I would wager that birth made her mother's eyes water and send the midwife into palpitations.

My mother, Mavis, and father, Sidney met out in Egypt where they were both in the armed forces (No, I wasn't born in Cairo in sight of the pyramids - the slightly more mundane Burton House, Stafford was the location of my debut). The first coincidence in this book - and there are many - Sidney was in the Royal Engineers; the same as Elgin's father. Mavis retired after the birth. I was obviously going to be a handful and that became indisputable very quickly.

Over my first eleven years on the planet we seemed to be always on the move; different schools, different addresses, no time to settle down, no friends. The phenomenon in the United States that children born to the many military service men is called "Zipper Blues". I think the term in England is, "Cor, that's one sad baby."

Three years later my sister Pauline was born, and my memory banks began to kick in about two years later. I remember my mother taking me down to the doctor's on Browning Street. I had an aversion to men with a stethoscope even then. Dr McBain was the doctor's name and I recall he was talking to Mavis as we sat on the other side of his desk. I'd got the hump over something and took my shoes off and hurled them one after the other at his head. He deftly dodged them both. He then informed my mother, "He's a very naughty boy!"

I think she concurred.

Now that little incident predated two memorable events in film and political history; in *The Life of Brian*. Those words of McBain were verbatim. The good doctor should have got a wedge of commission for that and the shoe-throwing was identical to the moment in 2008 when an Iraqi journalist fired two shoes at George W Bush's bonce in Baghdad, both missing the target - as did mine. But my effort predated the Middle Eastern one - so one went round the world and one was kept under wraps.

Then, without a word of warning, we were off to Aldershot in Hampshire - the military garrison town. I made no friends there. We were on an army estate. I can only recall two days at the Catholic school the name of which cannot be recalled. One day, I crapped my pants in the classroom; I got away with it, but they had to open all the windows. I was the picture of innocence. Was I embarrassed? Nah! - because I did it again years later as an adult. We all rock to the rhythm of the human bowels.

The one lesson I recall there was from a female teacher trying to teach me macrame. What a total waste of time that was - about as useful as feng shui years later.

I wasn't a happy kiddy though, and a year later Sid got a posting to Kingston, so we moved into his parents home in Hounslow. He wasn't a football man but he lent towards Brentford F.C., as did his dad, so just to wind them up I pledged my allegiance to Chelsea. We weren't there long and it was up to Wembley in North London next. I was now coming out of my shell ever so slightly. I joined the cubs... but only a month later I resigned. Bugger off, Baden Powell! I went to Barham Junior School - it's still there.

The best thing was that our house was opposite the front gate. You walked ten paces and you were in. I made my first friend there, Jimmy, and he was as mad as I was.

I've always loved steam trains, so we would go onto the railway lines high up which would criss cross all the main lines in and out of Wembley Station. For no other reason than we were simple, we'd throw stones and pebbles down from the top of the railway bridge onto all the trains passing underneath. We never saw any other people about because we were trespassing. It's only much later when your brain develops that you realise how bloody dangerous it was. We were the kings of the upper line and woe betide the trains on the lower main line.

We were rubbing British Rail up the wrong way. One day a steam loco came out of the station on it's lonesome - no freight, no carriages. We had never seen that before. It stopped at the bridge. There were three blokes on the footplate, shouting up all manner of abuse at us, so it was time for a tactical retreat. We stayed on the high line after that, but we still had time for some more derring-do. We found an anvil behind a workman's concrete shed, not full size as we wouldn't have been able to lift it. I guess it would have been about a third the size of a blacksmith's. I had the insane idea of putting it on one of the rails. Diesel trains used to thunder past about every half hour. We lifted it onto the rail, waited for the train and hid behind the shed. They take your breath when you are that close and we didn't know what would happen - eight year olds aren't logical or sensible in those situations. Looking back, it could have been derailed, careered down the hill and destroyed a dozen terraced houses that were 40 yards away with all the people in them. Thankfully it was like a mouse getting under the feet of an elephant. The diesel's wheel twatted it so hard, it flew 10 yards into a banked piece of land and such was the force of the impact, most of the anvil went subterranean: and that's where we left it for the workmen to retrieve.

No lessons learnt! I got in with a manky council house family down the road and we climbed onto the hospital roof one evening - me and three brothers - *why?* Don't ask! These were rough and tumble hard nuts, but the police were called. And guess who couldn't get down? It was the first time the old bill brought me back home... and it wouldn't be the last. It was a stern warning from them for the time being.

Wembley was alright when I was behaving. I can remember being on Wembley High Road when the cup final was on. Hundreds of supporters coming up from the underground when West Ham played Preston. A short while after that, Henry Cooper, the great British Heavyweight boxing champ, opened up a greengrocer's at the far end of the High Road from the stadium. No-one was nicking fruit from his shop let me tell you! My dad, who I was never that close to - we never really bonded - took me to the Wembley Indoor Arena to watch *The Harlem Globe Trotters* with the fab Meadowlark Lemon and also out on a mega day to Battersea Funfair in the morning. What a magical place that was! And then to Stamford Bridge in the afternoon to see Chelsea beat West Ham 6-2 - my very first match. I'll always be eternally grateful for that day, especially as they were few and far between back then.

So, happier times.

I remember going to see three films at the cinemas there. Mavis took me to see *Summer Holiday* with Cliff Richard (light and frothy, a 5/10). Sid took me to see *The Bridge On The River Kwai*, with Jack Hawkins and Alec Guinness. Even though this film was made in 1957, it was still doing the rounds. It went on forever - a long film for a kid. I think Sid took me as an excuse for him wanting to see it, but still a 7/10. And finally, a sneak in the side door with the manky family for an over-18 horror film with Boris Karloff and the ace, Vincent Price - *The Raven*. It scared me shitless! I couldn't sleep for weeks in the dark. A 10/10, but it put me off horror films for life.
I became a movie buff over time. I still love the work of the Coen Brothers, Scorsese and of course the great British 1950/60s monochrome films. There's nothing better than a cine masterpiece. So, on that happy footnote and in prime position to lay down some roots in sunny Wembley, it was suddenly all over. We were heading to Germany next. The zipper blues were kicking in yet again.

Auf wiedersehen, Blighty.

The historic city of Munster in Westphalia was where we were heading - North-west Germany, quite close to the Dutch border. Wembley was now a forlorn memory. I never made any friends here either, German *or* English. The devil still makes work for idle hands. The Royal Engineers barracks parade ground was the biggest in the British Army and I must have walked every last yard of it. A troubled lost soul with only my vivid imagination for company, drifting aimlessly around the hinterland on the army estate. There was a big lake by the woods that froze solid in the Winter, the ice must have been a foot thick. That's where my sister and I went. You could slide 20 yards with a good run at it. A big guy approached us one day. He loomed over us - he could have kidnapped us... or worse. God only knows where our mother was. You can't bring up kids like that these days. Yet, he only wanted to be friendly and shake hands. He had a woollen hat on and a big bushy moustache. Later on I realised he looked like Seth Armstrong from *Emmerdale Farm*. But apart from him being terribly cross-eyed like Ben Turpin, thank God, he was a kindly soul and had no evil intentions.

I wasn't so lucky another time in the woods on my own. Four German youths about twelve or thirteen years old grabbed me and were going to throw me in the Ems Canal. I turned on the waterworks and implored them, "Nein schwimmen, nein schwimmen!" They bought it hook line and sinker. I could swim like a fish, but that canal was filthy. "Danke, danke!" (I had a smattering of basic German language) Running home laughing my socks off, it was the first time I'd tried subterfuge and I was quite proud I'd pulled it off. Years later, I was the grand master at it.

The school was in the army barracks complex. I had a real shock when the lessons started, out of a class of 30, I was the thickest. Plumb last by some distance! These were children of officers and administrative staff as well as lowly rankers - kids like me. The previous schools I'd been to were pretty crummy, but I blamed myself, no application, no interest and no reason to learn. I would have got a B+ for apathy. To be fair I'd had no direction in my life. Neither of my parents had given me any advice on anything and I had roamed where I wanted, went missing for hours on end and was sulky and reserved at home. A young loner, looking for affection and love.

Yet the light bulb still went on upstairs in my napper; these other kids in class weren't brighter than me, they'd just had a head start. I started reading books and absorbing information like a sponge. I discovered that I had a fantastic ability to retain facts and information on those topics which interested me. I'd been a slow starter, but the tortoise can beat the hare.

Just before we were about to return to England after about a year on the continent, I disgraced myself again. I and another two lads off the army estate went onto a new building site at the back of the army buildings after all the workers had gone home. We caused thousands of deutschmarks' worth of damage, smashing ground pipes, windows, doors, plaster boards, in fact anything we could break - we did! It became a competition to see who was king of the vandals. We now had the German police coming round to our house - and pleased, they were not. From what I gathered it was only our young ages that prevented a trip to the cells. No one had to pay for damages and the building site swallowed the loss. My dad asked what was wrong with me and I seriously did not know the answer. We drifted a little further apart that day and this was something that couldn't just be put down to *boys will be boys*.

It was now post-West Germany. I was probably too young to appreciate how great Munster was. I learned later that the synthesiser pop group, *Alphaville* was from there, one of their singles, the all-time great 'Big In Japan' was a favourite of mine. We travelled the 60 miles down to Dusseldorf Airport by train. It was uneventful until we passed through the nearby industrial area of Wuppertal, which had an overhead suspension monorail (opened in 1901) which followed the route of the river. It knocked my socks off. Britain had nothing like it and I realised then that the Teutonic race were a class act. I was becoming a culture vulture with a later lifelong appreciation for great engineering, architecture and works of art.

Slowly the barbarian in me was being offset by a renaissance of enlightenment, which I kept to myself, as other kids might not be enamoured with this, but now I had the moral high ground and was improving and hungry for more. The pen is mightier than the sword and it was all coming together. Each day I became a better and more rational young man.

We returned to Stafford. I had been away half my fledgling life but I returned a good deal wiser at ten years of age. My dad left the army and became a fireman, but my mother was on the verge of a nervous breakdown. What had caused it, I never found out, but it couldn't have helped having an idiot like me for a son. St Patrick's Catholic School was my new seat of learning. I'd caught right up on education, especially at English and History, but still couldn't avoid upsetting the wrong people. Father Kelly, the parish priest, used to come in and give a religious lesson once a week - the man could bore for Britain! He used to throw his weight around and all the teachers including the headmaster were scared of him. One person who wasn't was my good self. I had his card marked. He was a vile, bullying, blustering Irish bigot who had no people skills. He would never be one of Kelly's Heroes in my young eyes.

One afternoon he was yammering on incessantly about something meaningless in the Old Testament, and me and another lad were playing the fool at the back of the classroom. He slammed his bible down on the desk, waking up half a dozen other dozing pupils and strode towards us with a grim purpose - he could be more than a tad testy when aggravated. He thrust his ugly boat race right up against mine; I could see the utter blind hatred in his eyes, his teeth were gritted and I could make out all the burst red capillaries on his nose that resembled all the minor tributaries of the Thames. He'd obviously been swigging more communion wine than what was advisable, bloody old sot.

"Go down to the headmaster's office and be thrashed." What could you say in mitigation? Not a lot. The headmaster, Mr Cooke was a decent old cove, "If it was down to me, boys, I'd let it pass, but you do realise I must follow through with what Father Kelly has decreed."

I thought he was wavering and suggested, "Listen, Mr Cooke, we won't say anything if you don't!" That fell on stony ground, but it did make him chuckle. We both got caned on the hand and *derriere* (he was a talented all rounder in the art of discipline). But from that day on, I hated Kelly with a passion - and his Catholic Church wasn't far behind. I've remained agnostic to the present day and the sex scandals of Catholic priests against minors and the cover-ups by the upper echelons of the Vatican hasn't strengthened their hand any. Thousands of priests were arrested and sent down - they can rot there for all eternity for me. I didn't have much longer to be around Kelly, the Eleven-plus exams were due but I knew in my heart of hearts, that they were coming too soon for me. I was a late developer. No grammar school, but Blessed William Howard Catholic Secondary School for me. *Oh goody gumdrops!* More masochistic religious zealot teachers!

It was time for ten Hail Marys.

Every teacher carried the cane. Some unorthodox masters would sling blackboard erasers across the classroom at your head - solid hardwood projectiles that could bring tears to your eyes. Mr Dobson, the technical drawing master, wasn't adverse to bringing a T-square crashing down on your head either. We used to go to the swimming baths once a week. We crossed the railway bridge on the Newport road on one outing - my mate, Noel, was misbehaving and a teacher called Mr Yarwood, a small Yorkshire guy who also taught metalwork and was universally known as 'Little Ray', smashed him straight in the face with the flat of his palm. His nose burst open and there was blood everywhere. Noel was a tough nut but I told him to 'go down'. Yarwood was panicking. "Get up lad, please get up." Cars were stopping and pedestrians milling around. Yarwood would have gone to prison these days, but of course nothing happened. Back then we were much more durable than the kids of today. We were used to the hard knocks. If you complained, you were a wimp and a snitch, and rightly so.

I had come right out of my shell, mainly through sport and ustilising the camaraderie of being a team player. I played for the school cricket and football teams, although I blanked rugby and hockey. And my 80 metres hurdles record stood for 22 years, so I was no slouch. I was also pretty speedy up to 400 metres, but struggled at longer distances. I played a flanker at the school cross country trials. After about a mile I was second last - the only guy behind me was a dweeb called Tony Hillman and he had made three attempts to get by me, but I punched him in the arm each time. It would only be a matter of time before he swerved past and gave me the ignominy of being last man home. I managed to come up with a plan. The course went by Stafford golf course and round the castle; it was four and a half miles long. I thought, "Sod this, I'll take a short cut", and I went through the back garden of one of the houses on Newport Road taking a mile off the course. I came in 7th. Mr Solly, the gym master, said, "Well run, Michael." As I finished, I nodded back nonchalantly like Steve Ovett winning at Crystal Palace. Had I come up in clover? Well, not really... worse was to follow.

The first ten home would be representing the school against Gnosall School on the following Saturday morning. Out of the twenty runners, guess who came last by about half an hour? Solly looked at me suspiciously with a furrowed brow, "Got a terrible stitch sir!"

They never asked me to run that far ever again. I'd even made the coach late for the return to Stafford. Hero to zero in a few days, but as the soap adverts used to declare, *well that's Lifebuoy.*

There was terrible bullying going on but I didn't experience that much because I found I could make a lot of people laugh. It was a moment of revelation. (Added to the fact I had sprouted up to six feet three at the age of 14). I was ahead of the game for the first time in my life, although there were precious few weeks when I didn't feel the sharp caress of the old bamboo. Academically, I was charging. Throughout the terms I was always in the first three in class in both English Literature and English Language and was an eternal number one at History. (When you know, you just know! Simples). I left Blessed William Howard School with 5 O-levels. Not bad - not Einstein, but a long way from the simple, ignorant kid I had once been. A lot had been achieved by sheer resolve and a willingness to learn. In my own mind, I was a success story.

That all goes out the window the day your school time ends. I had no desire to go to university as, at that time, there were many jobs you could simply just fall into but, like Elgin, I found dead-end work time and time again. I wanted money. And it was never enough. You only get your crap together when you become self-employed; you succeed or you starve. I'll go through a quick resume of the disasters that befell me which could retard any teenager working for a pittance and having people saying, "Have you got no respect for your work?" Not really, when you only got £5 for 40 hours graft back in 1971.

My dad got me my first job after leaving school. I was the worst person in the world with machinery and so anything electrical and mechanical was anathema to me. I struggled to change a plug without instructions. The old fire brigade station in Mill Bank in Stafford town was an eye opener. They took me on as a trainee mechanic (as if!). The foreman, Arthur Passe from Stoke, never trusted me one iota to do anything more complicated than sweep up or clean the vehicles. He was a good judge. He gave a speech one day after a spate of burglaries, "If anyone ever tried to break in ma house and endanger ma lady, he'd never walk properly again." I could see most of the mechanics biting their lips, dying to laugh - Arthur was the wrong side of 60, and five feet nothing tall.

He eventually gave up on me and sent me out with Cliff, another rotund old boy, in the breakdown repair truck which was assigned to all the other Staffordshire fire stations. I enjoyed this a lot more because most of the time Cliff was driving and I was reading the paper. We went as far as Mow Cop in the north and Kinver in the south. My first day out with him was nearly our last though. I hadn't passed my driving test yet and wasn't *au fait* auto-wise. He called everyone 'Shag', which apparently is a term of endearment in Cornwall. Why he did, I never asked. We came up to a really busy T-junction just outside Stafford, "Ok, Shag?" I thought he was enquiring about my disposition. "Yeah, fine." He pulls straight out and, God's honest truth, we missed a juggernaut going 60 mph by no more than six inches. To be fair I'd have definitely been a goner. Cliff probably, "FUCKING HELL, YOU SAID IT WAS OK!" I explained that I thought he was asking if I was OK. We both burst out laughing. More from blessed relief than comedic wit. He always looked both ways after that! I got more than a bit miffed he did that though. "You have serious trust issues, Clifford." We'd both agree to agree, "You're bloody right there, Shag."

Cliff was a good old stick and so were all the other mechanics, but it was time to move on. I was like a fish out of water. A mate, Nigel Shaw, said they had a vacancy in the stores at his dad's Mazda Car Showrooms, which was adjacent to Stafford Railway Station. I liked Nigel. I must have; I lent him my Status Quo album *Piledriver*. I loved that LP and I still have it today. I wasn't so keen on his dad, Fred, though. Another squat, porky guy who seemed like a bully and, whats more, I didn't like how he talked to Nigel.

I reluctantly went there and within a month I knew it was another blunder. They were selling new Mazda motors with the new revolutionary Wankel rotary engines. These cars never went wrong and instead of doing stores work which I would have been good at, all I ended up doing was degreasing all the new cars and sweeping up the workshops and showrooms. I was not a happy chappy. At home I was arguing every day with my dad.

My parents had bought their first house in Parkside - 14 Beton Way - and they begrudgingly let me stay under their roof. My granny had begged them to stay renting, "These houses are not for us, we are Labour voters, we don't belong in them." I'm sure you can you see now why I was a bit deranged having the same loopy blood as my relatives. I had great pleasure when I turned 18 of telling her I was voting Tory. I could be cruel sometimes, ha ha!

A fall out with Fred Shaw was an odds-on certainty. And it came swiftly out of the blue. I used to sweep the floors one-handed with the other one in my pocket. It doesn't look as good, but does exactly what it says on the tin. Shawry sneaks up behind me one day like a nimble fat mugger, "Use two hands on the brush,"

"I'm a frigging storeman, this isn't in my remit." I replied.

"I'm the boss, I pay your wages, you'll do as I bloody say!"

As the worst bloke in the world for taking orders and showing discipline, I begrudgingly went two-handed. Fred won the battle, but he lost the war when he retreated back to his glory hole. He returned from his office about 10 minutes later. I was on the other side of the workshops, non-ambidextrous again. "I TOLD YOU - FUCKING USE TWO HANDS!"

He screamed across the floor. All the mechanics stopped and turned around and I thought, *I'm not having that* and, with all my might, launched the broom like a crazy howitzer across no man's land. It missed Fred's head by about a foot, rattling against the wall behind him. I thanked God it was slightly astray. I was sacked of course, but he actually paid me off until the end of the month and wrote me out a blinding endorsement for my next unlucky employer. That was very, very good of him. I think he wanted a clean break. Nigel said it was never boring while I was around. He wished me well too.

Within a week I had another stores job in another garage. Jobs in the early 70s were like buses - you'd miss one, then three more would come along.

My next 'victims' were *Jones and Alcock*, situated on the Wolverhampton Road railway bridge. The big boss man, Aubrey Tipper Alcock, referred to me as 'Malcolm' throughout the six months I was there. I couldn't be arsed to tell him, *THAT'S NOT MY NAME!* (There's a hit record in that title... maybe). At least I got to do some stores work; it was a British Leyland franchise, but the other storeman, John, was a bit strange. He was 45, an only child and lived with his mother up at Rising Brook. I was bit wary of him as he didn't tick all the boxes. He was a massive fan of big bike motor racing, but came to work on a little moped and a 1950s crash hat. I started calling him 'Agostini', which he liked a lot. A bit of flannel never hurt.

The guy in the paint shop was another nutter from Blessed William Howard called Bruce Mayer. He was a year older than me. He would sing *Lady Eleanor* by Lindisfarne at the top of his voice while he was spraying cars in the paint bay. He rarely wore a mask - he must have had multi-coloured lungs. I can't hear that song these days without thinking of him. Alcock's second in command was a guy in his late 50s from upstairs called Edwin. He used to talk down to me. If that was how he wanted to play he wouldn't win. He had massive ears so I started calling him 'Chimpy'. It caught on and everybody started alluding to him as such. We had a showdown - he wanted to know why I called him 'Chimpy'. I said it was because he liked bananas. He said he wasn't that keen on them. It was getting surreal. If he walked into the room he looked like the FA Cup. There was nothing racial in this of course as he was as white as an albino in a snowstorm. He was still being referred to as Chimpy after I left. *15-love* there, I believe.

Bob Malin, the works manager and I, got on like a house on fire after I started. He used to laugh at all my jokes in the fine Telegraph pub next door during our dinner breaks, but our relationship soured over something trivial, culminating in him coming over to the stores hatch one day and slapping me round the lughole. I retaliated by punching him on the chin, but he was moving away and I only winged him. Aubrey came down and to my surprise said we were both as bad as each other and to get back to work. I did get the sack after that incident but over something totally unrelated. I won't spoil the surprise now - it's well chronicled later on.

RAF Stafford gave me a chance next. Someone with a warped sense of humour reckoned I could become a casemaker. I was fairly good at carpentry at school and this job entailed constructing the wooden cases that held ammunition, weapons and instruments: it all came with instructions and so within a few weeks, I was quite competent.

I actually now loved going to work, there was something really cathartic in hammering nails into wood. It never ever got less painful when I hit my thumb with the hammer though, but I was learning new things each day and for the first time since leaving school I felt bliss and satisfaction. Three months later a dozy foreman called Des rained on my parade, "I've recommended you for promotion."

"I've not put in for any," I replied.

"I've done it for you!"

"I like it here though..."

"You're too good for here. You're going to the clothing stores - it's another pound an hour."

"I hate stores work!"

"You'll love it there."

So that was that. I knew in my heart it wouldn't work. Des was trying to help and, in a way, he was instrumental in my quest for eventual success, but not in the way he thought.

The clothing stores were three nondescript wooden sheds tacked together. I was the newbie, the other guy was a weaselly little fella named Seymour. He reminded me of Uriah Heep. During the time I was there he was just about tolerable, but the 'erks' air recruits hated him with a passion. He played everything by the book; if they needed socks, trousers, tunics or caps and they were a day early in their request, he'd knock them back. There were terrible rows. He was called every name under the sun... and then some. He wouldn't budge though. Everything was black and white to him. He was a real Billy No Mates. I said to myself, *never behave like that*. The RAF wasn't going to fold any time soon, so if a bloke needed an item when Seymour wasn't there, he would get it, whatever the date. Being pedantic wasn't in my playbook and it never will be.

One day a dozen jungle warfare jackets arrived in stock. They were bound for Belize in Central America after some incursions by Guatemala looked to turn into a full scale invasion. The British Forces were backing Belize and reinforced the country with more men, weaponry and supplies. I tried a jacket on. The ample sleeve cuffs came over my fingertips. I was now 6 feet 5 inches tall and I said to the Group Captain, "What sort of military are you sending out there? I don't know about the poor old Guatemalans, but if they need jackets this large, they'd bloody scare me!" He laughed and said they intended to make the skirmish short and sweet. That, my friends, is back when we were respected all around the world.

I had now had enough of Seymour and the clothing stores. My one little perk before I left was to half-inch an Arctic Warfare Duffle Coat not used since the 1950s. It was sitting in the back store on it's lonesome, heavy, discoloured and soiled, but with half an inch insulated material making it the greatest defender against cold weather in the world. The hood of the coat was so voluminous that your head disappeared into a black void, making one resemble a mad friar on the way to the cemetery. It came home with me on my last day in a large dustbin bag. Winter's icy hand was approaching, and in conditions of minus ten degrees you were as warm as toast. That coat was better than any Armani jacket and I loved it like no other. I was gutted when it went missing; it was like losing a relative. You've never lived until you have battled Arctic conditions! Next up was my work at the builders merchants, Magnet & Southerns with my good pal, Andy Potts. (This is well-documented later)

And so, finally, to my very last salaried job - a year at GEC Measurements, aka MRI. Great people, but a mind-numbingly crap job. Yet with a lot of funny interludes, self employment was calling my name to 'do one'.

When I say they would take anyone on, I meant it. They employed me remember? In the 401 section (aka *Stalag 33*) it was like a prison to me, but a lot of great guys made a living there, some all their working lives. We had many laughs; Hughie, Baggy, Stan, Sully and of course Black Bart on the rumbling machines, a real dirty and dusty job, he wasn't Jamaican or African, but it seemed him and *Palmolive* were never fated to be together. He was a happy old soul though

There was a section of lady workers and one was absolutely gorgeous. She stuck out like a sore thumb; Jean - a strawberry blonde with a huge shock of hair. She would be be a pensioner now, but I like to remember her as she was, instead of a wizened granny knitting a pullover. It's cruel growing old, but your last breath is worse. If you are young, treasure every day. Thank you, stunning Jean, for raising my latent awareness of the fairer sex at that time. I'm only human you know.

Don Gruer, the charge hand, was another diddy man from Stoke. How did all these little guys get the head honcho gig? I had a nightmare one night; Don Gruer was wrestling a crocodile and had the reptile in a half-nelson. It was too painful to see the animal taking a pasting! Now, others of my age would be dreaming of copping off with semi-naked women but I was just wired up differently. I didn't let my vision go to waste though - Gruer became the crocodile wrestler in the 401 section and in honour of the great man, I started writing poems about it on the inside doors of the crappers in the mens as well. A week passed and I had graffitied every last one of the traps. It was some of my finest work! A saga *par excellence*. It went down in the annals of GEC as a fitting tribute to one of their finest sons.

People would go for a *number two* without taking a newspaper as they just wanted to read the legend of Don Gruer. Those who sneakily smuggled a *Sun* page three in for a crafty *J Arthur Rank* were disarmed with laughter. But people having a piddle outside were missing out on all the frivolity. Jack, the 401 union rep, who resembled Corporal Jones of Dads Army collared me one afternoon, "Hey, you've been here a month, why haven't you joined our union?"

I never did sit on the fence, "Because I don't believe in left wing Marxist crap!" And, by the look on his face, we wouldn't be bonding at his gaff, listening to Sergei Rachmaninoff's greatest hits at the Kremlin. He riposted with a cruel broadside, "It's cold on the outside."

He had walked straight into my bear trap. "Not if you own a 1950s Arctic Warfare duffle coat." And, like Halley's Comet, that one went straight over his head.

It was only afterwards that I realised Jack was a liberty-taker. I decided that he would have to go on the inside of the toilet doors with Donald. I had the two of them indulging in manly pensioner love *in flagrante delicto*. This was at a time when policemen were not averse to caving your head in with a *lignum vitae* truncheon if you were playing silly buggers in public toilets. Who says romance was dead? Jack got fed up with people laughing every time they passed him and he deftly reported it upstairs to Big Cheese, Alan Lees. He came down with a hand-picked posse of toady underlings. After reading one door, he came out to the mass ranks of 401 to give his decision. I'm sure he was trying very hard to suppress a grin. The doors would be repainted and anyone caught getting literate again would receive their marching orders. Now this was why Lees was paid the big bucks. The shocked look on Gruer's face suggested to me that he loved the current fame and attention that had arrived with it. He was retiring that year, but his alter ego, the crocodile wrestler, had gone first. That was only fair. Don was very adept with a vernier and slide rule, mind.

When I said GEC would take anyone on, I wasn't kidding. I looked up one day and spotted a guy who looked just like Irwin Whitlock. It couldn't be him though, he was as mad as a March Hare. But, oh it was! Irwin was not the full ticket. He came to school one day dressed in a Victorian frilly blue sailor suit. I told him he had some balls wearing that. One evening he climbed onto his house roof with a brush and tin of white paint and fashioned a big skull and crossbones. The council were thrilled. You must remember this was all before Banksy. Irwin was a trendsetter, someone broke the mould when he was born... *thank God.*

He was like a Midland Jim Morrison; he was obsessed with death. He had acquired his dream job that last year working for a funeral parlour, but they drew the line when Irwin who was running late, drove the hearse up the M6 at 90mph with the coffin holding the deceased rattling around like a pin ball machine. So here he was and I was close at hand when he greeted Don Gruer for the first time with an all time classic, "You'd look lovely in mahogany." That cracked me up. Forget Lincoln's Gettysburg Address, Whitlock's GEC regress was different class.

I now had itchy feet. I had those ten little tapping toes. It was a Summer's day like every Summer's day since Stonehenge became that season's next big thing. One day I drove down to GEC just like all the other days. There was a big roundabout outside the gates - and I went round it a dozen times. Onlookers thought *Hednesford's Demolition Derby* had come to Stafford. I went round once more for a bakers dozen. I couldn't go through the entrance - it was like an invisible force field stopping me. I said, *fuck it,* and drove up to the County Showground on the Weston Road. Mavis had made me some doorstop Cheese and Branston sandwiches. I had a big bottle of ginger beer and a Daily Mail. What else did I need? I parked on some grass, opened the windows for the currant bun to bathe me in golden rays and sat there contented like a blind squirrel finding his first nut of the day.

I had broken the curse of working for others. It was now time to be a winner.

That was my last salaried job. I'd burnt my bridges, so now I was going to have to stand on my own two feet. Mavis and Sid weren't very impressed. I wasn't looking for charity, and shortly after I moved out and never looked back. I started buying and selling antiques, furniture and vehicles; in fact anything I could turn a shilling with. You make many mistakes - you learn, you move on and you prosper. Within a year I had purchased a three-year-old Ford Capri mark 1 for cash. There was bubbles of rust coming through on the wings, but the garage were going to fix that and respray the silver grey livery. I gave them an extra 200 sobs and said paint it all *Le Mans Green.* A real poser colour, which of all things, I wasn't. It was just to wind people up and say, *Up yours, I'm climbing the ladder!* It looked the absolute dog's bollox though. Of course, the haters came out, "He's nicked that!" and

"I heard he's dealing drugs." It was a beautiful, beautiful motor. Most of the rabble only had push bikes, rusty old Escorts and knackered Hillman Hunters. The police also put their twopenn'orth in as the car was like green kryptonite to them. Most weekends I was stopped at night for something frivolous. It was nice to be wanted, but their concern was absolutely ludicrous. It's always the case though, that when you actually need a copper, they're never there for you.

Don't ever tell people you are struggling; 80% don't care and 15% are glad. People living a mundane life don't like success stories. I was the opposite; I would talk to winners, glean loads of useful information and generally wish them well. I would aspire to be like them and I learnt a long time ago, never do anyone a bad turn - karma will always come back to bite you where it hurts most. Common sense really.

Within seven years I had five houses. I don't say that to brag, just to let you know there is no glass ceiling you can't break through. Of course, not everyone can do it. You could fall short and have to go back and work for someone else, but at least you tried. You went for your dream. Nobody can knock you for that and if one person reads this and succeeds later on then I have played my part with optimism and panache.

I did most of my drinking in *The Sheridan* opposite the Borough Hall. Many years later when the brewery shut it down, the headline in The Newsletter was, ROUGH CUSTOMER PUB CLOSED. In all the years I drank there I was never asked once by the barman if I was a rough customer, although there was a rumour he'd implied it to a couple of tattooed lady drinkers. I'd only ever seen two people thrown head first through the front window. Most patrons were angels with dirty faces, but there was the odd devil who had showered and smelled of Kouros aftershave as well. Those were the blighters to keep your eye on.

Decades later I'm still in touch with regulars who drank there (mainly on Facebook); lovely Lorna Morrison, Fabulous Fred Randle, Andrew Wadham (*The Wad* - he turns up later on) and delectable Louise Gwyther - now Mrs Whitney, she moved to America donkey's years ago. She went for her dream. Her husband Jon won the lottery when he put the ring on her finger - although she votes Democrat and doesn't like the Orange Man much. She knows that I love her dearly and admire anyone that goes for a game-changer in life. She lives in Los Angeles and is now a vice president in a big company. Bloody fantastic and a credit to lil ol' Stafford here back in the sticks. I'm stopping now because her success is making myself and Elgin look like a couple of wallys... but we do love America!

Finally the late great Gina Till. RIP sweetheart. We lost her in the Summer of 2023. (I have tears in my eyes writing this). A special lady who loved *The Sheridan*. She also worked in the Coral Bookmakers on Salter Street. So I used to see a lot of her. She could smile for England and make you laugh without trying. God always takes the special ones first. He really gets on your nerves sometimes. But she is not forgotten and never will be. All of my memories of her are golden and nobody with all the money in the bank could be remembered for a better reason than that.

Lastly, I stopped drinking around the age of 30. One of the best decisions I ever made, but that decade in and around *The Sheridan* are indelibly etched in my mind, fondly and happily.

We are now nearly ready to rock and roll!

When myself and Elgin were in cahoots we were unbeatable. I really wouldn't recommend taking on a partner, as most times it ends in rancour and abuse. One partner seems to do most of the work and it all blows up into feral animosity, but if you get two guys on the same page with a vision, there is nothing better. Elgin was a far better salesman I could ever be, but we both brought something different to the table. A problem halved is a problem solved. So now, I'm going to fade into the ether and introduce you to the main man - without him there is no story, without doubt the best sales man I ever met in my life the incomparable *ELGIN HOUNDS*.

That was my early life. Elgin's follows later on in the book, but we start chapter one with Elgin as a middle-aged man facing the biggest dilemma of his life; the international law authorities homing in on him and his young wife in a foreign country. He had overstepped the so-called accepted boundaries - a rare misjudgement by a very shrewd, canny operator, but his back was against the wall and a very dark hurricane was approaching.

Ladies and gentlemen, we give you:

Working Class Millionaires!

The saga of The Staffordshire Two...

WORKING CLASS MILLIONAIRES

CHAPTER ONE

Beginning of the end

It was the moment Elgin Hounds and his new young wife's world fell apart. Four large FBI Agents smashed through the sapele hotel door with the destructive force of a quartet of hungry sumo wrestlers searching for a bowl of rice. They burst into the room, guns drawn and cocked, screaming, "Let's see your fucking hands!" They were dressed in casual plain clothes, so Elgin's first thought was, *It's a heist, we're about to be robbed, oh lucky me!* His open sweating palms were immediately pointing heavenward, each and every weekend there were local TV news bulletins of people being robbed and then mercilessly shot in their hotel rooms.

One of the intruders had a gun pressed hard against Elgin's throbbing temple, simultaneously another wrenched his arms back behind him and threw on a pair of chafing handcuffs, Out the corner of his eye he could see Bella going through the same ordeal, if this was all meant to intimidate, it was bloody well working, these couldn't be criminals, it was too well organised. The alpha male announced very loudly "I'm Federal Marshal William (something, some Hispanic surname, unsurprisingly forgotten in that moment of trauma.) Elgin Hounds, Bella Smyth, we have warrants for your arrests." He looked really pleased with himself.

At that precise second, Elgin was nonplussed why they had been detained, what did they know and why had they come for him, he'd done no mischief in the USA, not even a faulty tail light, but his answer came loud and lucid as the Marshal's next utterings cleared up any relevant misunderstanding.

"We are escorting you to jail, where you will await an extradition order to take you back to Lancashire, England." *BANG!* That hit Elgin as hard as if the dude had pulled the trigger. Bella had broken down and was crying hysterically. It was safe to say he'd had better days. All of his chickens had seemingly come home to roost. Elgin was in a daze, before he knew it, he'd been put into an orange jump suit, re-handcuffed and, just for good measure, shackled in leg irons. He was in a real shitty predicament.

Events had taken a turn for the worst.

It had been a mere six weeks prior, when he finally got his way and persuaded Bella, the new love of his life and wife of only eight months, to move back to Florida. It was a decision they both now bitterly regretted as they were incarcerated in the notorious John E Polk Correctional Facility in Sanford, Seminole County just North of Orlando.

He'd been trying to get Bella to move to Florida for the past eighteen months. Elgin had hated the previous three years living in Portugal. He'd had numerous business disagreements with Portuguese associates and he hadn't trusted them an inch and wanted away (It was ironic really, because years later his beloved football club, the mighty Wolverhampton Wanderers, had a plethora of them on the payroll. Of course, he subsequently mellowed and today is really fond of Portuguese folk... well, most of them anyway, but we are digressing - back to the story).

Bella loved Portugal with a passion. Her family were not too far away in England, although her mother Daphne was terrified of flying. It always took a great effort to get her airborne for the short hop over to Iberia, although they never had to go as far as drugging her like *Mr T* in the *A Team*. It's one of those phobias many people suffer from. Bella was pure 24-carat gold about moving to America, but her mother would never undertake a long haul flight like that, so she was basically putting Elgin ahead of her family. Of course the couple could always visit England whenever they wanted. That was the state of play running up to the arrests. Their recent lifestyle up to that moment had been God-given glorious.

The Hounds' lived a semi-hedonistic lifestyle. Bella had never experienced anything like it before marrying Elgin. Her life was on the up and she enjoyed every indulgent minute of it. They had a large luxury four-bedroom villa just outside Vilamoura on the beautiful Algarve. It was in the countryside and just far enough away from the madness of the British hordes in the Summer months, but still in close proximity to the upmarket bars and restaurants in Almancil, Quinta do Lago and Vale do Lobo. They had been extremely fortunate to have found a piece of paradise.

Elgin, as was his wont, liked to get away from Portugal and travel to new and exotic places. The previous year they had brought in the New Year on The Cape Verde Islands, an archipelago of ten volcanic islands just over 500 miles due west of Senegal on the North West coast of Africa and the following February just for good luck they flew over to Madeira for Valentines Day. In March, he realised one of his lifelong held ambitions by playing in a

World Poker Tour event in Reno, Nevada. This was the start of a six-week break which took them from the Western Seaboard of America, visiting San Francisco and Los Angeles, back to Las Vegas and then over to New York before finally stopping off in Florida prior to making their way back home. That caper certainly beat a wet weekend in Cleethorpes.

While staying at the Beverly Hills Hotel in LA, Elgin had won $14,000 playing poker at the casino, but he had made the cardinal error of mentioning his good fortune to his three fashion-mad daughters on his return. Needless to say they wanted a piece of the action. So when Bella flew back to England to visit her family, he whisked Emelia (24 years-old), Lotte (16) and Sylvia (12) over to Milan for some retail therapy. They made a bee-line for Via Monte Napoleone, an upmarket fashion area and touted to be the most expensive street in Europe. He knew this wasn't ending well as his three princesses had a field day. His credit card nearly had a cardiac arrest when the final total was tallied up. His three aces and two queens from Las Vegas were now a pleasant and distant memory, but the smiles on the young girls faces were priceless.

Elgin and Bella spent a romantic Whitsun weekend in Venice where they undertook the classic tour; a gondola trip under the Rialto Bridge, a visit to the Doge's Palace and sampled extortionately priced coffee in the Piazza San Marco. It really doesn't get much better than that. June brought a seven-hour drive to Benidorm. No sign of Johnny Vegas though. The Oracle could have warned Elgin to give Florida the swerve, but such is life. The wedding was set for September 2nd, so for a preliminary trip he took Bella and his two youngest daughters Lotte and Sylvia to *Gay Paree* in August for more shopping. They were now all set for the big day of matrimony.

The nuptial ceremony went without a hitch. It was a beautiful occasion, the bride looked stunning and late into the night after gallons had been dispatched and imbibed there was no sign of a punch up. Elgin's guests could certainly hold their liquor, it made you proud to be British. It was then time for the nine-week honeymoon. If you have wanderlust in your shoes, let the feet do the walking. Anyway, why should Alan Whicker and Judith Chalmers get all the fancy gigs? The newly-wed Hounds' were on a mission to visit all the world's hot resorts (They'd leave the cold spots for the Inuits, that was only fair).

It all kicked off in a Tuscany vineyard which came with a cookery course. Next was shopping in Milano again (he will never learn). Afterwards they flew over to Dubai to stay at their favourite sandy resort, The Jumeirah Beach Hotel. That was followed by having a great time in Thailand before flying down the Malay Peninsula to stay at the world famous Raffles Hotel in Singapore. The last leg of the touring extravaganza was three weeks flying round the length and breadth of Australia. It had all been first class travel and five star hotels. Had any young bride ever had a better honeymoon than this? Probably, but the lad could only give it his best shot.

Just before his birthday in mid December, he had a falling out with the guy who ran his strip joint in Vilamoura. It escalated into a scuffle and he was struggling to put the employee on the seat of his pants. Elgin came out of the altercation puffing and panting like an old dray horse. It was a good job he was up against an idiot or else he'd have been in real trouble. This was an apt time to put La Dolce Vita on the back burner, he would need to lose weight and regain his mojo.

He'd had a real wake up call, all the foreign holidays on top of the protracted honeymoon accompanied with all the rich food and alcohol had given him a somewhat sedentary stance on taking care of business. Elgin knew he had become sloppy and was determined to get back on the ball. So instead of the massive three-day drunken bender that would normally go hand in hand with his birthday, he wisely decided to get back down to his fighting fit, best weight, and what better way to do it than taking Bella skiing in the Pyrenees at the ski resort of Sierra Nevada. It was only a four-hour drive from their house. Bella had never been there before and was agog with excitement. As it turned out she was a natural, after just five days of practice she was confidently slaloming down the red slopes (These slopes are for 'intermediate' skiers). They returned trimmer, meaner and leaner. It had been a very enjoyable and worthwhile break.

Christmas was fast coming up on the rails, they had visitors, Emelia, Elgin's eldest daughter, another three from England, Bella's mother Daphne, step-dad Ralph and uncle Kelvin and best of all, a very special guest, Elgin's mum Eileen, who resided over in Spain. A memorable and pleasurable time was had by all in the Iberian Winter sun, Elgin now exercising daily and watching his calorie intake, he'd rediscovered the tiger in his tank, life was hunky dory again.

Another ski trip to *Espagne* was set in motion in the New Year.

Bella didn't need asking twice! The weight was tumbling off our athletic pair. Elgin was so proud of his wife. It was her 26th birthday at the end of January, so he flew her parents in secret over to Portugal for a few days, before they embarked on another five-week holiday in Florida, which included a week in Jamaica.

One could observe from a distance that these two people had the most wondrous life, but behind the scenes black storm clouds were brewing. Bella had scant knowledge of their ever worsening predicament on the European mainland, allied to the serious problems escalating back in Britain. It was all slowly morphing into a continual headache for Elgin. She was in the dark about anything untoward, but Elgin had plenty of dilemmas to weigh up. The day she agreed to move permanently to America, the worries of the world lifted off his laden shoulders. In early May they flew from Lisbon across the Atlantic Ocean to New York, their new life was just beginning. Yet more... *much, more* was to follow.

Once airborne, Elgin heavily exhaled with a equal amount of relief and contentedness, unknowing that the spider's web would still be closing in on him in the United States. For the time being he had dodged a bullet, but he would have to stay on his mettle to deflect anything the authorities would throw his way. At that precise moment he was still one step ahead of the game.

They normally stopped over in Manhattan for a few days when they visited New York and Bella liked to look around the shops, and they both enjoyed the theatres and restaurants of the vibrant, never sleeping city, but Elgin didn't want to take any chances of his name popping up on a wanted list and getting a pull through it, so they quickly caught a connecting flight straight down to Orlando.

Elgin had a lasting bond with Florida. He was comfortable there and had previously put down roots in the area. A few years earlier he had rented a villa in Orlando while waiting to complete on a house he had bought further down around the lake. Bella's uncle Kelvin was over on holiday and noticed that the villa opposite had a car on the drive with a Wolverhampton Wanders Football Club sticker in the back window. As both Elgin and Kelvin were Wolves fans they went over to investigate. Sure enough, a guy named Rob from their neck of the woods back home was indeed a Wanderers fan.

This is not bullshit! There really were three Wolves fans in close proximity in Florida, hard to believe I know, the odds must have been enormous, but all perfectly true.

Rob was married to Glenda and they ran a small property maintenance company, so Elgin hired them to look after the pool and house after he moved into his new property. They were also given the house keys when Elgin and Bella returned to Europe in the Summer months. Rob would keep the house spick and span and do all the odd jobs that needed doing while the couple were away. All involved became good friends, so on Elgin and Bella's permanent return to Orlando, Rob and Glenda were there at the airport to give them a lift back home, but not before setting off to their favourite local Irish Bar to wet their whistles.

John the barman welcomed them back, told them to sit down and he'd bring the drinks and menu over. Elgin had no need for the house options, he had already decided a fortnight ago what he was having that evening. The man was gagging for Prime Ribs and a pint of the black stuff. He was back in his element and this was the area he felt most at home. There's a lot to be said for someone who knows what he likes and loves and where he also gets his head down - *amen* to all that.

The two couples used to go out together a couple of times a week. Rob and Glenda would pop round, the two ladies would have some wine and get themselves ready to hit the town while the two Wolves fans would sit on the pool decking, have a few beers and, as the Americans would say, *shoot the shit*. Back home we'd say 'having a jolly old chinwag'. The correct description was perhaps somewhere in the centre. No wonder we had William Shakespeare and they had Mickey Spillane.

For the next few days, the new arrivals spent time catching up with old friends and shrugging off the jet lag. Elgin was euphoric about being a large Ocean away from all the detritus and *merde* that had been stacking up back in Europe. He was already planning his new life and everything looked so promising. Bella was really happy sunbathing by the pool, whilst Elgin played poker on the internet and watched the Fox Soccer Channel.

Six weeks flew by. Elgin was in the process of setting up a brand new business. He'd never worked in The States before - it had been his massive vacation playground, but the more he saw of the way trade was done there, the more he was confident he could achieve great success. He'd had a bit of a touch when he bumped into old pal Stewart in a restaurant. He was involved in a similar type of enterprise that Elgin was planning and the man had a shed load of useful contacts. Stewart was a diamond and even rented him some office space. It was amazing really because only a few years earlier he'd been down and out on his arse. So it was terrific to see him on the up and doing great things again. Perseverance is a trait not given to everyone.

Elgin, even at school, was a natural born entrepreneur. There is an old saying that *salesmen are born, not made*. Very true. It is an inherent talent that you either have or you don't. He began at a young age by selling chicken eggs and window cleaning... obviously not at the same time, but I wouldn't have put that past him. Afterwards he tried a myriad of jobs. A great salesman will know as soon as he finds his true calling, but the most legendary ones can sell almost anything; insurance, cars, double glazing or real estate. There isn't a glass ceiling nor a monthly pay packet large enough to hold the best salesman's wages. A lot of these special people are extremely rich and in my experience, they could lose every penny they have, start again and still rise like the phoenix from the flames.

Elgin was so excited and pumped up over his latest venture - putting together a killer sales force team courtesy of recruiting the very best faces about. He was training them into a well-oiled machine that was about to be released upon an unsuspecting American public. It had been weeks of tears, sweat and tough preparation, but by Friday 8th of June 2007, his squad were ready to rock and roll. They'd set the synchronised watches for the following Monday morning. *Cry havoc and let slip the dogs of war!* He could do no more - it was time for destiny to deliver.

He thought that merited a well deserved celebration (any excuse for a good drink). He searched the internet for a hotel in Cocoa Beach because the following night the space shuttle was taking off from nearby Cape Canaveral and the beach parties along there were awesome. They invited Rob and Glenda along with two other close friends, Greg and Lucy, around for the next day's festivities. It was all geared up for a blinding few days especially as Elgin was going to cook his speciality dish: Greek Lamb with Apricots. Was there no end to this boy's talents? He'd sell you something then make you a slap up dinner - what was not to like?

They all rolled up at the Cocoa Beach hotel at three in the afternoon - par for the course. It wasn't ready for them, so they walked down to an Oceanside bar and knocked some Margaritas back. Sitting on the terrace of the bar looking out over the ocean, they started to discuss one of their favourite topics - *where are we going for our dinner?* It was a unanimous vote for the famed eatery on the pier, which was about five minutes away, so they checked back into the hotel then walked along the boardwalk (promenade) to their destination. The pier restaurant was just starting its evening session.

They were shown to a great table overlooking the still-thronging beach. Elgin still remembers watching all the kids in the water thinking, *Why the fuck are those parents allowing them to swim in the sea at the shark bite capital of the world?* It was a good point: if a pair of great whites had rocked up, the sharks would have their *hors d'oeuvres* a lot quicker than Elgin would sitting in the restaurant. (For the faint of heart, no sharks or kiddies were injured that evening.)

For Elgin's last meal of freedom - not that he would have known this at that moment of course - there was roast alligator for starters, with swordfish to follow, with the mandatory two bottles of Pinot Grigio. That would have been in stark contrast to the slops they would receive for the next five weeks in jail. Suitably intoxicated, they made their way down to the beach. Spotting a bar with live music, they found a table and settled down with some more Margaritas eagerly expectant for the big shuttle launch. If only Sir Patrick Moore could have seen them. All those years of fronting *The Sky at Night* had paid off. His little English space cadets pissed up amongst the Yankees. I'm sure the great man might have shed a fond tear behind his monocle.

The atmosphere was crackling electric. It was still only seven o'clock, but the place was packed to the rafters and kicking. The launch time approached, so they took their drinks and moved across the beach to the water's edge. It was a magnificent sight. You first see the shuttle like a resplendent giant firebird soar into the night sky. Seconds later the deafening roar of the engines kick in nearly bursting your eardrums. WOW! No matter how many times you see it, the whole event is a dramatic, mind blowing extravaganza. It's just phenomenal to consider that half a dozen very brave people are strapped inside an aircraft attached to a giant cylinder full of thousands of gallons of highly combustible fuel. Unbelievable.

Bye-bye shuttle. It had just gone eight o'clock and they decided to have a couple more drinks at a strip club on the way back to the hotel. Elgin was right into the Tequila by then. Bella was really made up at the front door as the girl on admissions wouldn't believe she was over twenty-one. But after a friendly stand-off, in they went. The plan was to have a serious drink, but the venue was a disappointing let-down. It came over very tame and nobody could get in the mood. Not surprising really after watching that wondrous space launch. The strip club was a definite anti-climax. It was one of the few times Buzz Lightyear ever trumped Gypsy Rose Lee. Reluctantly they traipsed back to the hotel. Tomorrow would be another day when they could fill their boots to their hearts content. Little did they know that a lack of alcohol would be the least of their problems - grief was coming in the night.

    The hotel room had two queen-sized beds. Elgin had just bounced out of Bella's minutes before they got their early morning call off the F.B.I. It was unimaginable, a massive hangover and his worst nightmare unfolding in front of him. Watching his young innocent wife being manacled like a murderer. Once they had the cuffs on them and they were no longer a threat (as if), the mood of the good marshals changed. They were helpful and sympathetic, after all the couple hadn't committed any crime in America, they let Elgin make a few mobile phone calls and advised them both to leave any valuables in the car because they would go missing in jail. It was with a heavy heart Elgin loosened his wedding ring which Bella had put on his finger in Portugal not even twelve months earlier. He wondered if she regretted it now. The one and only thing he was ruing was using his own credit card to check into the hotel. *BLOODY IDIOT!* he thought. It was obviously how they had tracked him down. It was a rare and surprising lack of judgement by him. But we're all mortal no matter how sharp we are, anyone can have a moment of misjudgement.

    It was an hour's journey to the jail in the marshal's 4x4. He was trying to calm Bella down, but all she kept repeating was "My mum will kill you for this!" He wasn't worried about Daphne-in-law one iota, his main concern was a naive, reserved girl who had never crossed swords with the law, being banged up with a gang of crack-head lowlifes. He thought they would eat her alive, he had enough on his own plate, but it could tip him over the edge fretting for both of them.

    He had to stay strong. They were both heading for an alien existence and a torrid world of pain.

* * * *

CHAPTER TWO

Big house blues

Elgin was now a statistic in the American penal system. Not only did the United States have the largest prison population in the world - that figure vacillated just above and below the 2.7 million mark - but they had the highest per capita incarceration rate as well. It was a massive multi-billion dollar operation. He had seen dreadful, candid documentary films of the system in action featuring overcrowding, bullying, wounding, mayhem and murder. Believe me, when he got there, nothing had been exaggerated, hyped up or over-dramatised. It was *Welcome to Hell*. This would have to be a time for survival. He was entering a non-stop war zone.

It did absolutely nothing to alleviate his well-grounded fears while being processed at the reception desk, when he whimsically asked the guard for, "A no smoking room with a king size bed please". It was met with an icy glare and a helpful word of advice from one of the marshals, "Son, don't even joke with these people. Everyday, all they deal with are the worst dregs of society... they tend to class all inmates at that level." Elgin attempted to tell Bella to go into protective custody, only for the same guard to scream, "Shut the fuck up!" Jesus, this wasn't going to shape up like some of the cushy nicks back in England - the nightmare had truly begun.

There were tears in his eyes as they led Bella away. She turned and looked at him. She was terrified; it was the first time in their six year relationship that he was powerless to do anything. At that moment he hated himself. He could protect her in any other precarious situations, but here he was helpless as a babe. His innocent soul mate being taken away to the lionesses den, and all he could do was hope for the very best and say a little prayer.

He was informed that he was classified as a federal prisoner because there is a two-tier legal system in the USA: the state system is the regime we would all recognise over here, then there is the federal system, which is anything the government takes an interest in, namely serious criminality. Because the

British authorities had asked the FBI to conduct the arrest, it meant they were federal cons until they were extradited. It meant nothing to Elgin at the time, until he realised that although he was in a state prison, he was going to be put in a high security federal pod, in other words, a prison within a prison filled with the worst calibre of people.

As he approached the 'pod', he was still musing about Bella. He wasn't too concerned about his own personal safety; he was 48 years of age and over six foot tall, sixteen stone in weight and in the best physical condition for a long time. He didn't frighten easily. That was until he walked into that pod.

The metal door opened and he was pushed in. He swivelled round to ask which cell he was in. His answer was the door slamming shut in his face. Was he apprehensive? Well, you could say that! He was shitting himself. Every single person in there stopped what they were doing and turned to look at *the new fish*. His first thoughts were, "I might not get out of here alive."

He wasn't a bad judge.

The pod was a large area with eight cells running the length of one wall with stairs leading to an open walkway with eight more identical cells directly above the eight below. On the wall opposite was an unpretentious little window which was the hatch. This small orifice was the only connection to the rest of the prison and the outside world. Through this came all the food... and everything else for that matter. It was classic minimalism. The only other things in the pod were three metal tables, each with four metal chairs, all bolted to the floor and of course the shower behind a filthy curtain (the scene of some vicious assaults). The cells were small, having been originally designed for one man, but each had two bunks, one sink, one toilet and one light and, oh yes, the ubiquitous lights - really bright, all pervasive and spread far and wide, never ever switched off, and another pain in the backside.

The male prison population of America in terms of racial demographics is; white-Caucasian (including Hispanics) 58%, black 40% (from 13% of the general population) and about 2% Native American. But in Elgin's pod the seventy guys were predominantly black (about 85% in fact. And around 10% Hispanic and 5% Caucasian - which put him in a very small minority). He had been issued with an inch-thick mattress, a blanket and a brown paper bag containing liquid soap, toothpaste and brush. A Hispanic guy told him to put his stuff under the stairs, which he did and then sat down on the mattress. It was about 4pm on a Sunday afternoon and his thoughts turned back to the Greek Lamb dinner party he'd cooked up. He could forget about another of those for a while. Films of riots in American jails went through his head - the violence, the cruelty of the guards - the very things he would encounter and witness in the coming weeks. His heart sighed.

He'd been sitting alone for about ten minutes when a guy named Tom came up and sat beside him. Tom was a white supremacist who was awaiting trial for conspiracy to rob and other firearm offences. The FBI had been busy monitoring his activities for 18 months and had even infiltrated his skinhead gang, but couldn't get any race hate accusations to stick. So one of the undercover agents had suggested to him that there was a possibility of robbing a local crack dealer. Tom went along with the agent even though there seemed something odd about him. But the guy had been to all the parties, took drugs and seemed like one of the boys. The journey turned into a case of entrapment. On the way to the robbery there were elements of mutual mistrust which quickly escalated into a stand off. Tom swooped for his legally held gun nestling in the glove compartment when the guy attempted to brandish his own weapon. The agent's gun was discharged in the ensuing melee and he shot himself in the foot. Tom said it was like the Keystone Kops. He was pissing himself laughing, but the fed had to have his foot amputated a few months later, so they really wanted to nail him, he was looking at a lot of bird.

Tom had clocked Elgin's English accent and mentioned that he'd once met Nick Griffin, the head honcho of the British National Party. Although Elgin's politics were centre right, the last thing he needed was to be regarded as a racist. The best man at his wedding had been 'Big Colin', a Jamaican guy from Stafford. He started to wonder, could it all get any worse. He was locked in a cage with sixty huge black guys and he had a white supremacist trying hard to be his new best mate.

He was saved by the 'chow'. The food arrived in the nick of time, and so he queued up at the hatch. Elgin had next to no appetite and his stomach was tight like a Gordian Knot and after staring down at his prison fare it was extremely doubtful whether that would be an antidote. He sat back under the stairs picking at the tray holding his wholesome white rice and beans. No way Jose was he going to be swallowing that. He just hoped this was all a terrible nightmare and he'd wake up soon. But there was scant chance of that occurring, he hadn't even found a place to get his head down. It was heaving downstairs and someone with a warped sense of humour suggested he venture upstairs where it was hotter but less crowded. He approached the guys in the cells, but was met with mocking laughter and insults including, "Fuck off cracker!" (this was a derogatory term used by the blacks in the

South to describe white folk. It supposedly derives from a time when slavers had whips or Floridian cowboys used to crack theirs at alligators or predators moving in on livestock.)

There was no way anyone wanted an extra person sleeping on the floor of a cell, especially a white boy giving off more body heat. Elgin was getting desperate, he was running out of cells and hope, that was until he came across a guy named Corey two cells from the end. Without Elgin even asking he said, "Go get your belongings before they disappear, you can sleep on the floor here". He'd heard Elgin coming along, getting the knock back at each and every cell. On Elgin's return, he witnessed Corey having a full blown argument with his cell mate, Bligh, another huge black guy. "Why are you helping the white dude Corey, don't you think you should have asked me first?" Well, at least Elgin knew where he stood now. Never in his wildest dreams did he think he would be eternally grateful to be able to sleep on the floor of a boiling hot overcrowded prison cell with two black guys who were total strangers. Corey turned out to be one of the nicest, caring people he'd ever met in his life though. However Bligh, on first impressions, came over as a complete twat. He didn't disappoint on that initial observation, they never did warm to each other.

Corey was a born again Christian. He served in the US Army during the Afghanistan conflict where had got on well with the English troops out there, so he took Elgin under his wing as he was way out of his depth at the start of the incarceration. When he returned home after his stint abroad, he couldn't find any jobs so turned to drug dealing - seemingly the only way he could pay the rent and support his family.

A few weeks after getting to really know Corey, Elgin had a deep discussion with him. He thought that Corey hadn't needed to go down the path he had done, that perhaps there were other alternatives. Elgin had never seen any evidence of racism in Florida and put that to Corey, who retorted, "Well, you wouldn't have done Elgin, you're a white man. In your part of town things resemble all things like Disney. You wanna come down to where I'm from, it would open your eyes". He further elucidated that minimum wage jobs were the only openings in his area; flipping burgers seven days a week and still not having enough money to cover the family bills. This was an ongoing conversation during the time that Elgin was there. Eventually he was convinced that a lot of black youths from poor areas only had two real options open to them; join the army as gun fodder for the American war machine or deal gear. It was obviously not quite as simplistic as that, but opportunities for many, especially with a poor education were strictly limited. Perhaps the way Britain is now heading as well.

Elgin settled down for the night in the 'golden shower position' (the mattress next to the toilet). As people left the jail, bunks became available, but you had to be assertive to get one . He eventually managed to get one a few weeks later and so was up on to the next rung of the penal ladder. The bunk was sheer bloody luxury compared to what he had been having to sleep on. As we all know, you only miss the little things in life when they are taken away.

He was praying Bella was having a better time of it than he was, but he'd seen nothing yet of the proper Draconian jail regime in action - tomorrow would be his first experience. They certainly weren't being cruel to be kind.

At 3:30am sharp Elgin had a nasty surprise. He was sound asleep only to be awoken by what he imagined to be rifle fire. It was the moment of 'unlock' - that is, the time all the automatic locks simultaneously cranked open. All the cons jumped out of their bunks and started to get dressed. He had never been a man to copy others, but on this occasion he decided to follow suit.

"What's going on here?" Bligh condescended to speak to him for the first time face to face, "Breakfast, cracker. If you don't want it, I'll have it." He descended down to the hatch with no great presumption about the quality of the morning fare. He wasn't expecting Weetabix, strawberries and semi-skimmed milk, and so there was absolutely no anti climax when he clocked a powdered mashed potato concoction with spicy globulous gravy mix. This culinary delight was known in the pod as 'dog food'. If anything, it looked worse than the rice and beans he had refused the day before. He had half a mouthful and gave the rest to Corey, much to the chagrin of Bligh - but he was never going to be his mate was he? So he could go fuck himself, the vile fat bastard.

Elgin didn't actually eat anything for three days. It was a combination of the shock to his system, his previous eating habits and, last but not least, the shocking nutritional standard of the utterly shite food. After every breakfast it was impossible to get to sleep again. The guards had a loud tannoy system which was used constantly. Half an hour later they would call you down for soap. If you needed a wash you had to be down at the hatch. More often than not they would keep you standing there for up to thirty minutes, so once you had the soap you'd try to get some more shut-eye. Fat chance, off would go the tannoy, "OK you guys, toilet paper", and down you would go again. Back upstairs, just dropping off again and then, "Mail call!" Bastards. Handing out letters at 05:30 in the morning. But if you didn't go, you wouldn't get your letters for days and they were very important when you lived in a world of isolation and fear. As you've probably sussed out, most of these functions could have been implemented at the same time (maybe around 7am). A sensible, caring regime would have done that, but this was the huge American grind-them-down-machine in action. In essence, it actually facilitated sleep deprivation. It was all part of a game - a sly system to break people down.

Elgin quickly realised why they were doing it.

Most of the guys in the pod blamed this mental cruelty on the sadistic guards, claiming that they found it amusing and it got them through the day, but Elgin didn't think so because that would require a certain level of intelligence and many were lacking in that attribute, especially 'Napoleon' (more about him later).

Elgin was fond of conspiracy theories and had come up with a far more plausible hypothesis. Sleep deprivation had been used by the American military for a long time on prisoners of war, it was a form of torture to get information out of them. It has an alarming impact on your thought processes and concentration levels. A prisoner who has to prepare his defence plea whilst undergoing these major distractions has it all to do against a federal government who have a 98% success rate in the courts. Most people accept the plea bargain offered up by the District Attorney rather than run the risk of being found guilty and handed down an inhumane sentence.

Anyhow 'insomniacs anonymous' would go on until about 11am when chow duly arrived at the hatch. To say the food was bang basic was a gross understatement. The major staples were boiled rice and kidney beans. Elgin never saw any fruit or green vegetables while he was there - the head chef must have been a Scotsman. To survive, inmates had to buy food from the commissary. In the case of The John E. Polk Centre, a private company who sold substandard goods at inflated prices, they obviously didn't adhere to the adage of 'never kick a man when he's down'. Elgin used to buy packets of tuna or salmon to get some much needed protein. The food was very often out of date and sometimes rank. What could you do? The ombudsman wasn't an option. As Del-Boy once said, *"No income tax, no VAT. No money back, no guarantee"*. He even had to buy his own boxer shorts. They were $5 a pair. Christ Almighty, they were paper thin and fell apart after two robust washes. They'd have been available in the local Wal-Mart store for less than a dollar. The criminals were all on the wrong side of the wall, it was sheer unadulterated exploitation.

Only in America.

Even the phones were 'call collect' only (equivalent to the reverse charge in England). Actually, all local charges in America are free, that is, unless you were unlucky enough to be inside the *Big House*. The recipient of the call had to set up an account with an automated phone line and buy credit on their card, so Uncle Sam was deftly charging you for free calls. What a piss take! This was racketeering at its very finest. The cons were even charged for being incarcerated, a one off charge of $10 dollars for being processed on your first day, then $2 dollars a day just for the privilege of being detained inside! YOU REALLY COULDN'T MAKE IT UP!

After lunch everyone was wide awake. You couldn't hear yourself think - people talking, babbling, yelling and screaming like jack-hammers, all at the loudest decibel level. Sleep would be impossible until the evening. So Elgin had to find something to combat the boredom once he had acclimatised himself to life in the pod. His first acquaintance, Tom, had some books, but it was surprising how quickly he went through them when he was reading ten to twelve hours a day. He quickly began to ration his reading, taking a guess he would be stuck in there about a month.

The only other things to while away the time were playing cards or to chat to other inmates. There was always a long queue for the card games, but more often than not, someone would end up going down to *The Block* while the other guy took a visit to the hospital wing. Elgin gave it a swerve. He didn't fancy being on the wrong side of a beating and the block didn't sound very inviting, as it was a single cell where you're stripped down to your underwear, manacled by your wrists and ankles to a bed by an air conditioning unit which froze your nuts off.

He was left with the only option of talking to his fellow man which again didn't come without it's troubles. He could talk freely with the few white guys in there, but the majority of the black cons spoke with a deep Southern drawl - a brogue and burr - which he found great difficulty in understanding. They, on the other hand, understood him perfectly. It led to some thinking he was downright rude or even racist. This got him depressed because he had no way of explaining his dilemma.

The Hispanic crew spoke little or no English, their Spanish dialect was different from the Castilian language Elgin spoke, but he began to grasp what they were saying and the stories they told him were staggering. Many of them had been jailed previously. The sentences handed down by the American judiciary were God-given frightening. If you were caught with drugs and a gun in a second offence, that would be a sentence of 'natural life' unless there were mitigating circumstances. That would really make your eyes water knowing you were banged up until taken out in a coffin.

Some of the Hispanics had been caught importing cocaine from Puerto Rico and there had been suggestions in the local press that they'd executed several members of a rival gang. All Elgin knew was that they had a simple and basic plan. Puerto Rico is classed for immigration and customs purposes as being part of the United States. All they did was post half-kilo packages from home over to mainland America by regular mail. The authorities didn't intercept any of the powder packages, but their little game was halted when they were grassed up by another criminal. Being stitched up by one of your own is very common for drug dealers in America. No honour amongst thieves is so apt when someone else is looking at a life sentence and gets offered a deal to have many years knocked off their own tally.

The DEA (Drug Enforcement Agency) are masters at this - we've all seen *Goodfellas* and *The Sopranos* - a choice word in the ear of the accused, the suggestion he can go back to the wife and kids and have a new life in the Witness Protection Programme or spend every year until death in a spartan cell. It takes a special type of man not to be tempted to become a rat (as the 'supergrasses' are known in the underworld). They are all between a rock and a hard place. The main man in the Hispanic gang, Tony, son of an Air Force man who was born in Europe, had travelled widely and spoke excellent English. He told Elgin he was expecting natural life and if they gave him the death penalty for the murders, he'd much prefer that to festering away in a cell for fifty years. And who was to say that wouldn't have been his best option?

Elgin began to swap food with a really nice fella called Derek. He went to trial and was found guilty, receiving a sentence of 40 years for being caught with fifty grams of crack. It was his first offence and with no firearms involved either. Now bear in mind that prisoners in America serve 85% of their sentence, and Derek was 28 when convicted, meaning he'll be inside until he is 62 for just a handful of drugs. As you read this he has a lot of time on his hands before he comes out. People were getting twenty or thirty years in the courts - that would probably equate to three to five over here and some British cons can even apply for parole after serving a third of their sentence. A whole different world. Derek was badly depressed for two or three days after being sentenced, but then got back to his normal cheerful demeanour. They were tough cookies this mob, brought up on hard times.

A young white boy, Tad, didn't have to go down the same felonious avenues. He'd come from a good family background and had even been to university. At the age of twenty two he'd started up a crack house and gambling den. His brief told him to expect at least twenty years. Elgin found him to be excellent company and a real nice kid, but he couldn't feel sorry for him like a lot of the others in there, because he classed him as a volunteer. Back in England he'd had many opportunities himself to get involved with drugs, but he had always given it a wide berth. Sure, it's huge money for little work, but the possibility of a big prison sentence always put him off. It's a dirty game and most of the participants end up in prison or dead.

The more Elgin got to know the people in the pod, the more he realised that most had led a pretty shit life on the outside. He'd always imagined that everyone had the same chance to live the 'American Dream' - how wrong he was. He'd occasionally met some choice colourful characters in his local bar, but he didn't know anyone from a 'bad hood', so to speak. It quickly dawned on him that their philosophical attitudes to monster prison sentences were just extensions of the mindset they all grew up with. What had they to lose? To live in poverty or attempt to break free.

Access to good medical care was nigh on impossible. When Elgin was processed on the first day they took his asthma inhaler away. He was told that if he needed it, he should ask one of the prison guards. He was concerned to say the least. He could perhaps understand why they didn't want anybody to have an aerosol in the pod, but he was worried about not having it in his pocket as it went everywhere with him. His misgivings were realised on the Sunday when he was feeling breathless, so he asked the guard for his medication. This was met with an apathetic shrug of the shoulders, "You've missed the nurse", came the only response before he walked away. *Well, thanks a bunch for your concern.*

The nurse came round at 9am and again at 10pm, so Elgin had to wait ten hours or so to see her. He was in a real predicament. If he had a bad attack it could be a serious problem. He'd only had two major attacks before; once when he was in the army getting lost in the snow drifts on Dartmoor and the other when he ran out of medication a few years later. Since those ordeals he'd always make sure he was well stocked up.

Jersey (a Hispanic from New Jersey), didn't allay Elgin's nerves at all when he casually remarked, "England, they don't care if you live or die in here!" Elgin was starting to panic. Corey told him that it had taken one guy over a week to get his inhaler. That didn't sound too good either, and it suddenly dawned on him that he might actually be vacating the pod in a prison issue body bag.

The nurse came round that evening at 10pm - thank God for that. Elgin was struggling really badly. He started to explain his position when she cut him short and handed him a form to fill in.

"Hand it back in tomorrow morning", the nurse said. He told her that she must be joking, he didn't think he would see tomorrow. She gave a bland apology, "I'm sorry, but that's the procedure. Nothing more I can do".

He asked what would happen if his condition worsened in the night. She replied, "Tell a guard", then turned on her heels and left. She was one tough bitch. So much for being a 'sister of mercy'.

Elgin didn't know whether to laugh or cry. Unlike British jails there were no alarm bells in any cell. Thankfully his condition didn't deteriorate through the night. It was a good job really as he and Bella were up before the beak on Monday morning for the extradition hearing.

The drive to court was hair-raising. They all went in a vehicle the size of a large transit van - it had three compartments behind the driver. Bella was alone in one of them and the other two were crammed packed with male prisoners. The latter two resembled a pair of giant sardine tins. If there had been a crash or a fire they would never have got out alive. That said, the Feds probably wouldn't have tried to rescue them anyhow. To add to the trauma and entertainment, the woman driver up front displayed all the driving skills of a complete novice. She was breaking sharply on straight sections of road and accelerating on the bends. Other motorists were honking their horns. If she had been a civilian, she'd have clocked up more points than the Harlem Globetrotters. It was the final straw when they approached the bridge going over Lake Jessup. Elgin wasn't the strongest swimmer and if the van went into the drink they were all dead for sure. You could have heard a pin drop when they arrived safely at the courthouse. Facing the judge would be child's play after that excursion.

Fortunately Elgin and Bella were put in cells adjacent to each other in the courthouse, so they could natter away all day to their hearts' content. The first thing he said was, "Get yourself into protective custody". Again, "Why, why? I'm fine!" she replied. The bottom line was that there was no Federal pod for the woman's prison, she was in with all the State prisoners and it was a less harsh regime all round. The only difference was that Federal cons had to wear red jump suits and State cons had to wear blue. As she was the only Federal inmate in there, some of the other prisoners were wary of her in the beginning. By the time they all found out she wasn't the demon spawn of Ma Baker, she'd made friends with many of them. (Everyone, but everyone, loved Bella).

That was a big relief for Elgin - knowing his wife was safe - and not only safe, but in fact adapting a lot better than he was. When men are thrown together they vie for the alpha male role and there is a definite pecking order from strongest to weakest - it's all macho bullshit, but it exists in every country, society and creed. Women, on the other hand, seem to get on better under stressful circumstances. It's not universal, but on the whole it's a lot less violent and competitive. It surprised him how well she had settled down. He was very proud when she related that a woman had nicked her body lotion and she went into her cell and turned it over until she found it. That was amazing, as she was always non-confrontational on the outside. He had only seen her lose her rag once, and that was when she threw her drink over a liberty-taker in a Cypriot night club. The girl never retaliated because there were about ten other girls with Bella, but she felt really bad about it for days and even talked about trying to find her and apologise. That was the girl she was, no edge to her at all.

Their time in court was looming. Elgin had a bee in his bonnet: against his lawyer's advice (The Public Pretender, sorry Defender) had told him he would be in contempt of court if he brought up the subject of his medication. Elgin wasn't having it. He had nothing to lose. What was the worst they could do, lock him back up? The judge, to his surprise, hit the roof! She went ballistic at the marshals. They were ultimately responsible for his welfare. Not only did she demand he got his medication on his return to jail, but she also sent a strongly-worded letter to the prison captain in charge of Napoleon and the other guards. A letter from a Federal Judge has a lot of gravitas, so somebody was going to get a bollocking. It might make Elgin *public enemy number one* with the guards, but it was a win of sorts, even though it could turn out to be a pyrrhic victory. But he was on top at that moment. It was the first success he'd had for a while. It might even make the regime consider making some improvements to their medical procedure. One could only hope that pigs could fly.

It was a blessed relief to have a guy driving them back to jail in the van. Elgin hadn't told Bella about the crap he was going through as he didn't want to worry her. She had told him to look after himself. He thought, *Hello, shouldn't it be me telling her that?* Anyhow, it would be another month before they saw each other again. It was in stark contrast to the life they had together before their arrest. They had been inseparable 24/7 over the last six years.

On his return, Elgin's earlier triumphal mood had turned to a downer, his ankles were bloodied, bruised and swollen from eight hours of wearing the damned leg irons. It was barbaric for a space-age, super-technological country like America to be still using implements from the slave trade era. It was degrading and spiteful, but he couldn't see them ever going soft on crime. Thank God in four weeks he would be on a one-way flight out of there, he was counting the days.

The guards would soon be after his blood and try to make his life a misery in the short time he had left. Sure enough he got an inhaler within an hour of getting back to the pod, but even that was a piss-take. They wouldn't return his original one back to him. They coerced him to buy one of theirs and naturally he was over-charged for it! They just couldn't help themselves. If Elgin needed anything he had to put it on an application form. It became a pointless exercise; they ignored all of them. Bella had been given permission to write to him, but he wasn't allowed to reply back, because he hadn't got permission to do so.

He rightly figured out there must be a complaints procedure in the prison. There was - but guess what? You had to put in an application form to apply for a complaints form! It was classic *catch 22*. You couldn't win. What could you do! Anyway, Elgin hadn't seen anything yet, as Napoleon was just about to come into his own. A little man determined to erase the memory of his namesake at the battle of Waterloo and if he could, spread a little pain and suffering on one of old England's ex-soldiers.

It was time to draw bayonets.

* * * *

CHAPTER THREE

Napoleon So Low

There is a body of people, mainly men who, when given a whiff of authority accompanied with a badge and cap, become sadistic megalomaniacs with scant regard for all their subordinates. A sad summing-up of some pitiful human beings. Traffic wardens, security personnel, customs officers, traffic police and of course prison warders - the old *turnkeys*. There is good and bad amongst all these professions, but it takes a certain type of man to propagate more misery on someone down on his luck. A lot of these bullies are unsuccessful in other aspects of life, but when that cap and badge goes on they become kings of their own depraved realm.

'Napoleon', aka Officer Rodriguez, was the guard in charge of the pod. This posting would be the zenith of the man's humdrum career. He possessed neither common sense nor people skills. It seemed like he had been given the job with instructions to cause as much small-minded friction as possible. His regal promotion was to the loss of the diplomatic corps. The man could have started a civil war with the Amish such was his ineptitude and belligerence.

Elgin called him 'Napoleon' after the little French war hero, not because he had any tactical genius, but because he was short and squat. He also resembled Napoleon the rogue pig in Orwell's *Animal Farm*, not only in looks, but also because of his mantra that some were definitely more equal than others. He got an enormous buzz ordering around guys who were clearly intellectually and physically much more superior to himself.

Elgin had his card marked from day one.

He was responsible for organising inmates to clean the officers' toilets after lockdown. Nobody wanted to do it and he couldn't force you, so he used enticement in the form of meals from the officers' canteen. He was now in his element and he had men massaging his ego for a return favour.

He would organise 'clean cell competitions' to see who was on toilet duty that night. He'd be both the judge *and* jury. It was so sad to see people falling into his trap. There would even be daily motivational speeches coming out over the tannoy advertising that night's main event cleaning out the shitters. "Yo! Boooys be eatin' fried chicken on the bone tonight, make sho' yo' cells be clean!" Martin Luther King and Winston Churchill could only eat their hearts out after inspirational words like that.

Elgin didn't know it, but there were micro audio bugs scattered around the pod for intelligence-gathering purposes. Napoleon clocked Elgin slagging him off during one of his uplifting speeches. "I look after yo' boooys, what yo' say? Yeah, yo' England!"

Elgin thought *fuck it, I'm on his shit list, moving up it a few places won't make a difference*, so he went for it.

"I'd rather eat shit than be reliant on a control freak like you!" A huge roar of approval went up. The whole pod loved it! Elgin was only going to be there for a month, it was no big deal to call him out. Napoleon then completely lost the plot and couldn't get a coherent sentence out. The best he could manage was, "Yo! Yo gotta pay for tharrt, yo know tharrt, yo' probably gonna eat shit yourself boy!" That was the best the illiterate cretin could muster.

Elgin's street cred had gone through the prison roof. He enjoyed the cons back slapping and high-fiving with him, but deep down he knew retribution was just around the corner as Napoleon was not the type of man to let an inmate get the better of him. Elgin wondered what was in store for him. He waited and waited. The longer it went on the worse the suspense got. Three weeks passed.

When the 'payback' finally arrived - How sad it was! It came on the day of great celebrations in America, namely July 4th, Independence Day.

Americans traditionally have barbecues on that day, so the dinner was going to be hot dogs and hamburgers. Elgin kept clear of that sort of food on the outside, but after a near month of digesting slops it sounded distinctly *Cordon Bleu*. He queued up, only to be handed rice and beans by Napoleon. "None faw yo', England. Yo' country lost boooy... We kicked yo' outta arr great country."

It was no huge surprise at all. Elgin took it on the chin. He had plenty of retorts to throw back, but bit his lip - if that was the pathetic twat's best shot, he'd already won the argument. Napoleon had planned this snub for three weeks. Elgin simply made a tactical retreat and walked back to his cell to eat his consolation prize. A few guys led by Corey came in later and doled out half a burger here, half a sausage there. He actually ended up better off.

There was no segregation in the pod for paedophiles and other inmates *Not Of Normal Criminal Elements* (nonces). Elgin didn't realise this at first and started chatting to a Hispanic guy in his mid-twenties. He felt sorry for him as a lot of the other cons picked on him. He told Elgin he was in for 'computer crime'. Well, that was one way of putting it... It turned out he had tried to groom and pick up an underage boy on the internet, only for the young boy to be an FBI agent on the other end. Elgin gave the dirty bleeder a wide berth after he found out. Anyway, soon the 'law of the pod jungle' kicked in. He would obviously need protection, and he had to go to a guy called 'Big Will' and his henchmen who ran the pod. They treated him and a few others as pets and used them for oral sex. They were pimped out to other cons and these sorry individuals were regularly raped. Big Will would also get them to order up stuff from the commissary for him as payment for the 'protection' they were getting. These sex offenders were marked men throughout their time away. Elgin wouldn't ever offer out any sympathy for them as what they had tried to do to children disgusted him.

He was a loving father and in his eyes they deserved everything they got.

Big Will shouted up to Elgin one morning, "England, yo England!" That was all Elgin needed, a psychopath on his case.

"Hey Will, what's up?" It was bad news, "Come down stairs and bring your commissary sheet with you."

He wasn't going to do that and started to worry that the huge con was trying to coerce him into getting food off his account. Elgin needed to stall him, "Why, what's up?"

"You come down now and get blown by Juan." Elgin had certainly had better offers than that in the past.

"No thanks Will, I'm not bothered."

"Yes England, it's just like a woman." Elgin defiantly stood his ground, insistent that he had no interest and eventually Big Will gave up the ghost. He saw many weaker men succumb to this. Once you were a fly in the spider's web you never escaped.

Extreme violence was commonplace. People fell out over a wrong word out of turn, but the main catalyst was gambling debts. Sharpened toothbrushes being the weapons of choice where cons were 'shanked' by these improvised blood-letting implements. This behaviour wasn't confined to American jails, it was a problem for penal institutions worldwide. The Marquess of Queensberry rules were seldom adhered to in a confined space full of *desperados* with nothing to lose.

Elgin never had a problem with bully boys because he made a stand first time of asking - don't forget he was representing Great Britain. It happened in the initial week of entering the pod when he received his commissary goods. Another very large black con called 'G.A.' from Savannah, Georgia, (the 'G.A.' being the abbreviation letters for the state) tried to 'tax' him. It was vital at that moment to set a precedent. Elgin told him in a very unfriendly way, "You are welcome to try and take it if you wish, but even if you succeed you will have great difficulty seeing with a toothbrush sticking out of your eye."

The big man walked away laughing. Elgin had called his bluff. He turned out to be a chancer, but other people wouldn't be as strong. If anyone showed any sign of weakness they were finished - it was a *dog eat dog* existence.

More than a few in the pod couldn't stick up for themselves. Amongst that unhappy bunch was a white guy called Kris who had been training to become a doctor before the FBI turned up on his doorstep and arrested him for tax evasion and money laundering. He was a very reserved fella in his early thirties who thought he was happily married until he asked his wife to tie up some loose ends. If you get a court bond (bail) in the US you have the choice of either fronting the whole amount and reclaiming it when you surrender your bail and appear in court, or you can pay a non-refundable 10% fee to a bondsman who is liable for the other 90% if you fail to show up in court.

After Kris was arrested he made bond for $70,000. He immediately called his wife to come down to the jail with a $7,000 cashiers check (a US equivalent to a UK bankers draft.). That didn't materialise. He then heard nothing for month until divorce papers arrived at the jail and fell on his lap. Not even a *Dear John letter* explaining her behaviour. She wouldn't answer any of his calls or reply to any of his letters, so his lawyer investigated the lack of communication and discovered she'd cleaned out his bank account, sold his motor and was in the process of selling the house.

Silence is never golden when the woman you love decides she wants everything and *you* can go to hell. The upshot was that he had no wife, and no money to buy out the commissary - and on top of that he was allergic to most of the slop coming through the hatch. Tom had him in his cell, he couldn't see one of the white guys unravel in front of his eyes. Being this close to Tom was the only stroke of luck Kris had because he was extremely frightened of any form of physical violence. He rarely even stepped out of his cell. The man was a broken shell. Elgin tried to help by giving him some of his commissary every week, but he'd be going back to England very shortly. What a miserable existence poor old Kris was living, but what could you do?

Another guy to whom the environment was totally alien was 'Greece'. Now, you may have noticed a pattern here - 'England' from England, 'G.A.' from Georgia and 'Jersey' from New Jersey. Yes...you've got it! 'Greece' was from...Miami! Ah, but he was born in Greece, so that was his moniker. Anyway Elgin was pretty sure one of the black guys was named Miami, so if Greece wanted that name he'd have to take it up with him, but as he only came up to his belly button it probably wasn't advisable.

Greece had been an extremely wealthy car dealer but was another poor sap with woman troubles. His demise started when he traded his wife in for a younger model. This is never the smartest move, especially when that woman was the reason you were the proud possessor of an automatic Green Card. This documentation is simply priceless in America; it enables you to own and run a business. Ordinarily you have to invest an awful lot of money into your business to qualify or you can take the easy simpler option of 'marrying' for your Green Card.

He had sold plenty of motors and became a success story, but forgot how he got his easy start and left his wife for a trophy girlfriend. Bad mistake! Hell hath no fury like a woman scorned (when will we learn?). Anyhow, the wife teamed up with her cousin (a cop), and planted a fair smattering of drugs down at his garage. She then anonymously tipped off the local police force by phone and said that cars weren't the only things being moved down there and poor old Greece got banged up.

The man was very aloof and actually talked down to some of the inmates, a dangerous practise in a confined tinder box full of violent cons with hair-trigger tempers. Elgin used to let him tag along with him against his better judgement. One day they were having a cracker meeting in Tom's cell and Greece started bitching about the food and the heat. Tom sensibly replied, "It's the same for all of us" only for Greece to come back with, "Yeah, Tom, but I'm better than you." Elgin saw Tom's face drop and dragged Greece out the cell before Tom could react. It was quips like that which got you hospitalised. Greece's problem was that he believed everything he said, however, it was simply not the best place to be so opinionated.

Elgin had a cellmate called Alvin. Greece enquired what the guy was in for, and he was told "Guns and drugs". The horror on his face was a picture. He shouted, "GUNS, GUNS, what do you mean guns? I've never seen a gun except on a cop! What was he doing with guns? Oh my God! He must be dangerous!"

It was one of the rare lighter moments for Elgin, Greece's response was one that a child would have come out with. Once Elgin had finished laughing he told him straight, "This is a jail you know, not the fucking golf club! There's some really nasty people in here." He looked petrified at that and Elgin saw the chance for some fun and told him about every bloke in the pod who had committed a nasty or violent crime. Greece looked like he would faint. Elgin hoped it would be a wake-up call for him to not take liberties with the wrong people, but it was like water off a duck's back. Nothing changed with him. Although, if anything he got worse. He started to become a dangerous liability and it got to the point where a couple of the main men in the pod warned Elgin to 'sort Greece out', insinuating that he was his fellow European's mentor or henchman. So Elgin started to distance himself. Greece wouldn't heed any advice he was getting. Here was a man totally oblivious to the perils of copping some serious injury.

A tad later when Elgin was on the point of leaving, the case against Greece was collapsing. His wife's badged cousin could control a police enquiry, but not a full-blown federal investigation. Elgin just hoped Greece could beat the charges after he'd gone. If he could wind up the normally composed Tom, it wouldn't take a lot to provoke some psychotic nutter in there. Hopefully he did get out with all his teeth and vital organs intact, but you'd not wager the crown jewels on it.

Another light moment - and they were few and far between - was Tom's 'Secret Project'. He'd been brewing 'hooch'. He called in a trio of lucky pals and offered up a plastic bottle full of what resembled milk. He'd boiled water added bread and sugar and put it in a plastic bag to ferment. A month later he'd supplemented it with commissary apple juice and bingo it was all ready to launch.

Just the look of it put Elgin off. Tom was advocating, "Never mind what it looks like, get it down you... it's just like Baileys."

That clearly hadn't convinced anyone but Elgin took the plunge and was first in. "Fuck me!" he shouted. It was putrid! It tasted like out of date mouldy bread flavoured vodka... and that was being kind. Back in the British prisons it's often called 'brew' and it's done differently. They make a culture out of Marmite and sugar, dissolve it in a little boiling water and feed it sugar solution every couple of days. You then add orange juice and let it ferment. It takes the lining off your stomach, but it's far more palatable than Tom's 'Baileys'.

Kris and Tad followed Elgin with a polite sip each. No-one wanted seconds though and it was all left to Tom for his own 'enjoyment'. He only went and drank the lot. He had a quaint American saying for the after-effects of the hooch, "Jesus, I was sure well fucked up after that!"

Seeing was believing and he confined himself to his cell for three or four days, not taking the chance of moving more than a few feet from the toilet, but when Elgin was leaving, the mad bastard had got another batch on the go.

Then it was all over as quickly as it started. Over the tannoy came, "England, pack up your things." Elgin thought, *I don't think so*. He was walking out with his paper bag full of his legal papers and a few personal possessions. He'd been in a few scrapes, nothing too serious, but he had survived the ordeal. He gave his friends, Tom, Corey and Kris everything else he had left. Elgin genuinely wished them well - they would need all the luck in the world to stay safe, but his own problems hadn't gone away. He was jumping out of the frying pan into the fire.

A guard took him round to the stores to hand his prison garb in and collect his own clothes and belongings. He turned the corner and there she was... Bella, with a big flashing smile on her face. She was fine. Elgin never thought he'd be happy to see the Old Bill who'd come over to re-arrest him, but a wave of relief washed over him to see something familiar again, something quintessentially English.

In a perverse sort of way these good people had come to make sure Elgin got back to England safe and sound. He was in noted company, following in the footsteps of Freddie Foreman and Ronnie Biggs, fine fellows who came home early too. There was one female officer to escort Bella back and five big burly coppers for Elgin. A bit of overkill perhaps - he didn't have the reputation of Hannibal Lecter - but you could never be too careful in an international extradition, especially if a two or three day jolly away in sunny Florida was involved.

Bella and Elgin were cuffed up and put in two separate Federal vehicles which were driven by the marshals to Orlando Airport, where they were kept in a holding cell for an hour or so. Then there was the part Elgin was dreading, walking through the never-ending terminal in handcuffs, surrounded by a plethora of British coppers and American marshals. The tourists and holiday-makers were staring and pointing, like they were prize exhibits in the zoo.

Elgin mused that whenever he used to fly from Orlando and was travelling on the monorail between the terminal and the gate he always used to say to himself, *I wonder when we'll be back here again.* He had a rough figure in his head, which was more than a good few years and his heart sank a just a little, the enormity of what he had done was starting to hit home.

They were flying back on Virgin Atlantic and if they weren't conspicuous enough to begin with, the authorities had pre-reserved the last ten rows of economy class. They sat Elgin in the middle of the back row with two cops either side of him with Bella was sat in the row in front between the female officer and the remaining copper. Then there was a big gap to the other passengers, a sort of no-man's land... *enter at your peril.* A few chancers tried to make themselves comfortable, but the officers took great delight in informing them that they were the Old Bill and that *they should hop it*! (remember the old cap and badge adage)

Elgin noticed that some of the returning holiday makers were shielding their children's' eyes as they passed by to go to the toilet. They must have thought Bonnie and Clyde were aboard. Bella had her handcuffs taken off once they were airborne. Elgin had no such luck - they must have thought he was a black belt in origami or something. Anyway, the shackles were staying on. He needed the toilet about half way over the Atlantic. It was *no dice*! Has anyone ever tried to wipe their arse with handcuffs on? A bit tricky, but there was a rumour Houdini could do it.

He asked the head plod for his legal papers after getting back from his toilet trauma, only to be told they didn't have room for them and that the marshals were posting them on. That was a bummer for Elgin, as he'd written some very important coded phone numbers on the back of them. The wankers hadn't changed their illegal tactics in the 15 years since he'd last had the pleasure of their company.

Bella talked with Elgin all the way back. They hadn't seen each other in over a month and God only knew when they'd get a chance again. They spoke of the nightmare they'd just been through and their concern of what the future held. Bella had undergone a lot harder time than she had relayed to Elgin in her letters, but she didn't want to worry him - how very considerate and pragmatic. Bella came up with an amusing fact; since she'd been with him, she said, "My first football match was England playing in the World Cup in Japan. My first casino was Caesar's Palace in Vegas. My first cricket match was England bowling out West Indies for 45 in Jamaica and my first prison was the John E Polk." She was ready to return to a normal life. Well, not many folk have had debuts like that, Elgin was obviously spoiling her.

It was amusing to witness the cops trying to stay awake, their body clocks were still on UK time. It was obvious they were under instruction to note down anything that was said that could be useful to the authorities. The Head Plod kept suggesting to Elgin, "Why don't you get your head down?" It didn't happen, "No thanks, copper. I'm going to have years with nothing else to do but sleep."

The flight passed quickly, but just as they approached the coast of Old Blighty, the *Fasten seat belt* sign came on and Bella got a bit emotional - not knowing when they would see each other again, I mean, at that moment, who could say? As they broke through the clouds they got their first sight of England. It was a typical Summer's day - it was pissing down. Elgin started to ponder; *How the fuck has this all come about?*

Profound words indeed.

* * * *

CHAPTER FOUR

Dumped!

Elgin was born in the same year as the Munich Air Disaster - in 1958. He popped out in right good style on the 12th December, just in time for his Christmas presents. He was the eldest of three children born to Dennis and Edith Hounds. His brother Ivan followed two years later and baby sister Angie turned up last but not least five years after Ivan. His parents had been childhood sweethearts and married soon after his dad came back from fighting in the Korean War. Elgin knew from the very few occasions he mentioned it, that he'd seen some pretty horrific sights out there - the conditions by all accounts were atrocious. He was involved in some vicious hand-to-hand fighting at times and had lost more than a few mates out there to the 'red horde'. That was enough to mentally scar any man, but Dennis was a tough customer who could readily take his knocks.

By the time Elgin turned up, his dad was sailing on calmer waters. He was working as a factory hand. He was obviously thriving in a much less frenetic occupation, but he still kept his wits about him as he passed the Chinese chip shop walking home from work. Mother Edith was working at the local Royal Mail Sorting Office. They were a normal couple working hard and were ready to start a family.

They all lived at 257 Sandon Road in the county town of Stafford in Staffordshire. The numbers 2, 5 and 7 coincidently were the same as the siblings' ages when the parents broke up. Elgin had little or no recollection of living in a large post-war semi-detached house on the Northern outskirts of the town - in fact his first vivid memory was the day his mother left his dad - a traumatic thing for a young kid of seven to take.

It all began when Edith told Elgin and Ivan they could have a day off school - music to any kid's ears. She said they were all going on holiday (not dad though, someone should have smelled a rat). The boys were well excited, but little two-year-old Angie was non-committal - she just went with the flow. They took a thirty-minute drive down to 'Silver Trees', a modest holiday park of a dozen or so chalets and a few caravans in the middle of the sprawling woods of Cannock Chase. Elgin clocked this as a tad unusual because they normally went to sunny Ramsgate on the Kentish coast - a jaunt that took the best part of a day to get there. Underwhelmed wasn't the word, but all was revealed minutes after they disembarked. It was going to be the first time they met 'Uncle Charlie'. The three kids were too young to fathom out what was going on, but they were out of school, free and on the loose.

Telephones were not a common commodity in the mid-1960s, so not to be in contact with their dad never entered the young boys minds. Elgin nearly gave his mother a heart attack though when she intercepted a postcard he'd bought from the site shop and innocently wrote on the back of it, 'Hello dad, this is where we are staying, love Elgin xx.' It was safe to say that it never got posted. Somehow, that piece of incriminating evidence turned up fully intact many years later in his father's possessions when he died in 1994. It is amazing to think that the postcard meant such a lot to his dad and is a really touching spin-off at a really bittersweet moment.

How long they were there and what they did is lost in the murkiness of a child's memory, but one incident Elgin remembers vividly was little Angie falling in the swimming pool and Charlie managing to pull her out - he will always be grateful for that. Events then took a turn for the worse. Elgin has never been able to work out the reasons for his mother's actions - why she did what she did - but suffice to say, no child should have experienced the mental turmoil that they all went through.

Unbeknown to the youngsters Charlie was sent to prison. It was not entirely clear what the circumstances were at the time, but years later, Elgin's gran on his mother's side said it was for driving offences, but his dad always maintained it was for embezzlement. Charlie actually worked at the sorting office with Edith, so he could well have been *half-inching* postal orders, credit cards or parcels - that sounds a lot more convincing than driving offences which very rarely meant a custodial sentence unless you killed someone under the influence.

Elgin reckoned that Charlie was purloining so he and his mother could amass enough money for a cunning swerve to some place further away where Dennis couldn't find them (Elgin witnessed the reason they wanted to 'do one' a little while later). So, with Charlie banged up Elgin's mother decided to... err... well, dump him and his brother at their grandparents' home.

She booked a taxi and they drove to a street where she pointed to a house, told them to jump out and knock on the door - no goodbyes, no nothing. There was no one in so Elgin turned round only to see that the cab had driven off. The rain was pouring down so the two brothers sat on their cases in the porch nonplussed as to what was happening.

Edith, the mother, has had little contact since and none on her own initiative. Even today Elgin doesn't know if she is alive or dead and he doesn't really care, but what comes out of this sad episode is terrible parenting skills and a perverse desire to put a relationship with another man in front of the upbringing of your own flesh and blood. The sad thing is this sort of behaviour is not a rare isolated incident, it has become a lot more prevalent over the last fifty years in a fragmenting society.

Elgin to his credit doesn't apportion blame either way as far as the divorce was concerned, he wouldn't imagine his dad had been an easy man to live with, but what has puzzled him ever since is what could a seven- and five-year-old have done to warrant that at such an early age. It must have affected him growing up psychologically to some degree, because he's never trusted a woman who voluntarily leaves the full time care of her offspring to someone else. It's a controversial subject, but Elgin opines that he has rarely been proven wrong. The most positive thing to come out of the marital schism is that Elgin would never blame the rejection if he had fucked up his adult life. Too many people use this scenario as a convenient crutch for a reason to fail. The do-gooders out there will always give you an excuse to flunk out; "What chance did they have with one parent? Aw, poor them."

Total bollocks. It should make you much stronger. Anyone unhappy about how their life has turned out, look in the mirror for there lies your answer. The politically correct liberal elite now rule the roost. 'Snowflakes' are the new norm, spawning a generation of spoiled and indulged wannabes who don't understand the word 'no'. The poor live in the real world of ours, people who try and strive will succeed.

Eventually gran turned up and the boys were over the moon to see her. She was laden with shopping bags so they ran out to help her carry them in. There was good news at last and she said, "Your dad's here as well." It didn't come any better than that. Inside, she dried the boys off in front of the fire. She was anxious to know the whole story. Elgin could tell she was very disappointed with what she heard. As she made them dripping on toast with two hot steaming cups of *Rosie Lee*, Elgin caught her wiping tears from her eyes with a hankie. The boys loved their gran and she loved them too. For the time being at least, they had stability in their lives.

Home was now *The Rockeries*, a cottage on a private road that overlooked the rolling fields at the back. It all sounded grandiose, but in reality it was just old servants' quarters that had once belonged to the big house at the end of the road, a sort of 'upstairs downstairs' on the same level. Elgin was extremely happy living there, especially as gran was one of the best cooks he had ever known.

The highlight of the week was always on a Saturday, when dad and grandad used to take Elgin and Ivan to Molineux to see the mighty Wolves (Wolverhampton Wanderers). All four of them were fanatics - Elgin still is. If they were playing too far from home, they'd go to watch their second favourite team, Wolves Reserves. These were the days before all-seater stadiums. The young boys used to have to stand on boxes their dad had made just to watch the game. The atmosphere for the boys was just magical with 30,000 supporters all chanting for their team.

Apparently Elgin went to Molineux even before he was born. His gran told him Dennis had taken his eight-month-pregnant mother to the match only to find they were locked out, so he made her climb over a turnstile with him to get in. Who says romance has died out? These were the glory days when every game was a sell out. Grandad never used to tire of telling stories about the time all of the England half-back line (midfield) was entirely made up of Wolves players. He would reel off the names of all the great players: Billy Wright, Ron Flowers, Jesse Pye and Johnny Hancocks who had won major honours like the Football League Championship and FA cup.

By the time Elgin started to go solo, Wolves were in decline and looking to emulate some of the past success, but like all good football fans you stick with your team through good times and bad. It made little difference to him as he still had his contemporary heroes, Dougan, Richards, Knowles and Wagstaffe, all excellent players who would be worth a fortune in today's money-crazed game.

That first Christmas at his grandparents was the time Elgin got his best ever present - a Wolves shirt. This was long before the wearing of your club colours on the terraces became fashionable. No one else in Stafford had got one, not even Nicky who lived in the big house down the street. He never took it off. All of his spare time involved kicking a football on both grass and concrete. The shirt was responsible for Elgin's nickname of 'Ozzy'. It had gradually changed from 'Orangey' over a period of months (Wolves shirts were old gold in colour) and stuck for life. When he was in the army some officers called him 'Ozzy' instead of 'Hounds'. His brother was and still is referred to as 'Little Oz' by some people.

Around this time something quite significant happened, but didn't seem so at the time. Elgin was about eight when he decided he wanted to go home early from school one day. So he hatched a plan, telling the teacher he had a doctor's appointment. He was let out of school and went home. He told his gran he'd been sent home because he felt ill, but she was better than Columbo and she rang the school and got the truth. The incident was blamed on his mother leaving suddenly, but it had nothing to do with that, he just simply wanted a day off. He had pulled his first stroke, but more importantly he learned from his initial mistake and wouldn't let anyone catch him out so easily again.

They periodically saw their sister Angie when Dennis brought her home for the occasional weekend. On one of these pick-ups the boys saw another side to their father they hadn't encountered before. They used to go with him down to Cannock Bus Station to collect Angie. One day Dennis clocked Charlie sitting in his car - he must have just got out of the nick - so Dennis went over to give him a coming out present. He dragged him kicking and screaming through the open driver's side window and knocked him senseless all around the bus station. It must have been months of pent-up frustration and aggression exploding outwards in one almighty blow-up.

It was pay-back time for all the shit he had gone through when Elgin's mother had done a runner and took the kids away. The fact he wouldn't have had a scooby of where they were or if they were even safe were obvious factors in his reactions. It had frightened the boys at that moment, but as time went on and Elgin began to understand the circumstances behind the ferocity of the attack, he quickly realised why people didn't take fucking liberties with his old man.

About 18 months after the boys moved into *The Rockeries* their dad met a woman named Eileen who would become their step mum. She was a schoolteacher from Stoke who already had a son of her own Andrew. He was about four years older than Elgin. The parents became inseparable, they were actually together right up to the time when Dennis died. Every Friday he would pick the boys up from school and dash over to Stoke for the weekend. They even had to eat their tea in the car as he was an eager beaver to get over there as fast as possible. It was a great adventure for the boys who had been left to their own devices most weekends previously. To be fair they hadn't been any trouble or got into any mither up until then. That was all about to change dramatically when they started knocking about with the boy about town, Andrew. He was older but definitely not wiser.

The first scrape they got into was shoplifting. Andrew was appalled to see the boys about to buy sweets with their pocket money. After he asked them what they wanted, he proceeded to casually snaffle it all into his pockets before buying a penny chew and walking out. He was quickly followed by his two new open-mouthed apprentices. At that moment he was the Mr Big of the chocolate stall. "OK lads we can go to the pictures this afternoon now," he said with a smug look on his face like he'd just pulled off the Brink's-Mat bullion heist. The three amigos returned to the flat for their lunch - mum was the word, loose lips sink ships, the best laid plans of mice and men oft go astray... Well, guess what? They did here, thanks to a dozy pillock named Ivan.

Lunch was served and as they waited for dessert Ivan let it slip that they were off to the pictures afterwards. Why would he announce that? Dennis was on it like a Bengal Tiger, "If you spent your money on sweets, how come you have some left for the cinema"?

Andrew came up with some nonsense about finding some money on the pavement, but that didn't ring true at all, so Dennis went for the weakest link - Ivan, aka the world origami champion (he was great at folding under pressure). Not only did he come straight out about the shop saga, but he also blamed it all on the two other boys. It was a sign of things to come from Ivan. Elgin wished he had taken notice of the hard lesson that day, it would have saved him an awful lot of money and aggro in the future.
It can be costly sometimes to keep giving people the benefit of the doubt.

Dad grounded them for the rest of the week and, not only that, they were all locked into the shared bedroom as well. Andrew was nominated head of the Colditz escape committee. He went for the classic three bed sheets tied to the bed leg liberation method - always a winner that one. Five minutes later they were out about and at large. On finding a large bag of what looked like flour, they decided it would look good on the neighbour's tortoiseshell cat. Unfortunately it turned out to be quick lime. Oops! They honestly didn't know. Kids of that age do stupid things, but thankfully the cat only suffered minor burns to it's skin, but it was enough to get them a debut taxi ride home in a police car.

Eileen answered the door, she hadn't even realised the boys had done a bunk. Dennis was seething. Elgin was sure they were going to get a good hiding, but a scolding was the maximum that was dished out. This was only the prelude though to the regular sessions of tanned backsides. They'd all swallowed their naughty pills and it was going to take more than a stomach pump to extricate them. They were on a roll and the jolly japes just got larger and larger. *Spare the rod and spoil the child* has never been more apt, but even the notion of bigger and harder wallopings couldn't stop the wild bunch. They were on a mission to *Misbehaviour City*.

The weekend after, the police were rattling the front door again. They were putting the Jehovah's Witnesses to shame. There was a big search going on for a missing child; *No officer, we haven't seen him!* (Of course they hadn't). Andrew had put one of the younger kids down a manhole. The crux of the plan was that he then crawls along the storm drains and emerges out at the brook. But unsurprisingly he stayed exactly where he was dumped. They returned and swore him to secrecy before letting him out. He grassed straight away, and so it was back to Camp Colditz for some more corporal punishment. The Hounds' were guilty by association. It was a life lesson for Elgin, and he was to find out a lot later that it wasn't just your concerned parents who lock you away without properly investigating the matter either.

They didn't always have to go out to cause mischief. Eileen and Dennis were out shopping one day and the boys had clocked a big box of fireworks secreted away on top of a double wardrobe. Bonfire Night the week after seemed a long way off, so it probably wouldn't hurt to ignite a few while they waited. Andrew smoked so they had a box of Swan Vesta matches which was all that was needed to get them another lacing. They didn't really think it through, and it was all over after the first jumping jacks burnt Eileen's new carpet. Dennis didn't disappoint, his consistency was one of his painful strong points. Let's say it was a good job they left the rockets in the box!

Probably the worst thing the trio ever did was on holiday at Ramsgate, and this occurrence scared Eileen to death. They had decided to clamber up a sheer cliff face, Chris Bonington-style. It was crazy really, one loose step or poor hand grip and the resultant fall would have been fatal, as the rocks at the bottom really didn't look very inviting at all. Thankfully they made it to the top where mum, dad and the omnipresent police were waiting to greet them. Elgin's parents were trying to build a fledgling relationship under this sort of duress. But eventually they did and a strong and unbreakable bond it was too.

The inevitable happened, Dennis and Eileen got married, and soon they bought a house in Rowley Street, Stafford. It was a smart terraced abode that backed onto a new council estate. Andrew was now old enough to leave primary school and go to Trinity Fields Comprehensive. Ivan and Elgin started at the John Wheeldon Primary Church of England School which was on Corporation Street and universally known as 'Corpo'. Not half a mile away was the Roman Catholic School, St Patrick's, seat of learning of Micky O'Rourke (me, myself, who will be flitting in and out of Elgin's life throughout the book).

In Elgin's first year, he finished top of the class. He says he cheated because when he was asked to write a story, he just copied one he'd read earlier and his essay gave him the edge over another pupil called Ian Henderson who was vying for first place. There's nothing wrong with plagiarism - especially if you don't get caught. Always try to get an edge in life, it will take you a long way. Elgin got weighed in with ten bob (ten shillings - or now, 50p) - a nice amount then - from his father. What a result!

Events were happening at a rapid rate. Andrew wasn't destined to live under the happy Hounds' roof much longer. He was about fourteen at the time. Mum and dad suspected he was hiding a secret, but they couldn't put their finger on it. Andrew was up to something alright, all the way up to his nuts. Dennis followed him from school one afternoon and caught him *in flagrante* with a bloke of about 35. He did his considerate stepfatherly thing and smashed the dirty bastard to bits. But Andrew had a go at him, saying that he loved the guy. He was shipped back to Stoke to live with his real dad. That was for the best for all involved. Elgin's boyhood hero had now flopped down to zero, they didn't see much of him after that. It was quite remarkable that years later he got married and had children. Peoples' sexuality is a complex subject, especially these days when both the sexes are under threat from gender neutral and transgender *believers*.

The world's gone mad.

The very last time Elgin saw him was after his dad died. He hadn't been in contact with the family for many years. Elgin thought now would be an ideal time for him to rebuild a relationship with his mother as she was her only child. He tracked him down to a shithole in Reading. He relayed to him that his mother had moved to Spain seven years ago, but was now isolated, living on her own and struggling to cope - not financially in a larger sense, but with the everyday mundane things like paying utility bills and such. Elgin's dad had done everything for her previously so she could relax and enjoy her life in Spain, but now he had gone some company would help her greatly. Andrew made some excuse about not being able to afford to go, so Elgin told him he was going over in a few days and he would pay his passage and expenses. You couldn't get fairer than that. He refused to countenance it again, so Elgin walked out in disgust. No one ever heard from him again, so it was good riddance to bad rubbish.

It would have been a great fillip if Elgin's behaviour had improved after Andrew was jettisoned off to 'The Potteries' (this is the industrial area encompassing the six towns of Burslem, Fenton, Hanley, Longton, Stoke and Tunstall, which is now the 'City of Stoke-on-Trent'). He initially showed some promise - but it was the lull before the lightning storm. He was still playing football right up to leaving for senior school where he found there was more fun to be had indulging in some extra-curricular activities. A whole new world opened up for him. He started to hang around with a different crowd.

His two best mates were John Morrissey and Paul Sandford; the latter was a bit of a hard case and had just moved up from London. John had three brothers, Steve, Neil and Danny who formed part of the so-called *Stafford Posse*. At that precise moment who would have thought one of that bunch of six ne'er-do-wells would go on to international fame and fortune. Amazingly, he came through after being at the bottom of the layer cake as well.

Neil Morrissey went on to appear in the 1984 film *The Bounty* starring Mel Gibson and Anthony Hopkins. He played 'Rocky the Biker' in the TV series *Boon* with Michael Elphick and 'Tony' in *Men Behaving Badly*, but his most lucrative role was surely being the voice of 'Bob The Builder' for donkey's years.

His early life hadn't looked so promising. He was taken into care after breaking into the local Women's Institute. In hindsight, probably the best thing that could have happened to him was getting out of Stafford. He attended three Stoke Theatre Schools and also was taken in by a foster family. If Elgin's mob would have found out they'd have given him serious grief for doing something so sissy.

Today he has a pub near Stafford, *The Plume of Feathers* in Barlaston and was the former owner until recently of *The Old Bramshall Inn* in the quaint village near Uttoxeter where Elgin actually lived for a while. Even Neil has had his ups and downs over the years, but best of luck to him in the future, he has earned it.

The gang used congregate round at the Morrissey residence every Tuesday, Thursday and Saturday night. The parents both nurses at the local psychiatric hospital would be out socialising. The house wasn't the most salubrious in the area, there was chip pan fat all over the cooker, clothes strewn everywhere and nicotine stains on the ceiling. Elgin never saw a hoover, but it probably had mud flaps on it. Hey, what did they care? Laurence Llewelyn-Bowen was unlikely to turn up for an episode of *Changing Rooms*, so it was their little club house and it was a lot better than freezing your bollocks off on a street corner. This was the location of where Elgin got his first ever tattoo - he was 13 or 14. Somebody brought in some needles and a bottle of Indian Ink. They all decided to have *a Simon Templar (1960s* TV's 'The Saint') motif tattooed on their arms. Once it had all been committee-approved there was no going back. They were all as thick as shit in those days.

Dennis clocked Elgin's 'artwork' a few days later. He went bloody ballistic and hit the roof. How was he to know his dad couldn't stand the sight of Roger Moore! This growing up lark was a steep learning curve. Every now and then you'd tread on a dog turd. Successes were few and far between, but Elgin was a quick learner. Every mistake was 'money in the bank', each an experience of what not to do again.

It would all come good in the long run - he was getting a real taste for *wonga*.

Steve Morrissey was a sound fella, his life appeared to be the antithesis of what his brother Neil had gone though, but he looked like he was going to be a success in whatever he did. Years later, him and Elgin would go out drinking down town on the pull together. After leaving school he worked as a life guard at the local Riverside leisure centre before going on to marry a real nice girl, but sadly it never went on from there. Soon, drug-taking reared its ugly head, and the two pals gradually drifted apart. Steve had started smoking *puff* - nothing wrong with that if it's a recreational sort of smoke, but he went along an escalating path of stronger and even deadlier narcotics. Elgin actually heard that he was self-injecting lighter fuel in prison. That couldn't have been be a good idea. He was sad to hear of his demise, but he was helpless to intervene.

The last time he saw him was in 1991 when out of the blue he suddenly turned up at Elgin's double glazing unit, which was just over the road from where they used to live as kids. He was only a shadow of the man he used to be - he stood there in a shocking state, emaciated and sallow and on top of that, he was incoherent. He'd been ravaged by self-administered chemicals. Steve offered to sweep up for a tenner, but Elgin gave him a *pony* (£25) and told him, "Forget the sweeping and get some food." And with that - he was gone. A few years later he was found dead in a grotty flat. He'd been there some time, and no one had missed him. It was inevitable really; a sad lonely end, the needle and the damage done. RIP Steve Morrissey.

Just after the tattooing debacle, three of them joined the army cadets. They had some fantastic weekends away together and it became the beginning of a love affair for Elgin that's still ongoing today - namely cooking. He went on a week-long cookery course with Paul Sandford and his brother Ivan, courtesy of the Army Catering Corps at an army base in Donnington near Telford in Shropshire.

They all had a great week, cooking by day and drinking in the NAAFI at night. Elgin was sold. From that moment on all he wanted to be was an army chef. Back home they would all walk down to the army cadets building - Kitchener House - on two nights a week, but on the way back home the old bad habits were still a strong magnetic attraction away from their more sensible side. They would stop at the St Georges Social Club and creep round the back where they found they could put a screwdriver in the valve of a beer barrel and pour it into a jug they kept nearby.

This got Elgin pondering. They needed to find a pub or club that kept bottles outside as well, that way they could take them away and drink them later. Hardly the crime of the century, but a nice piece of lateral thinking. The beer bottle investigation hunt was on! They came across a hotel called *The Turnpike* which kept all its barrels and bottles locked up at the back of the premises. *There was a God.* The only thing keeping the fox from the hens was a small combination lock which was cracked in less than twenty minutes. At this stage Elgin showed his undoubted leadership skills which would stand him in good stead for the rest of his life. As Yogi used to say, "Smarter than the average bear!"

Most young teenagers would have half-inched the lot, but Elgin said, "The combination must be kept secret, when we have drunk a few bottles each, return them to the crates so as not to raise suspicion. Hopefully the hotel management will not miss the few taken. If we don't take the piss we can return here week after week and nobody will be any the wiser."

Forget about The Gettysburg Address, there wasn't many about Stafford with a head on their shoulders like that. Although he wasn't academically brilliant, Elgin had something you can't teach. You are born with it either - he was STREET WISE. As sharp as a tack. He'd now begun to leave his past errors behind him. He'd still make the odd cock-up here and there, and he was certainly no angel, but his star was definitely on the rise. This was his first personally-conceived business, venture. They stopped drinking the beer and started selling bottles of Double Diamond at school along with jars of sweets that mysteriously went missing from Mr Swinson's shop, and also cigarettes from Old Man Preece's shop on the A34.

The teenage black market had come to Stafford.

They never got caught because they were meticulous about picking up and taking away all the empty bottles and sweet wrappers. Most kids would have left a pile of dubious-looking and possibly incriminating litter. By this time Elgin had realised the work ethic could also bring financial rewards, he started a window cleaning round and also worked part time at Fowell's Butchers.

A roving eye was still being maintained on the quest for pubs with rear bottle stores. A foray by John Morrissey into the back of *The Cottage by the Brook* on Peel Terrace opened up another money stream. Initially he shouted back over the wall, "Nothing here lads, just a load of crates of empty pop bottles." Paul told him to come back, but Elgin shouted, "NO, pass them over!" This was a time that pre-dated recycling and 99% of pop bottles were refundable when you returned them to shops or pubs. A lot of inns had an off-license on the premises in those days. It was *winner winner chicken dinner*! As long as not too many bottles went back to each shop, you simply took from the back and got paid out the front... *simples*.

The boys had a good format, they always split the money equally three ways. Paul was the 'enforcer' - he made sure they didn't get ripped off or had anyone move in on their scams. Elgin was the 'ideas man' - always on the lookout for bigger and better dodges, and John was *Raffles the Cat*-like - a bold and fearless stock-mover. Together, they really were a formidable team of brawn, brain and stealth.

Elgin's 'big earner' was his egg round. He used to buy eggs wholesale and sell them as free range, delivering them on his butcher's bike. He was on a roll, but a woman had his pants down on one occasion. It was an experience he would come across many times in the future as a salesman. There is an expression in the sales game called 'BUYERS ARE LIARS'.

The respectable lady told him that one of last week's eggs had a dead chick in it. Now the hens that laid these eggs had never seen daylight let alone Foghorn Leghorn the cockerel. He begrudgingly gave her half a dozen eggs as goodwill gesture. He knew she was trying it on, but as he was selling them as free range he yielded. Who says you can't con a conner.

School was now actually getting in the way of all the free market enterprise. The boys would turn up for assembly - it was Groundhog Day each and every morning - and Mr Procter, the deputy head would call out, "Hounds, Morrissey, Sandford, in my office after assembly." They knew what was coming, but they were always well prepared. They'd be in deep shit for one reason or another and these were the days of corporal punishment where the short, sharp, shock of rattan against flesh was the ultimate deterrent. The boys would have numerous pairs of underpants and tracksuit bottoms on under their trousers. John even had a copy of the famous boys' comic, *The Hotspur* down there one day. Procter seemed to get a cheap thrill out of it all. It's odds-on that the pervy bleeder would have probably visited ladies of ill-repute after school to have his ample botty spanked and pay for the privilege. Compared to some private boarding schools though, the boys would have got off lightly. There were some evil bastards about in the education system at that time and atrocities are still coming to light, but many were hushed up.

After they had had their daily beating, they would get marked in for attendance on the register and, later on the morning break, knock out all their ill-gotten gains to a crowd of willing buyers. Forget about Alan Sugar or Branson, these lads were naturals! Once all the merchandise was distributed they would be away to Paul Sandford's house as both his mum and dad were full time workers so they had the run of the home. Even if his parents had discovered they were skiving there wouldn't have been a scream up as they were lovely people with Paul seemingly being able to do anything he pretty well wanted.

With an abundance of contraband and spare cash, Paul and Elgin started to attract some female attention (John struggled in that department, sorry mate, you've either got it or you haven't, but last time Elgin saw him recently, he was happily married. There's someone out there for everyone).

Elgin started to go out with a girl called Denise Godwin and, just to make it cosy, Paul was dating her mate, Sue Baker. Denise was Elgin's first proper girlfriend. She was good fun and they were together for about twelve months which is quite a long time for a fourteen-year-old. He bumped into her again in a pub by chance in the early nineties and they had a nice drink and a chat. She had married, had kids and still lived in the same street! People like conformity and continuity - and where better than home.

    Elgin had his heart set on joining the army, so his parents' relief was greater than the one at Mafeking. They had real concerns for his future as he had been an embarrassment with his troubles at school, notwithstanding that Eileen was a teacher herself. He spent his money on drinking, smoking and going out with girls... and just wasting the rest. What sort of life was that? (Don't answer!) Off he went to Harrogate Army Selection Centre. Mum and dad were over the moon. He spent the first few days taking aptitude tests, but it didn't all go to plan. They decided in their infinite wisdom after reviewing the results that Elgin's mathematics were not up to scratch. He wouldn't be baking any cakes in the Army Catering Corps. Here was his chance to serve Queen and country in his chosen corps, The Royal Engineers.

    It was a curious arrangement by all accounts. A few months later he was required to work out how much explosive was needed to blow up a steel girder bridge and estimate a safe distance away from the volatile material. This took hours of calculations - a bit ironic that the test panel hadn't considered his maths to be of a standard to weigh out a pound of flour. But maybe they had too many cooks. The bottom line was he was all set to join up on the 6th of May 1975.

    Elgin was set to leave school in the April, but at the onset of March the headmaster called six or seven *desperados*, rascals, rogues and vagabonds into his office and he made them all an offer they couldn't refuse. *Leave right now and don't set foot onto the school property again.* They obviously didn't want any drama in the last knockings of the school term... they knew it made sense.

    That freed up Elgin for a couple of months. He was legally entitled to take up some work and earn a few more bob before joining up, so he got a job at *Jeff's* - a haberdashery outfit. He started in the basement selling carpets with two other lads. He'd only been there a short time before realising that moving on all the rugs and accessories out of the door was coming so easily to him. (no, he was selling these items, they weren't walking out the building after hours!) Every customer he cornered was leaving with something under his arm... and a lighter wallet. He enjoyed it that much that he seriously considered staying there and giving the army the *bum's rush* as he was earning a nice few quid and improving his selling technique daily.

    He broke the news of his latest plans to his dad. The look of horror on

Dennis's boat race didn't bode well for a career in the textile flooring industry. He vowed that if Elgin didn't join up he would raise his weekly board and lodgings up to a level that a young member of the Rothschild family would struggle to pay in instalments. Elgin couldn't blame him as he wouldn't have wanted someone like himself living there either. So, it was time to move on. Next stop would be the Old Park Barracks in Dover.

He was still a young guy and unsure of where his destiny lay.

* * * *

CHAPTER FIVE

The Lost Years

Before joining up and failing dismally to measure up to former military stalwarts like Field Marshals Kitchener and Montgomery, Elgin needed to set the record straight about the absence of sister Angie throughout his teenage years. It was like a bad dream that manifested into a cruel, dark nightmare. For the first few years after the divorce, relationships were pretty normal. Angie would regularly visit, brought there by her mother. This arrangement carried on until she was about four, then without any prior warning the visits ceased.

Charlie and Edith had moved down to Essex. The logistics of bringing Angie all the way up to Staffordshire must have been a factor in the no-shows, plus it was doubtful Charlie would want to bump into Dennis again any time soon as he was still licking his wounds from their last encounter. It was the classic situation of 'out of sight out of mind' - long term detachment was going to be the order of the day.

Late one Friday night Elgin fell out of a club drunk as a skunk. He would have been about 17 at the time and on leave from the army. It's a strange phenomenon when a belly full of beer makes you a lot more philosophical than Jean-Paul Sartre. He needed to know and he needed to know right there and then why his own mother didn't want to see him anymore. He deftly persuaded his drinking partner, the equally inebriated Mickey Beardmore, to join him on his heroic quest into the heartlands of Essex to seek restitution.

They boarded the 3am train down to London. It wasn't long before Mickey fell upon a guy drinking a large bottle of rum. The three imbibers soon got chatting away and the rum bottle danced a merry jig between the trio's appreciative quaffing, but it sadly ran out long before they pulled into Euston Station. They poured off the train and eventually made their way to an enchanting merchant seaman's club somewhere in the East End, wherein they had another good session, before crawling onto another train to Billericay, just in time for the local pubs to be opening. Of course it would have been remiss not to sample a few more pints of *Watney's Red Barrel*.

The deadly duo turned up at Elgin's mother's at about 4pm three sheets to the wind, taking three steps forwards, one sidewards and two back. They managed to negotiate the tricky garden path and in due course rattled the front door knocker. For obvious reasons, Elgin has little recollection of what took place that afternoon, but through the alcoholic mist and beer goggles he seems to recall his mother pleading with him not to tell his sister who he was. She couldn't get rid of them quickly enough and after making them dinner, took them back down the station, promising to straighten everything out. It was an unsatisfactory result all round.

By Sunday Elgin had sobered up and told his dad the 'full SP', who then went for broke on the dog and bone to Edith, giving her an ultimatum, "If you don't agree about stopping the maintenance payments, I'm coming down today with the boys to let Angie know the whole story."

She immediately ceded, so really the only thing achieved was that his dad saved himself a good few quid. But Elgin was even more confused than before. Whenever he brought the subject up his dad would always say that his sister probably thought Charlie was her dad and it would upset her to find out the truth, so Elgin sensibly pushed the muddle to the back of his mind. He had enough pressing problems of his own without all the banal amateur dramatics playing out.

His dad never saw Angie again.

In hindsight, it could have been resolved so much better, but relationships don't always end hunky dory.

Just after Lotte, Elgin's second daughter, was born in 1990 (he would have been about 32 at this juncture), his younger brother Ivan reappeared. He hadn't been sighted for many a good year - in fact the only occasion he would make contact was when he was *brassic lint*, so it didn't bode favourably that his luck had changed and he was about to spread his new found wealth amongst his loved ones. No, true to form he was utterly potless again. But while he was around he would at least come in useful as back up - for Elgin wanted another crack at seeing his sister again.

This time, they went down four-handed; Elgin and his partner at the time, Lucy, (she comes into her own later on) Ivan and Trish, (his wife). Destination: Halstead in Essex. Charlie and Edith worked on Lord Butler's estate, a huge 1,500-acre arable farm where he was the handyman and she worked in the kitchens. They soon located Charlie. Elgin told him he wanted another talk with his mother and they weren't going away without some dialogue. Charlie locked the door behind him. He'd take them to where she was. Edith was actually working in a local restaurant that lunchtime, so they jumped in their car and followed Charlie's motor to the eatery.

She was serving behind the bar. Her face turned a deathly pale when Elgin strode in, just like she had seen a ghost. After gaining her composure she suggested they all go upstairs where they could talk in private. Elgin laid it on the line, stating he wasn't interested in a relationship with her because she most evidently didn't give a toss, but he would like to rekindle the past contact with his only sister. He demanded that she return home and tell Angie the whole truth or he would come round himself and do it. She nodded in agreement and said to call round the house at 3pm after she'd finished work. Elgin and Ivan were pleasantly surprised that the family could be reunited so easily after all the years apart. They all went round in a very optimistic mood and spent a couple of hours making small talk allied with some friendly chit-chat with everyone promising to keep in touch from thereon in.

When it was time to leave Elgin felt something still wasn't quite right. He suspected his mother of somehow playing a flanker... maybe telling Angie beforehand that it was her cousins that were visiting.

But events took a turn for the worst after that visit.

Not too long after the last attempt to reconsolidate, Elgin's gran (Edith's mum) died. She had been the only remaining direct link to his mother and sister. They didn't even find out until three weeks after the event when Lucy's mum saw the memorial in the local rag announcing the death with the funeral being held in Essex. Elgin tried desperately to contact his mother on the phone, but the number was never working and two handwritten letters were returned - "Not at this Address." He was clearly flogging a dead horse. It was absolutely pointless carrying on, so he decided enough was enough. He was morphing into a bitter and twisted man, and therefore he reluctantly severed all ties.

So back to the main story... Elgin joined the army on the sixth of May as arranged, but with the biggest hangover in Western Europe. So nothing new there! He thoroughly enjoyed his first three months, loving all the training and soldiering. It was all coming so easily to him - like taking strawberries off a donkey, with the added bonus of sporting opportunities at which he excelled.

From thereon he was rarely in uniform as his tracksuit was the apparel of the day and as great as the life was, he began to get disenchanted after observing how some of his older mates in their thirties seemed to be just going through the motions. The army does everything for you; thinkers and non-conformists are anathema to it, so Elgin started to look for a way to bail out. He didn't want to turn out like a lot of the others; he realised there must be more to life than that. He'd had a great time and made good friends, but after 18 months he'd had his fill of it. He could have coasted the next twenty years, but it just wasn't his style.

He tried one final futile attempt to join the Army Catering Corps again, but after getting another knock back, he decided to go AWOL (Absent Without Leave,) to "work his ticket." The notion was to stay absent for over 28 days which would escalate the charge up to desertion which would then result in serving a short jail term followed by the obligatory army discharge. Little did he know that he'd taken a flawed course of action, he had over-elaborated and would soon pay the price for it.

Whilst Elgin was away on his unofficial holiday, a new commanding officer had taken over and brought with him his new broom to sweep clean any unwanted detritus. He wanted changes and he wanted them from day one. The man in question was Colonel John Blashford-Snell, the world-famous military man and explorer. He was handing out discharges like confetti to anyone who didn't want to be there. It was just Elgin's luck though - he could have walked straight out of the gates if he had only stayed around instead of bumming about for a month, getting drunk and turning into the pub bore. It would have fallen right into to his lap.

With time duly served away from the barracks, he handed himself in at Stafford Police Station. It was a fair cop. He was whisked back to receive his 28 days detention and then a discharge. He could do the time standing on his head. All he needed was peace and solitude. It was going swimmingly until he had an unexpected visitor, it was the *Big Cheese* himself, Blashford-Snell. He tried to talk Elgin out of leaving. He told him he was a very useful soldier and offered him a proposal. "I'm in the process of organising an expedition to Ethiopia in the near future and I need a good fellow to take care of the pack mules. What say you, Hounds ?"

What a truly brilliant incentive that was to stay - clearing up donkey dung in torturous heat. Mindful of the fact he could get a good few extra days for saying what he was really thinking - even a euphemistic, "Sod off, you dozy twat," might be pushing it. He politely declined the offer saying his mind was made up. The C.O. trudged out disappointedly. His trans-African safari would need a new shovel man. Elgin was going home, and so Addis Ababa, the insufferable heat and the millions of flies would simply have to do without him.

On his return, his father was mortified to find out he was back in mufti. Dennis was utterly convinced Elgin's exit was the catalyst for big trouble. He couldn't understand that he wanted a lot more out of his life and refused to let him return to live in his house. Well, thanks for nothing! Elgin now knew exactly where he stood. Thankfully his grandparents welcomed him back with open arms. In fact they couldn't hide their disgust of what Dennis had done, but these little things do make you stronger.

The first job to fall in his lap was working as a trainee at *Dewhurst's* (the butchers) - not exactly what he had in mind, but adequate enough until he worked out what he was leaning towards new career-wise. He quite enjoyed it, if the truth was known, but the money was shite and the prospects were slimmer than an anorexic eel. He couldn't bring himself to do what the rest of the lads were getting up to either, that is nicking meat and selling it around town. He couldn't have looked old Mr Langford in the face. Elgin knew he wasn't Goody Two-Shoes, but these people were paying his wages. Since he had left school, he had never stolen off anyone that he worked for and he made a personal promise to himself never to do it in the future.

A short while after starting at *Dewhurst's* he met a really lovely girl called Helen Firkin. They started dating and before he knew it, they were engaged. Elgin needed to hunt around for a much better paid job and dropped onto a position at the *Venables Timber Yard* on Doxey Road in Stafford. Not only was it nearly twice the salary, but an added bonus was working with a great set of new workmates. He would have been about 19 at that time, the rest of the lads were early to mid-twenties, saving up for a house and getting married - all except 'The Wad' - Andy Wadham. He had his priorities right with beer, betting and pool.

Elgin got drawn into that comfortable mindset - he was beginning to think that this was the way, going out with the lads on a Friday night, taking Helen out on the Saturday and playing for the works football team on a crisp Sunday morning. It was a routine a lot of his colleagues lived to work for. After 18 months he thought he was contented, all about him were telling him he'd cracked it, he had a great job and a stunning girlfriend to boot. Although he enjoyed the close companionship of Paul Noddles, Baz Milgate, Terry and Josh, the Wallace brothers and of course 'The Wad', he still mused there was something missing. What it was, he didn't have a clue at the time. These feelings were never relayed to Helen.

Elgin worked overtime at night and at most weekends to earn some extra money, but it seemed to him he was knocking himself a lot out only to be able to save a little. What was it going to be like when he got married? Would it be like Baz Milgate's sorry situation? Baz was a really good bloke, but permanently skint. He didn't want to go down the same road as another workmate, Frank Duffy, an educated, articulate guy who was surreptitiously smuggling out materials under his employer's nose. He had dropped out of university and was working on the yard whilst looking for another job and, in the meantime, he was liaising with a lorry driver and, between them, timber had been slipping out the front gate for quite some time.

It was truly ironic that Frank landed a really good posting as a manager at *Applied Acoustics*, a subsidiary company, owned by *Venables*. They were giving him the whole shooting match, a massive wage rise, expenses, money to move to London and a company car. The day he was due to leave, he got caught. Whether he got grassed or the books were audited, nobody knew, but Elgin clearly remembers him crying outside the offices after he'd been sacked. He actually went on to great things - he later resigned as a managing director of *Dr Martens* the footwear people and bought into *Scholl Shoes*. No one's CV is ever pure and lily white.

Itchy fingers must run in his family though. Years later Elgin had a significant run-in with his younger brother Tim, who was on the take. The consequences of that misdemeanour would be a lot more serious than a few tears shed.

One Saturday dinner time sitting in *The Bear Inn*, a hostelry in Stafford town centre, Elgin got talking to another mate, John Jillings, a local brick layer who was on the lookout for a hard working labourer. He and his mate needed someone to mix the sand and cement throughout the day, the beauty of it was, the harder they all grafted the more they got paid, including the labourer. That sounded much more like it and against everyone's advice, Elgin packed up his job at Venny's.

The first job they all worked on was building Stafford's new police station and courthouse. The really funny thing about that was Elgin couldn't think of anyone that was working on that job who wasn't eventually locked up in the cells they helped to build. That was with the exception of John Jillings of course, who was real lucky, but that can't be brought up here - seeing as he became a screw at Stafford nick a few years later on. What would the governor have said!

Elgin was earning a fair bit more than he was while he was at *Venables* and John was a really great bloke to work for, but he was still bloody frustrated that something was missing. As Bono of U2 so succinctly crooned, "And I still haven't found what I'm looking for."

Friday evening was still lads night out. They used to have a well travelled pub crawl around the town. It would begin in *The Bear*, continue across the road in *The Swan*, then back over to the old *Sheridan*, then down to Mill Street for *The Nag's Head* before finishing off at the bottom of the town at *The Grapes*.

Yet Elgin was tiring of the same routine, seeing the same old faces in the same old places. He was getting frustrated with the tedium. He still turned up every Friday though. He even came out early this one evening, standing on his lonesome in *The Bear* waiting for all his mates to turn up, when he clocked someone he knew chatting to two nice looking girls. Although this guy, Ashley, was a bit of a slimeball and not really a friend, there was nobody else to talk to, so he sidled over to where they were standing. Ashley introduced him to the girls, Philomena, the one he was sniffing around and Katrina, a tall attractive blonde. Now, Elgin and his Helen hadn't been getting on that well over the last few months and bumping into the very delectable Katrina wasn't going to improve it any.

It was lust at first sight. Who said romance was dead? It was also the start of a relationship that would produce a truly wonderful daughter and a not so wonderful son.

Things were starting to heat up.

* * * *

CHAPTER SIX

Into The Damp Game

Katrina turned out to be married - not happily - and on the verge of splitting up from her husband. She actually left him about six weeks after meeting Elgin. His first priority was to break the bad news to his engaged-to girlfriend, Helen. He certainly hadn't covered himself in glory, but he felt it was best to make an early clean break, rather than get married with his head up his rear. They'd been together a couple of years, the wedding was booked and they were near to completing the purchase of a house. It was a pretty shabby state of affairs. He was ashamed to say his only real defence was that he was too young to commit after being swept along the route to matrimony. He was quite insensitive towards her feelings at the time, not realising the psychological shit he was putting her through. He met her many years later and apologised profusely. She was happily married to the butcher at *Sainsbury's* - a really nice bloke who thankfully became her knight in shining armour. A super result.

Elgin didn't know Katrina's husband, Paul, but they both had a lot of mutual friends that were caught up in the middle of it all, causing a bit of a kerfuffle in a town like Stafford where everyone knew each other's business. He felt no guilt of being with Paul's wife because she had told him of his errant behaviour towards her. A few years later he was older and wiser and realised there were always two sides to most stories. Paul was another guy he would meet years later and thankfully there were no hard feelings. He seemed a decent bloke on the face of it who, to be fair, hadn't done any disservice to Elgin - if anyone had been wronged, it was him.

After two months of courtship they made the move together to a small flat in Oxford Gardens. Yet, even early doors it wasn't a normal, loving, trusting relationship. For a start it wasn't monogamous; Katrina would see other blokes and Elgin would hitch up with different ladies. People they knew were only too willing to tell either party the salacious misdemeanours of the other. This would inevitably end up in a ferocious argument - classic tit for tat - but they always seemed to come to a hard-fought compromise and stay together... for that week at least.

They were both too young for a stable relationship. There wasn't a lot they had in common apart from a purely physical attraction for each other (That was when neither was 'playing away from home'). Elgin found Katrina attractive and seductive, while he was a smart looking 'Jack the Lad'-type character, the sort some women love - like the James Bond-style character, the 'Milk Tray Man' from the 70s and 80s *Cadbury's Dairy Milk* television adverts.

On the work front, Elgin was about to meet a man whose influence would totally change his life forever and it came right out of the blue. He was having a drink with his pals Richie Geoghan, Gappy Cookson and Ant Hancock in *The Bear* in Stafford, when Danny, one of the Morrissey brothers ambled in looking rather pleased with himself. He asked Elgin to change a £30 cheque for him (at this time if the payee endorsed the back of the cheque, it could be paid into any account). Elgin was curious to know what Danny had done to get it, and he was told 'canvassing'. Elgin was still nonplussed so he sought further clarification. Danny explained that after some initial training he'd gone out to 'knock on doors' asking any prospective house owner if they were interested in a free 'damp survey'. If he got a favourable response he'd then book an appointment for a 'surveyor' to come round post-haste. Elgin remarked, "That's not bad dough mate. £30 a week for just walking about?"

Danny, (who was actually jacking the job in) retorted, "No, Ozzy, that's not for a week... it's for an hour."

Elgin wasn't on a bad screw himself at the time - 50 sobs a week on the building site - how much could he earn if he applied himself to a week of canvassing he wondered? Danny gave Elgin the contact details. He was out of the door quicker than Billy Whizz! There was no time like the present. Procrastination was the thief of time in his eyes. He was putting business before pleasure that day.

He steadfastly rocked up to *The Albridge Hotel* on the Wolverhampton Road. He was looking for a guy called Kevan Murphy. The premises was called a hotel, but in reality *The Albridge* was a small, nondescript bed and breakfast in a row of terraced houses. One star might have been doing it a favour. Elgin soon located the 'Duke of Damp', informing him Danny had peaked and retired and he was interested in applying for the situation vacant. Kev duly filled him in on what was involved. It was more or less what Danny had said in his communication in *The Bear* - apart from the caveat at the end which decreed, 'Commission-only wages.' Elgin sought a lucid explanation for that term. It came back as. "If we don't sell, we don't eat."

Far from being downcast about the pay structure, it actually stirred Elgin up. He was never one to shirk a big challenge. Kev wanted to know when he could start. "How about this minute?" was the response. The new applicant was keen as mustard and very eager to learn the ropes. There were no flies on Ozzy.

Kev's first instruction was for him to nip out to the shops, buy some strong mints to mask his beer breath. On his return, he underwent an hour-long, crash course of training and was soon ready to 'start knocking'. Kevan suggested that he try his luck across the Wolverhampton Road where there were half a dozen side streets full of privately-owned terraced houses. He duly kicked off in New Garden Street. The first few doors who answered were met by a mumbling, bumbling novice, but as he progressed down the street he sharpened his 'pitch' up. He was fine-tuning it as he went along. Elgin wasn't the kind of person who worried about messing up his lines, his attitude was; *fuck it, I'm never going to see these people again, so just carry on.*

After knocking a score of doors, jackpot! Elgin got a 'lead' (an appointment). He was so excited that he exchanged friendly banter with the punter for about 15 minutes. He didn't know it at the time, but this was one of the cardinal rules of a salesman - creating a warm and receptive atmosphere is a huge part of selling any presentation and, amongst many other things, it installs a bond of trust.

The punter even asked if it was possible for Elgin to pop back when the surveyor came round. He told the guy that this wouldn't be a problem and sprinted back to *The Aldridge* to give Kev the good news. The main man was happy as Larry until Elgin added that the customer wanted him there as well. He was quite adamant at first, apparently canvassers never got to see what happened next, but he relented and took Elgin along for the ride. Maybe he saw great potential in him.

For the next hour and a half, Elgin was spellbound as Kev weaved his magic and signed the punter up for a damp proof course worth £500. He took a nice substantial 'dipper' (deposit) and soon it was all done and dusted. Elgin had never seen anything like it in his life. Only two hours ago the punter had been sitting in his house, unaware he was going to have a survey, buy a damp course, hand over a dipper and have all the work done the very next day. It was all very impressive.

Kev was an old shrewdie. Back at the hotel, he handed Elgin his commission - £30 in cash. He had obviously spotted the raw talent of the young bloke standing in front of him, and the prompt payment was an encouraging enticement to get him away from the building site. He explained to Elgin his company's procedures: they would blitzkrieg an area for two or three weeks, knocking each and every door. Stafford's turn was coming to an end and the company would be operating in Preston next week. He added, "You won't be able to go though will you because of your job?" Elgin smiled, "What job was that, Kev?" He was now officially in the damp game.

Over the next twelve months, Elgin worked as a canvasser and a very good one too. They would meet up in hotels, mainly in the North of England on Monday afternoons. There would be about 25 of them - fitters, canvassers, salesmen and the bosses. It all worked smoothly; the canvasser would take the lead and the salesman would come in after and sell it there and then. Never, ever was a quote left - it was either sold on the first visit or not at all. Then the fitters would install the job the next day. It was a well-oiled, mean machine, primed to make the optimum use of time and effort. Everything was accomplished in a double-quick way.

The merry band toured the country. In every town and city there was a chance to make more money and once you'd visited them all you went back to the places where you'd been two years earlier and started the whole process yet again: a never-ending circuit of opportunity. In a sense, it was very similar to the painters of the Forth Rail Bridge in Queensferry, Fife who move along from the Southside up the Northside slapping on all that red oxide paint. Once they've painted the very last piece of steel, they'd start again from the Southside. A job for life for sure, but what a tedious task... *no thanks!*

Down in Cardiff, Elgin once took a lead at eleven o'clock in the morning. It was sold by the salesman at midday, the fitters were bang on the job early afternoon and they'd all been paid before tea time. Most of the canvassers only worked evenings when most people were at home, but in some areas, Elgin would work a few hours in the day to catch the shift workers. Salesmen usually had two or three canvassers working for them, but Elgin took enough leads to easily keep Kev going on his own. At this stage of his career he was regularly earning over two hundred pounds a week. And the building site became a old friend that wasn't ever being re-visited.

Most days started at 4pm. The hours prior to this time consisted of trying to find a winner or two in the bookies or playing cards - two great British pastimes for young men on a mission for glory. They worked until about 8-30pm, the salesman an hour later, then they all went to a restaurant or a pub before going on to a club or casino. What a life for a 21-year-old who was quickly becoming utterly streetwise.

The other guys in the upper echelons of the business were larger than life characters. The two big bosses, Jimmy Johnson and Bill Craig, were of that ilk and gambling mad to boot. Elgin once witnessed them having a £500 bet on which one of two raindrops running down the car windscreen would reach the bottom first. The most amusing anecdote about them was that they had first met at Gamblers Anonymous. That institution obviously didn't wean them off the big buck-wagers.

One early afternoon they were all in a small independent bookies in Swansea. Jimmy decides he wants to wager £3,000 on a 'win double' (both horses have to come first). The guy behind the counter shit his pants. He probably didn't take that much all week so he nervously said he'd accept the bet if he could lay most of it off with one of the bigger bookmaking chains. How exciting was it to be around these sort of guys. Elgin's maximum bet would be about a score and now Jimmy was attempting to bet the equivalent of over three months wages earned from canvassing.

Jimmy had another almighty barney with his wife during the previous weekend and she'd left him for the umpteenth time, so he'd emptied their joint bank account on the pretext if he lost she wouldn't get any of the money, but if he won, he'd be sitting on a small fortune. They could all hear the desperate bookie on the phone to Ladbrokes trying to lay it off, but after a long hiatus he came back and the bet was struck. All that had to happen now was the hard bit! Both horses would need their heads in front at the winning post. The sun was shining on Jimmy that afternoon. Both steeds won their races. The return was a colossal 54 grand. He demanded his winnings in cash - *fat chance of that* - he was told to return the following day, when he was paid out £10,000 in readies with an accompanying cheque for 44k. Very nice indeed!

This happened in back in 1981 when the average national wage was about 70 quid a week. The damp crew worked hard and played hard as well. Fair play to Jimmy, he took everyone out that night - no expense spared. It was the start of another long love affair for Elgin; life all started to make sense - *Dom Perignon* Champagne, the camaraderie, the excitement, the gambling and money in the pocket - it all felt like the pieces of God's jigsaw were falling into place.

Jimmy originated from Blackpool, and before meeting Bill he used to run one of those mock Dutch auctions from an open-fronted shop on the sea front, knocking down five or six boxed electrical items into a black bin liner and then offering them out to the crowd of mugs for a pony (£25). It's a strange phenomenon how humans witnessing a sea of hands going up to pay for some so-called mega bargains get totally immersed in the situation themselves, wanting frantically to grab a piece of the action. Many of them would have returned back home, more than a shade disappointed with their bag full of Taiwanese tat worth no more than a Lady Godiva (£5). Still, you should all live and learn in this unscrupulous world of ours.

Bill was a cockney and as sharp as a butcher's knife. He's dead now, but that wasn't the greatest shock, smoking eighty Silk Cut and drinking a dozen pints and a bottle of scotch a day - not exactly the breakfast of champions - so he was never going to be an octogenarian. All the guys had the *live for the day* ideal - that is, spend loads of money, race fast cars and burn briefly like flaming meteorites in the night sky. They were not remotely interested in the endgame and all that sorry tedium about saving a percentage of their hard-earned cash for a rainy day. They didn't give a flying fuck about the coming week, month or year, they were urban warriors of the *here and now* and, even if they weren't around for longevity, they were never forgotten by the *hoi polloi* who encountered them during their divine mission of profligacy.

One of the best things about the job was meeting the great British public. There's nowt as peculiar as folk and they seldom ever disappointed. One really crap week in Trottersville (Bolton) was coming to an end, and it had pissed down all week and the last thing people wanted to do was talk on the open doorstep with a force nine gale blowing a small rivulet down their corridor, so a wee strategic swerve was forthcoming in the shape of a retreat down to the more clement climes of the Midlands. Elgin and Kev usually went home on a Thursday night, but the Bolton experience had laid that plan to waste, they needed a deal or two to salvage the week.

Elgin was normally dropped off in Stafford by Kev, who would then proceed to motor down to his gaff in Kent. All bets were now off. On the Friday morning Elgin went canvassing down the killing fields of Tithe Barn Road, determined to get at least half a dozen strong leads which was close enough to being assured of a deal. The currant bun was majestic in the cloudless, azure Staffordshire sky... what a bloody difference a day made! After only ten minutes on the knocker he hit pay dirt. The woman was an absolute 'raver' (a client who is extremely keen to spend their hard-earned with your good self). He made the appointment for later that evening when the good man of the house was home from his day at work. Phase one had been accomplished, it was time for Kev to bring home the bacon.

The gentleman of the house worked at Stafford Hospital which actually backed on to the top of Tithe Barn Road, so there wasn't ever going to be a 'no-show'. Known nationally as Mid-Staffs, the hospital has been in the news for all the wrong reasons in recent years. Over a thousand unwarranted deaths, the word scandal had been used more than once or twice, but even before that cover-up, it was the scene of an outbreak of Legionnaires Disease in 1985 when 22 people died, which was fucking ridiculous as the nearest desert must have been at least 2,000 miles away.

Elgin gave Kevan the scores on the doors; he was on a big downer after the dismal week and he said, "With our luck, he's probably a brain surgeon, as sharp as a lancet!"

Elgin had to snap him out of it, "I doubt that Kev, she's got a better moustache than Craig Stadler and I don't think Pledge, Mr Muscle or Fairy Liquid have made many trips there from the supermarket shelves. Kev was getting his *Eye of the Tiger* back. They had three decent leads, but this looked the one with most potential. To make certain, Elgin went round again to confirm and check out the guy. The woman answered the door, bad news, the husband had retired to bed feeling somewhat under the weather. Elgin wasn't having that, "You'll have to get him up, the surveyor is on his way round!"

She apologised and went upstairs to rouse him. Elgin returned to Kev in the motor. They gave it 15 minutes and returned two-handed. It was going to turn into one of the most remarkable deals ever witnessed in the history of door knocking.

The woman let them in, the husband was down the hall in the sitting room. Kev introduced himself as Mr Murphy and stooped down to switch off the television. This served two purposes; to get the customer's full attention and also to gain a degree of control on the situation. Elgin was standing in the hall way door and all he could see of the bloke sitting in a high-backed chair was the back of his head - which actually turned out to be the preferred slant on things.

"Would you mind putting some clothes on sir?" Kev implored. Elgin was none the wiser until the guy stood up and turned round. He was starkers apart from a pair of socks and an ill-fitting vest which just covered his belly button. So this fella thought it was acceptable to rumble up to greet two complete strangers with his todger on show for all the world to see. He sashayed past Elgin with his cock swinging left, right, left and off he went back upstairs to hide his false modesty. Elgin was killing himself laughing, while Kev had a blank astonished look on his face that said, "Brain surgeon, my arse."

They were dealing with a right pair. If his wife thought that his skimpy outfit was suitable attire in which to discuss a damp course then they were both as mad as each other, nutty as fruit cakes. The sale was a formality though. It was a really good deal for all and went some way to compensating for the dire week. It's worth mentioning at this point that if money or lack of it was brought up as an objection, then the company had a finance facility in place which covered the criteria of being employed and owning your own home no matter in what sort of rancid state it stood. It could all be paid off in easy stages... what was there not to like?

While they were conducting the survey, Elgin spotted a sitar on the wall and asked them about it. The wife said, "Oh that, I brought it back from India for him when I was on my honeymoon out there." This was getting choice, it was better than Fawlty Towers. "Didn't he go on honeymoon with you then?"

"No, my father paid for everything and wouldn't let him go because he was on the dole."

Jesus... talk about kicking a man when he is down! The poor bugger had no job, no wonga and didn't even get his leg over on the subcontinent because he wasn't there. God knows what the Indian people thought about it all. No wonder we lost the empire.

An hour later with all the paperwork completed and the dipper deftly tucked away for safe keeping, Elgin had one last request. He brought the sitar down off the wall and immediately had them both arguing who plucked it the best. He eventually got the oldest swinger in town playing it in a Ravi Shankar style (not) with her crazily caterwauling away like a demented banshee. Bloody hilarious it was, melodic had gone for good... but all was well. *Once upon a time in the Midlands.*

A small footnote to all the previous gay banter was as follows; Years later Elgin read in a local rag that our *Nature Boy* had been arrested for nicking ladies underwear off clothes lines. He was bang to rights when the police searched his house and found the freezer crammed full of knickers and bras - it was a fair cop. Our hero can still be seen today cycling around Stafford on a pushbike cross dressed between a white Rastafarian with dreadlocks and a Greenpeace supporter. His noble quest from his base in Stafford is to *Save the Whale* whilst being high on ganja. We wish him well - the Lord Almighty can only surmise what 'er indoors is currently up to!

After many months of watching Kev in action, Elgin was now clued-up on the art of closing a deal. While the other canvassers had been nipping down the pub after work, he had been going into houses with the company salesmen and absorbing their every word. He was ready to make his opening gambit and rise a few rungs up the ladder of opportunity. Kev and his wife Ange were about to go off on holiday to Spain, staying at his father's villa. Elgin and Katrina were due out there a week later to meet up, but Elgin was determined to make the week of Kev's exodus a profitable one for himself. He was going to ask Kev to leave him his 'pitch kit' to see if he could do some deals while he was away. Elgin knew he wouldn't be too keen because if he showed an aptitude for selling, Kev would be losing the best canvasser he ever had, so the timing of the request was crucial. He waited for boss Jimmy to be within earshot when he made his move. While Kev was stuttering and prevaricating, the head man butted in, "Give the kid a chance, Murph!"

Kev reluctantly agreed. The ploy had come off a treat. Elgin was very excited to be given the chance of selling. The following week in Lloret de Mar, Elgin gave Kev the good news - he'd done three deals and trousered £560. Not bad from a guy who'd been knocking himself out on a building site a year earlier for 50 sobs. Kev had a sickly grin on his face. He knew he'd shot himself in the foot, but you can't keep a good man down - although Elgin would have to find him a half decent canvasser as an adequate substitute to fill his boots before he could kick start his selling adventure.

Elgin soon found a replacement. He recruited one of Katrina's best friends - an attractive girl called Sharon who was also the sister of his mate Ant Hancock. He was also mindful of the fact that Kev and Ange were just about to get divorced, so he had to keep an eagle eye out for her in case Kev got any feelings of amorous affection post break-up. Luckily, Sharon didn't want anything to do with him outside work. It was another weight off his mind because she was good at her job and Kev couldn't come back at Elgin for deserting him in his hour of need.

He started off his first official week as a salesman the same as he had a few weeks previous with three cracking deals, but these had been bigger properties and he had cleared over £650 quid. Not only that, he hadn't risked taking on an untried canvasser either, he'd worked his own leads as well... double bubble, with a nice few bonus sobs to boot.

Yeah, he'd made it! He was zooming to the top, or so he imagined. On the second week he sold nowt... *nada, zip, not a sausage*. This was another important lesson learned as he honed his path through sales. He had foolishly gone home the previous Thursday evening and drunk the weekend away, with spirits and champers flowing like water from a tap. He felt that the only consideration for the second week would be to simply turn up and go through the motions. Wrong on so many levels! The first week had been sold on enthusiasm which had rubbed off on the punters, but the second week when all the euphoria had abated was a shocking wake up call.

Week three was another stinker, but at least he had come out of it with a deal. It was what they call in the trade an absolute 'kick in' (an easy transaction that virtually sells itself). If life was a series of kick ins it would turn to heaven on earth, but the salient truth soon revealed itself - the journey could be a long hard road from here, although it was much better than working for peanuts at a company in Stafford. Katrina meanwhile, was already having serious reservations about his decision to be gallivanting away all week, especially after a few duff pay days. She told him if he packed it all in, her friend could get him a job at *Evode* (the local glue factory). Whoopie-doo, put up the bunting, what a head turner!

That comment and the following conversations made him realise for sure that they were growing in different directions. She might have been happy for Elgin to work in a glue factory for a few decades, but it wasn't going to happen any time soon. He had his sights focused higher than that. If they were both looking into a crystal ball, they were seeing the outcome very differently. He wasn't Nostradamus, but there was no way his future was going to be stuck in adhesives.

For the next six months he carried on as before, working the week away and coming home weekends. Some wages were good, some were poor, but it was all part of the territory of sales. He actually went out on his own most weekends. They never really had any big rows or bust-ups, but it was obvious they were slowly drifting further and further apart, so much so that it had got to the point where he was about to leave town. He had met another girl while working down in Swindon. They had gone out together for two months and had talked about the possibilities of moving in together. He was at another crossroads in his life.

Her father was a wealthy business man who offered Elgin a job and financial help moving down there and buying a small property. It seemed like a brand new start away from his present trials and tribulations. He was just about to take the plunge when Katrina hit him with a bombshell, she declared herself pregnant. After the initial shock he asked her what she wanted to do. She told him she'd like to get married. So Elgin agreed for all the wrong reasons apart from the right one to stick by her. He was only 23 at the time. He hadn't really thought it through - a new baby could bring them together, but on past form it looked a real long shot.

He was now in a situation way beyond his control. He had to reluctantly cut ties with the other girl in Swindon, which was in hindsight a thoroughly tragic decision that would have fatal consequences in the future for the poor girl and all her family.

* * * *

CHAPTER SEVEN

For Better, For Worse

Katrina and Elgin married at the Stafford Registry Office in the February of 1982 in circumstances that singer Roy C would proclaim as a classic 'Shotgun Wedding'. The following summer Mr Stork delivered a beautiful bouncing baby girl Emelia, Elgin's first, and a child of the relaxed *laissez-faire* eighties. During Katrina's pregnancy, her father persuaded Elgin to leave his work and embark on something with a bit more 'respectability'. Was there nothing that he couldn't turn his hand to? His new calling could have been just what the doctor ordered.

He found himself working for a company called *Hambro Life*, selling insurance or, as the PC brigade put it, masquerading about as a 'financial advisor'. This should have been right up his street because from time immemorial, as the old saying went, *Insurance is always sold and never bought*. Well, that was the theory anyhow! He hated it all from the onset. Too many poncey fly boys driving around in flash, hire-purchased speed machines, pretending they were something special, but couldn't actually sell to save their lives. In the insurance industry it takes a long time to set up a favourable position to earn the big bucks, and the top hitters are the bods who pull the strokes, failing to pay out legitimate claims for any scurrilous reason going - a real snake pit of iniquity. He quickly gave himself some sound financial advice; *BACK TO THE DAMP GAME, LAD!*

He'd really missed his old work mates, having been gone a year and just to make matters worse, his relationship with Katrina had reached rock bottom again so a change was good for the soul... and his earholes. There was another spring in his step - he was going away on tour again.

The fickle wings of damp course fate took him down again to Swindon a few months later. His long hours working away hadn't improved any of the ongoing marital strife back in Stafford, so he decided to re-contact the girl he'd so nearly set up home with on his last sojourn down to sunny Wiltshire.

He nervously rang her house and her dad answered the phone. He hadn't seen or spoken to the girl for over a year and was half expecting the father to tell him to bugger off, but judging by the tone of the guy's voice, Elgin could sense something different was amiss. He asked Elgin to come around to the house and he'd explain everything. Elgin pressed him for an explanation, but one wasn't forthcoming. On the journey over, he was convinced that there was another little Hounds on the loose and he was just about to meet it. No such luck.

If only it had been that...

The father solemnly told Elgin his daughter had got married six months after they had split up and the new husband had murdered her.

That shocked him to the bone. There was no rhyme or reason to it. We are all pawns in the great game of life but this was a terrible revelation. He comforted and apologised to the father, who rightly told him, there was absolutely no fault attached to Elgin.

He left the house a little wiser, but a whole lot sadder. He wished he hadn't found out the whole awful truth and it stayed with him for many years. He knew that certain people could be selfish and vile, while others were naturally friendly and caring, but this was the first time he had crossed paths with really dark evil intent and it didn't sit well in his comparatively sheltered world.

Whilst he was at *Hambro Life*, there was no way he could earn enough money to put down a deposit on a new house for him and his new family to own, but back in a job where he had the potential to make a lot of money quickly, nothing was out of the question. In the meantime it became a reluctant move to a council house, but Elgin was a proud man and ambitious to boot, and he started doing something which had once been totally alien to his thought processes - saving money. He'd earned some decent money in the past, but had spent it just as quickly. But now he had new pressing responsibilities, and it was prime time to get more than a few quid together smartish.

Elgin was starting to fill his war chest with gusto (and wonga) over those long hard weeks. He and Katrina had even commenced house-hunting when another huge setback manifested itself - his beloved gran passed away.

Her death came like a steam hammer blow to him. He was utterly devastated. It took the wind right out of his sails. He knew she would have wanted him to keep fighting and moving forward, but all was not as straightforward as he would have liked - other health issues had to be taken into consideration. It wasn't going to be easy striking the right balance.

Some little time before, his beloved grandad had suffered a stroke and with him fast-approaching his 80th birthday, his circumstances could not remain the same because he couldn't adequately look after himself. Elgin's dad and his Uncle John (his grandfather's only two offspring) decided it was 'best' to put him in a home. But, best for whom? Yeah, that's right, best for them. Take the easiest option, the path of least resistance and shunt him out of sight, out of mind. Either of them could have quite easily accommodated him, both in terms of space and also in getting him the care he so obviously needed.

Elgin wasn't having that at any price. Here was the man who had offered him love and a home in the past on two separate occasions. Now in his moment of need after losing his partner of more than 50 years, his two sons were adamant that he was being put out to grass. After consulting Katrina, they were both united in their decision that grandad should and could come along and live with them.

It was a magnanimous gesture by Katrina, as her own relationship with Elgin was fraught with difficulties and differences which were quite considerable at that tense juncture. It wouldn't be a cakewalk bringing up a toddler and looking after another person's relative on top and this was something Elgin would always be eternally grateful to her for. Most people would have probably baled out. They went over to Dennis's house (grandad was staying there temporarily until a home was found) and announced their righteous intentions. Grandad was overjoyed.

Dennis told Katrina she was placing herself into a bleak nightmare situation, but her mind was made up. Out of the blue came a stunning payback from grandad when he told them, "We can all live at my house and when I join your gran, it's all yours and Elgin's."

That went down like a lead balloon with his dad and uncle, but what did they care? The odd visit at weekends or whenever it suited them to go round the home wasn't the answer, and this way grandad still had a few golden years ahead of him. It all felt right because the man could now live and die in a dignified manner.

History was repeating itself. Elgin now had a hat-trick of moves back to the glorious *Rockeries* - he couldn't keep away from the place and quite right too - but was it all sunshine and roses? Was it heck as like! To go with grandad's stroke the 'powers that be' hit him with the 'Big C'.

He was diagnosed with inoperable cancer.

Elgin had a very profound adage when things were turning to shite; "When you are at you're weakest, they come for you." Who or what, we'll never know, but the lad was a working class philosophical giant, probably not on Nietzsche's lofty level, but right up there with the most erudite drinkers in Stafford town centre.

The poor old boy was in a fair bit of pain most days and his cure for alleviating the constant aching was a nice bumper of scotch. He had enough pills to shake rattle and roll, but he never quite had the dedication to his medication. There was nothing he enjoyed more than a single malt of gold watch. Grandad also liked to have a daily yankee bet as well at his favourite William Hills bookmaker shop at Rising Brook. Elgin and Katrina had murders keeping him out the adjacent Royal Oak pub though. Why do so many bookies build their shops close to a boozer, surely they don't think sensible drinkers will fritter their hard earned away after four or five pints do they? We all know the answer to that, been there, done it, got the obligatory t-shirt.

Katrina had a devious plan to get him to go at 10 o'clock when the bookies opened their doors, as that meant he had two long boring hours to hang around twiddling his thumbs before the Royal Oak opened at midday. They were hoping he'd get fed up and give the pub a swerve. Fat chance of that! The old bugger would stand around talking to the three till girls Rennie, Erica and Pammy for an hour then pop over the road to a parade of shops opposite for a peruse and pie for another sixty minutes. The man was a *tour de force* - he had it all down to military precision.

Katrina and Elgin were shopping in one of the aforementioned shops opposite the bookies one fun-filled afternoon, namely the *Rising Brook Co-op*. Could it get any bleaker than that? You betcha it could! Grandad appeared out of thin air and asked if he could tag along. The Wild Bunch had been reunited by the pick and mix. It didn't take long for the old bugger to come up with his ulterior motive, "Do you fancy a drink in the Royal Oak, son?" He had Elgin at "do", but one glance across at Katrina with steam coming out of her lugs was enough for him to deftly knock back the kind offer. He didn't need a lot of persuading in those madcap days, but a wise strategic withdrawal was probably a better bet than kicking off World War Three.

They got to the checkout without any further ado. There hadn't been a warning of a total eclipse that day, but a huge shadow blocked the sun - a massive store detective loomed over the three of them. He alleged that he'd been watching grandad walking round the aisles chewing gum which hadn't been paid for. Not exactly grand larceny, but it earned the three of them a long walk of shame up to the managers office. Nudge nudge, wink wink, the attending Co-op clientele were in their element. The huge captor was giving out the old nonchalant nod to the crowd every ten yards like he had just busted the Jesse James gang.

Out of sight from their adoring public, Elgin was the voice of reason, "He's old and confused mate, if he's taken them it was unintentional." He was on a roll until grandad butted in, "But Elgin..."

He was cut short by his learned brief, "Be quiet grandad, leave this to me and perhaps we can stop them nicking you."

"But Elgin..." Katrina weighed in this time, "But nothing grandad, let Elgin sort it out, you stay silent."

That did the trick and he was as quiet as a church mouse. Elgin carried on and eventually persuaded the 'tec that it wasn't really in anyone's best interests to prosecute, adding with subtle mediation how grandad's afflictions were affecting him adversely and vowing to make sure he never came in the shop again unaccompanied. He later swore that he saw a precious tear roll down the cheek of the big man. If it wasn't already in the bag, it was clinched back at the checkout counter - firstly by him paying for the stolen contraband and then ostentatiously lobbing a pound note into the charity box. The stuff of legend. Justice was seen to be done that day.

The conquering hero then goes outside to see a sheepish looking Katrina standing by grandad whose head is bowed down like scolded schoolboy. Elgin had been worrying that maybe this was the onset of Alzheimer's or something worse and was only going to give him a mild rebuke, but Katrina said he had something to show him. He held up a receipt, he'd been in the shop earlier bought a paper and the gum, gone out, spotted them going in and decided to join them. "Why didn't you tell me that when you got arrested grandad?"

"I tried son, but you kept telling me to shut up!" Elgin could have throttled him, but felt so guilty he took him over The Oak for more than one or two. So, who says it didn't turn out well for all? Katrina must have wondered how the three of them ended up in the pub all afternoon. But as Elgin knows, God will move in mysterious ways.

Grandad's local doctor had specified that it was perfectly alright for him to have a few beers now and then, but "Try to wean him away from the top shelf optics". Elgin mused, "Thanks for that doc, mission impossible, especially with the guys I drink with socially."

He used to take him up *The Highfields Club* on Sunday lunchtimes where his mates were drinking. Ronnie Marsden, Johnny Pope, Paul Ashforth and one of his best mates Neil Williams (Wiggy, and no he wasn't a slap-head). They thought it was hilarious to buy him double scotches when Elgin's back was turned, telling him to sink them before Elgin clocked their nefarious deeds.

He was a happy character for someone who had serious medical problems, and everyone loved him for that. He was the life and soul of the party and it was a joy to watch him living life to the full. Yet, Elgin would be in so much shit some days, especially Sundays when the pair of loons returned home to Katrina, with Elgin holding him up as they came or fell through the doorway. Like clockwork, once lunch was eaten, he'd be straight up to bed and that was the last you'd see of him until the next day. He wasn't trying to keep out of Katrina's way though - the lad was cream-crackered through copious amounts of alcohol and pills a plenty. He'd sleep for England with sweet dreams of *more of the same next week gaffer, I could get used to this*.

Elgin was doing fantastic therapeutic work, it wasn't textbook, but it was bloody good fun.

He might have had a stroke and was slurring his words which was making him hard to understand, but he was as *compos mentis* as a glacial mountain stream; crystal clear and always going with the flow. He knew the time of day, he'd pull up any barman who short-changed him and could play cards better than Doc Holliday. There was no evidence of any cognitive decline, in fact he was as sharp as a samurai sword. He played in the same crib team as Elgin, whose lame excuse was that although it seemed a bit sad to be playing in the crib league in his mid twenties, it got him out the house for a drink. I've added dominoes, darts and quiz nights as well - he was an all-rounder. Anyway I digress... Grandad knew every possible combination at cribbage and was a cheating sod at pegging as well. He seldom got a pull if caught red handed because of his advanced years. But it did help to have a team of psychopathic nutters behind him who were always ready for a tear up when liberties were taken.

It's a game with pent-up emotions. Many a pub has witnessed a punch-up over the turn of a card. The Germans call a deck of cards,

The Devil's Prayer Book. Never play with strangers and never play for money. Next time you watch a Western, get ready for the card game, somebody is going to taste lead. It's amazing how many times the poor old dealer gets carted off to boot hill. The best mild-mannered gentlemen become raving lunatics if they can't pick a hand up. If you are offered a seat at the table, carry on walking - you *know* it makes sense.

Well, that's the etiquette of the game, and grandad was the star player. Elgin hated being paired with him because if he made a mistake grandad would remind him about it all week. He loved those fifty two little rascals with a passion and would always want to play against other senior citizens on a Sunday at *The Highfields Club* while he was getting sloshed for free. Ronnie Marsden's mother, Mary, would always accept the challenge and they had some epic battles. Highfields was a working class estate, not the most salubrious in Staffordshire, but the people were golden, diamonds in the rough. You knew they were loyal to their friends, they would always have your back. Mary Marsden was one such wonderful woman and she recalls a story which is gospel true and one of the best tales of all time.

Mary was up in her native Scotland at a relative's wedding a few years later. She got talking to a group of really nice young men who were guests there. They asked her where she was from and she said that she was originally from Glasgow, but for many years she had been living in the Midlands at the county town of Stafford. One of the guys said that they played in a band and that he was Marti, the lead singer, and they had a gig in three weeks in nearby Birmingham, would she like to come and see them play? She said, "I can do a lot better than that Marti! My husband Ron Senior is on the committee at our local working man's club. If you give me the exact date, I'll wangle it to get you a spot the next evening at *The Highfields*. It's a shame to come all that way for just one performance... at least it will help with the petrol money."

That was followed up with, "If you ever become famous you need to steer well clear of drugs." She had a few pictures taken by the wedding photographer of her and the boys at the reception which she brought back to Stafford.

The four boys turned out to be *Wet Wet Wet* and the lead singer was the great Marti Pellow. They had released 'LOVE IS ALL AROUND' earlier that year which went on to be British number one for a record 15 weeks. It's doubtful whether the lads needed the petrol money, but it was nice to know they had something to fall back on at the *Highfields Club*. Mary only cottoned on when she showed friends and family the pictures back home.

All the young girls were drooling and jealous of Mary for being so close to their pop idols. A wonderful, true account of different generations getting their wires crossed with hilarious results.

Wiggy was really good to Elgin's grandad, but he was a hard man to read. He'd often do things that would have you scratching your head, like the time he said to Monica, his wife, "Just off to the shops my love, and while I'm at it I'll cash that tax rebate cheque... kill two birds with one stone."
At this particular juncture Monica thought they were happily married. Wiggy proceeded to disappear off the face of the earth for 18 months. He had actually travelled to Paris and joined the French Foreign Legion. He never rang home once, but calmly turned up one day back in Stafford like he'd never been away. This must have stuck deep in Elgin's subconscious because later on in the book he has a dabble himself. If it's any consolation to Monica if she ever reads this bit - Grandad really missed Wiggy as well.

As is the author's prerogative, I will say that I knew Wiggy well. He would come with me and several other lunatics following Chelsea's away football matches in the North and in the Midlands - always lively days out, and some might say *dangerous*. He recalled a comical conversation he had with his platoon sergeant in the legion which tickled me for it's absurdity. Gunter Schultz was six feet, nine inches tall, but a friendly guy who would chat to Wiggy in English, but in a really heavy Bavarian accent - a bit like the German officers in the TV sitcom *Allo Allo*. "Hey Wiggy! You're a big football man, who do you follow? I have much admiration for your hooligan element."
"Well, I like to go and watch Chelsea."
"Oh yes, the famous *Chelsea Headhunters*. I have read many times about their exploits in *Bulldog* - the English National Front magazine - I never miss an issue." Wiggy politely asked who Gunter supported, thinking it would be a top German side. "Me, I'm a proud supporter of Birmingham City. Maybe one day we can both go together to see Chelsea play Birmingham... what do you say?"
"Yeah, terrific..." said Wiggy, moving in the general direction of away.

It never just rains in periods of life, every now and again a jungle monsoon will announce itself when one imagines blue skies are forming. Little Emelia fell ill a few months after the Hounds' repatriation of *The Rockeries*. At first the worried parents presumed it was flu. The local quack who visited came up with the same diagnosis, but a few days later it became apparent to Elgin that something a lot more serious was afoot. She didn't have any mobility with her neck and head, and any room lights left on irritated her as she lay on the sofa under a quilt. Katrina got the same doctor to return who still insisted it was the flu. Elgin said that reasoning was unacceptable and informed him he was taking her to the hospital. He was told that he was wasting his time from the medic who had taken umbrage at the suggestion he was wrong.

Katrina wrapped her up, put her on the back seat of the car and off they went up to the hospital on the Weston Road. She was examined straight away, then had tests done. The parents waited two hours until they were summoned to a lady consultant's office. She sat them down; *MENINGITIS*.

Elgin had heard of it, but didn't know a thing about it as the disease wasn't high profile in those days. In one sense, they were perhaps both fortunate to be unaware how bad it was in infants - it could quickly affect the areas of the brain and spinal cord. They might have badly panicked if they knew how virulent the disease could be.

The consultant gave a hopeful summary that it was something they could treat, but her prognosis that it could just as easily go either way left them both in a state of shock. Elgin was of no use to Katrina - or anyone else for that matter - he was badly traumatised. One of the worst nightmares in life as a parent is to have to bury a child - compassion and prayers go out to anyone who has endured that pain. He took to grandad's universal cure for all ills - more and more scotch, and the bigger the bottle the better. There were two other children in the same ward as Emelia, both with Meningitis - one died, one survived, but with brain damage.

It was fast coming up to Christmas. Elgin and Katrina had an agonising sleepless two days, but little Emelia pulled through with no long term problems except a slight loss of hearing in one ear. It was the best present ever, but you had to feel for the other two sets of parents who lost out to that evil disease that is still taking young lives in our modern world today.

Elgin didn't recover quite so quickly. Emelia had come home and was fine, but even two months after all the anguish, Elgin was still in the gutter with a drink problem. He didn't have an answer either for why he had reacted the way he did with all the dangerous negativity. Even to this day he can't explain why he allowed the demons to manipulate his mind. He started drinking to block out the bad consequences that could have materialised with Emelia's illness, but even after the all clear, he couldn't put the bottle down.

At this stage Jimmy had stopped trading, so Kev and Elgin had set up on their own, but Elgin was only going out to work once or twice a week - and that was only when he was desperate for money. Kev eventually gave up on him after a spate of no-shows. He couldn't contend with all the unreliability and returned to Kent to reignite his working partnership with his father... and who could blame him.

Thankfully Elgin woke up from another alcohol-induced miasma one morning and started berating himself, "What the fuck is up with you, get your bleeding act together." He checked into an alcohol dependency clinic that very morning and stayed there for a month. It probably saved his life. He stoutly fought back and triumphed over a dangerous addiction.

Elgin, through some periods of his life, had been a heavy drinker, not unlike a lot of other folk who enjoy the odd session or two, but after he came out with a clean bill of health from the clinic, he then went on to abstain for a further 18 months. Not so much as a sherry trifle or a packet of wine gums! It was an ability which has stood him in good stead throughout his life. He knows that if he over-indulges in any addictive pursuit, he can put it to bed and keep it on the back burner for long periods of time. Sometimes the most potent word in the world is *no.*

Now when Christmas comes around it is even more special than ever because it reminds him how much he could have lost that fateful day when meningitis raised its ugly head. It's a time of year when he loves being really close to Emelia as well as his other children - in hot or cold climes it's always a family fiesta.

A few Yule-tides later he went to Wolverhampton races on Boxing day. It had become a recent tradition for a big crowd from Stafford of like-minded degenerate gamblers, *ten bob-a-race merchants* and *stick-a-pin-in desperados* to partake in the holy pilgrimage to Dunstall Park. Katrina and, unbelievably, the king of bookie-bashers grandad himself, had given it the swerve so Elgin was in his element. He was as free as a bird on the wing. This was a race meeting indelibly carved into his diary and, on top of that, his mate Graham Cork, an accountant at *Evode* the local adhesives factory, had inside information on a horse that was running that day. Corky was pals with the managing director at work who had just purchased a horse called *Grundy Glow.* He had placed the horse with the trainer Jenny Pitman who had just saddled the winner of the Grand National that Summer - the very talented *Corbiere* - her star was on the rise and her judgement was very well respected.

The horse had arrived at her yard unfit and out of form, but she'd managed to sharpen him up and have him in the right condition required to win a moderate novice hurdle. In Elgin's eyes this was a sign from God. The stable had laid him out to win the third hurdle race at Wolverhampton on Boxing Day. About twenty good and true men had turned up to cheer it on... and try to drink the bar dry as well!

Win or lose the lads were on the booze.

The more they quaffed the ale, the more they talked up the horse's chances and by the time the race came round, it was already home and hosed in their minds. This horse could have given *Arkle* a head start... and a beating. They emptied their pockets down at the massed phalanxes of their mortal enemy - the on-course bookmakers. The 5/1 odds on *Grundy Glow* disappeared and were replaced by 4/1. In fact on the off some bookies were showing 7/2; they were all running scared of the Pitman hurdler. Now all the horse had to do was the hard bit, win the bloody race.

It was all over when they turned into the straight, he was ten lengths up and going clear, all he had to do was jump the last hurdle. I'm trying to build up some tension here, but there simply wasn't any! He skipped over the final obstacle and coasted home thirty lengths clear pulling a canal barge. The Stafford mob were going berserk. A few local members were tut-tutting, but a big win was a marvellous thing to behold. Elgin had been teetotal this time over Christmas so a few drinks were now well-deserved, even if more of the beer was going onto the carpet than down the old imbibing hatch. This was a time when the old racecourse was very run down. The facilities were shambolic. It was nothing like today where the old jumps course has metamorphosed into a multi-million pound, state of the art, all-weather flat racing venue, which also incorporates a hotel and conference centre.

Does Elgin ever get nostalgic and miss the old track? Well, probably about as much as a mangy dog misses the fleas.

The racing committee decided that with pockets full of the folding stuff and the town centre pubs full of Christmas revellers, it was time to make a move to the bright lights of the metropolis. They were still despatching the beer at an alarming rate of knots when Roger Crutchley mentioned that Monmore Green, the local dog racing track, was on that early evening. Elgin hadn't been before so was right up for it. Roger's dad raced dogs, so surely the son would be on the ball. Err...no. Wrong! After six races on the ten race card, Elgin had lost most of his *Grundy Glow* winnings. He was on the cusp of spending some of his own coinage.

He was seriously the worse for wear by this time. He slumped heavily down onto a bench next to two elderly ladies. One of them leaned over and said, "What's up son, are you doing your money in?"

"Yeah, you could say that." He slurred back. "Have a few bob on trap four in the next race, you might do yourself some good." she added. Elgin reckoned that she must know more than a posse of lagered-up imbeciles, so stuck a fiver on it. The dog won half the track. He sobered up in an instant. He brought them back two gin and tonics and said, "Thanks for that last dog, any thoughts on this next race?"

"Don't have a lot on, but trap six looks good for this."

He was off and running, sure enough trap six wins going away. Elgin was straight up the bar ginning the old birds up, doubles this time. "Oh, you are a nice boy, trap five should win this next race. But trap three is a big danger."

Elgin rushes off and tells the lads. "Five and three, five and three!" But they're like a brick wall, no response. They are wrecked. It's doubtful if they know whether it's Boxing Day, Shrove Tuesday or Sheffield Wednesday. Elgin backs five dog and puts it in a reverse forecast with three dog. Trap five only goes and beats trap three in a photo... JACKPOT! He's right back in the game! And one race left for glory.

He returns to the Stafford Bushwackers, "Lads, I can get you all out of trouble in the last race."

The whole lot of them are paralytic drunk, and his kindly offer of redemption is met by scorn and derision, "Get stuffed!", "You're full of bullshit" and an old classic, "Go take a long walk off a short pier!" - always very hurtful that last one especially if you aren't a strong swimmer.

Just at that moment *The Wad* (Andy Wadham, Elgin's pal from the timber yard), comes around the corner, "What do you fancy in the last race Elgin?" The Wad was a sensational drinker, ten pints was just wetting his whistle. He didn't bother with the top shelf though - he was a beer man through and through. He must have sunk 25 pints that day - child's play to him. Elgin fills him in on the golden girls and off they both went. They found the good ladies, who were delighted to have a last race nightcap of double GT's... "Trap two should win the last boys." Say no more! The lads were gone in a flash down to the row of bookmakers.

They bet with every bookie in sequence, going down the line with bundles of notes aloft. Elgin suddenly thought to himself: *What a plonker he was going to look if trap two got beat.* The Wad would go apoplectic. He hadn't been on any of the previous three winning dogs, yet still his intent was pure. What could you do ? He should have had no such worries, the striped jacket of trap six had briefly led coming into the home straight, but trap two nailed him just before the winning line.

"Never in doubt!" Elgin proclaimed as he puffed his cheeks out. But that *was* too close for comfort he knew, but he had God and the two ladies in his corner... what a holy trinity that was.

In his drunken stupor he couldn't work out if Christmas had come a day late or that he was in the middle of a phantasmagorian pantomime with the old dears playing the geese that laid the golden eggs. But really, it was all much more mundane than that. The ladies had been going the dog tracks for donkey's years and got to know all the trainers who would very kindly mark their cards before a meeting, knowing full well that they were only wagering 20p stakes on the Tote. Elgin, to be fair, had had slightly more than that on. He looked like he had robbed a bank. There were notes bulging out of every pocket.

One of the ladies said to Elgin, "Do you ever go to Hall Green dogs in Birmingham?"

He thought to himself - *Not really, but I do now.*

"Well, we are going Thursday, perhaps we might see you down there!"

There was no perhaps about it, Elgin had been converted overnight. The next day as he finally got his brain into some semblance of normality, he was trying to piece together what had happened the day before. It definitely wasn't a dream because he had wads of serious money hidden in various places of concealment around the house. It was a placid Wednesday, so he had plenty of time to organise his run to Brum the next day. He decided to ring up his old boss, gambling mad Jimmy. It took Elgin a while to convince him it wasn't a big wind up, and that it was 100% kosher. Jimmy said he'd be up at dinner time, no small feat in those days from Bournemouth as that was a time with few motorway links from the South Coast.

You lot don't know you're born these days.

It took him over five hours to reach Stafford and another hour for good luck for them to schlep back down to Birmingham. The small, happy crew were getting more and more excited as they planned their winning strategy. Just past Wolverhampton Jimmy had already in his mind put a large deposit down on a villa in Marbella. Nothing wrong with a positive mental attitude, but that might have been slightly premature thinking. As they reached the track, Jimmy asked Elgin what the two golden girls looked like, "I've no idea mate, I was rat-arsed all day and night, but I know they were both er... *old.*"

That didn't really convince Jimmy. The master plan was perhaps unravelling, although Elgin was still confident though that they could hit pay dirt.

They looked around the bar area, not a sign of any geriatrics. It was full to the gunnels with young totty. It's bloody marvellous ain't it - you're looking for a couple of septuagenarians and all you can find is very attractive blondes and brunettes... how unlucky can you get?

They changed tack, going outside to search the rest of the track. Things were looking up. There were plenty of older ladies in groups and pairs, but Elgin hadn't an inkling what they looked like. Jimmy started to get impatient and arsey as the first race was fast approaching, so Elgin went for broke. He approached every woman over fifty, "Oh hi! Nice to see you again!" hoping for a reaction. All he got was odd looks from the women and dirty looks from blokes close to them. They never found the women and of course they bet off their own volition... and of course they did their bollocks. Jimmy wasn't amused. Elgin wasn't getting a lift back to Stafford, as Jimmy sped off down to Bournemouth without waving a fond farewell. Elgin caught the train back home. It wasn't his finest hour, and Jimmy has never let him forget it up to this present day.

So it wasn't all wine and roses. Far from it. Elgin's on-off relationship with Katrina was reaching breaking point. They'd been here before, but they were now leading different lives. Elgin was still working away week after week. And even when he was at home, Katrina used to take Emelia to visit her parents in Lancashire, leaving Elgin to look after grandad on his own. He didn't mind that, but the marriage was clearly a sham. He was going to confront her to have it all out into the open...

That was until two separate occurrences changed everything again.

* * * *

CHAPTER EIGHT

Continental - We've All Gone Mental

Elgin was woken up by some dozy bugger rattling his front door early on a Sunday morning. Katrina and Emelia as per usual were up in sunny Lancashire. He had a throbbing headache courtesy of Bass Worthington.

"It better not be the Mormons," he snarled through gritted teeth. It suddenly became irrelevant who was knocking - there was poor old grandad spread-eagled at the bottom of the stairs. Elgin thundered down the flight. Grandad was stone cold dead. He'd been gone a good few hours.

It had later emerged that he'd had a massive heart attack. Hopefully he hadn't suffered and had gone quickly. It was probably for the best that Katrina had taken Emelia away on the Saturday because she had a tendency to get up early on Sundays to watch the kids programmes on TV. No small child should encounter unexpected brushes with the work of the grim reaper. Elgin was more than thankful for that.

He was ready to break away from Katrina after she got back, but bit his tongue. It felt that it would be better to sort out the arrangements for the funeral first and to get all of grandad's affairs into some kind of order. Elgin was going to come clean the day after the funeral, but Katrina gave him a bombshell after they got home from the crematorium. "I'm pregnant again."

Bloody hell, he thought, *every time I'm about to make the break from this relationship I get sucked back in again.*

Whether it was through misguided loyalty or just wanting to be seen to be doing the right thing, he decided to stay, even though over the next few months nothing was changing for the better, he wasn't excited about the oncoming new arrival. He was an unhappy man.

The new arrival was soon just around the corner. Katrina was taken into hospital a few days before it was due. Elgin had casually made other arrangements to go hitch-hiking with a pal, touring the resorts and sunspots of continental Europe around the same time. These weren't really the actions of a rational doting father, but he now had zero interest in playing happy families any longer.

He was at the hospital one day as the birth was imminent, checking to see if Katrina needed anything - she did - it was a doctor and midwife. As she was being rushed out of the ward, Elgin told her that he had parked up on double yellow lines, and that he would nip downstairs, park up properly and come straight back. As porkies go, it was a whopper. He sped off down to the railway station to meet his old mate, Sean Parkinson - a bit of a rogue, a ne'er-do-well and a geezer you wouldn't trust with your last tenner, but as he was the only dude in Stafford to fancy the grand tour with him, he was unanimously selected to partake in the adventure. But, if only Elgin could have foreseen the future, he would have made a beeline back to maternity.

As it was when he returned home a month later, battered, bruised and potless, the unflustered Katrina asked him, "Where on earth did you park that car?" It was a very profound question that was never suitably answered, so we had better fill in the activities of the missing thirty days. Thomas Cook fine style it was not...

He met up with Sean outside the station at the taxi rank. He had no contrition, he was as free as a bluebird, the world was his lobster... as Arthur Daley would say. Their plan was to conserve as much money as possible on travel and accommodation and save most of the wonga for essentials - that being alcohol and 'fun time'. They bought platform tickets and jumped on the London Euston train on platform one. It was a text book start. They started as they meant to go on, you couldn't fault them. These boys were real Jack the lads. Neither of them ever had any trouble chatting up the opposite sex - the ladies always love a bad boy. (Girls, what are you playing at?) So, it wasn't a great shock when they sidled over to a table where two young lovelies from Telford were sitting on their lonesomes. They were away for the weekend on a great package deal, which included staying at the Kensington Palace Hotel and taking in a top West End show. If you ever read mystery or whodunnit novels, then you can guess where this one is going, double sharpish.

It was the ladies first ever visit to the capital so our debonair men about town told them they would show them around all the bright lights of the city. That was an offer no discerning female could ever turn down. Of course, there were ulterior motives at play, namely to stay the night in their hotel room, sample the mini bar and maybe get lucky in their quest for some horizontal jogging. They all had a good evening out and the room slept four occupants that night, but not before Sean had decimated the drink allocation in the fridge. It got Elgin thinking that was a bit of a piss-take, as he'd only had a couple of bottles himself after they got back. Sean though, was wading through champagne and spirit bottles like a rampant Oliver Reed. There would be a princely sum to be paid for the room service bill the next morning and he would not be in the vicinity to pay. Neither would Elgin, but he was now having second thoughts about his travelling buddy. Actually, he'd seen nothing yet. Sean was only in first gear. The best - or indeed worst - lay ahead. It must have made Elgin rather guilty as he went out and phoned Stafford Hospital for news of the birth. It was a baby boy, more importantly a healthy bouncing new arrival. But it all simply washed over him, he was in another space and time dimension. He was only fully focused on one thing, leaving it all miles behind and heading for the European Mainland.

The next day the lads caught the train to Folkestone to catch the ferry to take them across the water. This was a time pre-channel tunnel when a lot of ferries sailed in and out of Folkestone. Once the tunnel was built though it killed that trade stone dead around the time of the millennium. Naturally, there were zero direct rail links from London to Paris either. Things were a little harder then, but who is to say that for all the hi-tech advances, everything has been wholly beneficial? So, after a pleasant, incident-free voyage across a mirror-smooth, becalmed, English Channel, they arrived in *La Belle France* at the historic port of Boulogne. It's only a journey of thirty three miles across but if the fickle Wind Gods ever get grumpy and decide to heartily blow, it's akin to rounding Cape Horn. Old sea dogs euphemistically call the conditions 'a bit of chop' (choppy waters), but for most green, legless landlubbers it resembles twenty foot waves from a perfect storm. There is plenty to recommend a nice swathe of *terra firma* after a turbulent maritime adventure.

The boys hopped on the Paris train at Boulogne station. They didn't even bother with platform tickets here - that was for amateurs! In those days of draconian checks and regulations, it was possible to ride buckshee. Their only enemy was the dreaded ticket collector, but even if he suddenly appeared, he could be stymied by a quick swerve to the toilet or buffet car, where checks were never done. These areas were like kryptonite for the 'clipper men'. The train was heaving. Believe it or not, the only two seats available were on a table occupied by two absolute stunners. It was like a beautiful dream where you didn't want to wake up. Elgin politely asked if they could share their table and the boys sat down opposite each other, watching both ways in case they needed to evacuate their seats in haste.

The young ladies, like the 'Telford Two', were English, but this pair were pure class, well-educated and speaking with upper class accents. It was all too good to be true. They said they were going back to study at Bologna University. Sean piped in, "But we've just come from there." They burst out laughing, and Elgin had to kick his shins and say, "It's in Northern Italy, you cretin!"

Sean blushed and said, "I knew that, didn't I?"

The girls were fascinated by the naivety of the Staffordshire posse. They'd never before in their sheltered lives come into contact with a right pair of working class wallies before. One girl's father owned a luxury apartment in Paris city centre. They were going to stay there for a week as he was away working in New York for the United Nations. After that they planned to head across to Italy. Jackpot! All the ducks were now in a row, the chickens had come home to roost, God was in his heaven with the angels, a fanfare of trumpets with copious amounts of nectar and ambrosia... and the lads wouldn't be far behind.

Elgin didn't even have to look at Sean to know what he was thinking; they had fallen upon the precious mother lode, but he knew his mate still had a profound ability to fuck up any favourable situation put on a plate before him. An hour later in Paris proved his point as Sean came out of a supermarket, arms aloft triumphantly holding two bottles of basic red table wine which he had shoplifted. He had risked getting arrested and lying in a piss-ridden police cell, instead of a week in a luxury flat for the sake of a couple of quid for cheap plonk. In life, there is always a universal truism - for every dodgy deed expect to pay the consequences or, as the prison warders will tell you, "If you can't do the time, don't commit the crime." That small peccadillo in Paris proved to Elgin his mate wasn't playing with a full deck.

All things being equal, the boys now had their feet firmly under the table in this amazing luxury flat near the Gard du Nord railway station, but they had only been there a few hours when Elgin's heart sunk yet again. One of the girl's casually remarked that she needed to get her hair cut a little shorter because of the oncoming Summer heat in Italy. Sean pounced on it like a famished Bengal Tiger, "I'm a hairdresser!" Elgin grabbed his arm and took him aside out of earshot of the two girls, "Don't be a twat, mate, we're bloody laughing here if we behave like normal people."

That advice fell on stony ground. Sean was on a drunken roll and when the girl who was more than slightly inebriated herself, unbelievably decided to go for it, all bets were off. Elgin looked into the very near future with them both back on the mean streets of Paris within the hour.

Can you picture the situation? Mr Teasy-Weasy goes into the kitchen and comes back out with his implements of choice, the girl probably spent more on hair care than most people earn in a year. Her beautifully conditioned tresses were about to come into very close contact with an imbecile wielding pinking shears in one hand and bacon scissors in the other. Elgin was pleading with him to leave it out, but off he went. He was hacking bits here, snipping bits there with gay abandon and he was prancing round the back of her showing off his handiwork courtesy of her dad's shaving mirror from the bathroom. Elgin was bracing himself for the expected fireworks and torrents of tears, but all she said was, "Sean, you're not a real hairdresser are you?"

He said, "No, not really." and then burst out laughing and, do you know what? So did she and her mate. Well, this was a turn up, especially as he had left her looking like a mad monk with alopecia.

They stayed with the girls all week. They couldn't put their hands in their pockets, the more outrageous they were, the more the girls loved it. You couldn't 'go Dutch' if you wanted too. They had a simple and man-made recipe for success; ply themselves with alcohol and repeat frequently. That strategy never failed. The week came and went in a blur and Elgin sensed it was going to be the Nirvana period of the holiday. He wasn't wrong. The girls dropped them off at the Gare du Austerlitz, where the boys could catch another train heading South. They promised the ladies that they'd look them up in Bologna because they wanted to introduce them to their university friends. What were they like! Then they were gone... *Bonne chance, mesdames.*

They headed for Bordeaux, having great expectations of earning mucho wonga grape picking, but the nearer they got to their destination, the more the realisation of back-breaking work in an open field under the cruel blazing sun started to arouse a reluctance not to go along that particular career path, especially in an area where wine was flowing like water. Common sense came bursting through to take up the running. Fuck it, they'd just get pissed. The vineyards weren't put on the back burner, they were officially dismissed as no go areas.

Luck was still with them though as they bumped into a local lad, Marcel, who spoke excellent English. He seemed to know the ropes and all the right people and took them to a restaurant owned by an old lady who was a stellar name and celebrity in the area having been an active member of the French Resistance in the Second World War. She was multi-lingual. Elgin sat with her and was fascinated by her reminiscing of war-time accounts and adventures while Marcel and Sean were up the bar caning the stock of booze. It was happy hour, and the old lady had decreed that 'none would pay'. They were guests and no money would change hands.

By the time they had left, Sean and Marcel had become firm drinking buddies. So much so, it seemed as though they had formed a new *Entente Cordiale* and had come up with a plan to make money. Elgin was all ears, agog with excitement over this Anglo-French alliance of genius. Sean was the spokesman, "We're going to mug the first geezer we see that looks like they are carrying a few bob."

Marcel was well up for it, but Elgin told Sean he wanted nowt to do with it, and that he would wait at the railway station for two hours, and if Sean didn't turn up, he was going to make his way back home to England. They weren't that skint to warrant caving someone's head in for a few francs.

He'd been sitting at the station for about an hour, when Sean turned up sheepishly, apparently he'd fallen out with Marcel over something trivial and clumped him. So much for 'friends across the channel'. Of course they were now both sitting ducks by the train tracks, Marcel knew where Sean would go, he might turn up with a gang of like-minded French nutters or even get the not-so-friendly gendarmes involved. It was time to cut and run. Elgin knew that if Sean had clumped Marcel, he'd have robbed him for sure as well.

The next train leaving Bordeaux was heading for Perpignan near the Spanish border, and Elgin suggested they both board it and vamoose out of the vicinity before they became *persona non grata*.

Once safely on the train, Sean quickly sobered up and they discussed their next plan of action. It was unanimously agreed that a pilgrimage to Northern Spain was the order of the day and with that in the locker they both conked out, joining the Greek God Morpheus in his dream world of what was or what could have been. It was the end of a long and eventful day.

The grand awakening coincided with the train pulling into the station of the large historic city of Perpignan. Lovely timing that, but there was no time for sight-seeing, they literally fell over a bus going to Girona (provincial capital of the Costa Brava) and from there they hopped onto a local bus heading for the popular seaside resort of Lloret de Mar.

(At this juncture Dear Reader, your author adds a small piece of personal coincidental data... Not being the greatest sun-worshipper from

Blighty, I have only ever been to two places in Spain - you guessed it Girona and Lloret de Mar.)

My only interest in entering Catalonian airspace was for financial gain as a few of us would fly from East Midlands Airport in the off-peak season to Girona, courtesy of Easy Jet and catch a taxi down to Lloret. After a night in a very decent hotel we'd stock up with cigarettes and pouches of tobacco and head home again. We weren't taking the mickey out of the customs like having a van full, but I'd bring back about double what was suggested in the official 'your having a laugh' draconian guidelines. I was stopped many times, but always stuck to my guns that it was for personal use, the customs always retorted with a warning, " OK, but don't come back for three months!" An instruction which I accepted gracefully. It wasn't that long ago when you could fly to Spain or catch the ferry from Dover to head for Adinkerke in Belgium, a town awash with smoking stock and paraphernalia and turn a profit. Very happy days when you could pay for a plane and hotel, have a short break and have a couple of hundred quid more in your sky rocket afterwards. As a man who has never lit up a cigarette in his life, I can never condone smoking, but if I could help people who liked their tobacco acquire it for a lot cheaper than they could in the shops, then I was your man.

The British economy has had thousands of years of smuggling and I was proud to keep all that great tradition going. I was never in Howard Marks' class, but he actually lived near Stafford for a while so a bit of his lustre must have rubbed off on me.

Anyhow, I only digressed to really say that Elgin had taken the exact same route as *moi*, but many years earlier, so in more ways than one he was a trailblazer for what followed. They say it's a small world, but not if you have to paint it... and on that profound note we'll carry on with our intrepid duo's sortie from France to Spain.

They'd led a charmed life so far, and I'll wager that some of you are now gagging for it to all go *Pete Tong*. It's inevitable really I suppose - and perhaps just a question of where and when. But you know it's coming, just like *The Great Escape* on TV every bloody Christmas.

Lloret was very popular with the British tourists: they came in their thousands. The lads had enjoyed a great week sponsored by many young female holidaymakers who had graciously kept them in clover with free booze, nosebag and accommodation, but they were now down to a few measly coins between them. Elgin, ever the voice of reason, suggested getting a job in one of the many vibrant English bars there. Sean more than pooh-poohed this rational idea, "Fuck that mate, why don't we rob one instead... or even better, let's mug a really drunken holiday maker."

It was becoming crystal clear that Sean wasn't averse to being taken away in handcuffs. Elgin, though, had no intention of visiting a Spanish nick (he would see the insides of one eventually, but that was some years away yet... cor blimey!).

The bottom line was that they had a bit of a fallout, but they soon stopped arguing when two lovely looking French girls came out of nowhere and sat on the wall next to them. Even when they were penniless and out of sorts they had more charisma than a lottery winner trying to spread the wealth. They escorted the girls around all day as per usual, and that evening they ended up on the beach for some slap and tickle and a session of smoking puff. The girls could hardly speak any English so Sean, ever the opportunist, announces, "On the count of three, let's grab their bags and do one." Elgin tries to tell him to behave himself, but he shouts three, grabs a bag and hares up the beach. Elgin is up, but can't run because he's laughing that much, he's just standing there with tears rolling down his face. Sean has to return crestfallen pretending it's all just a jolly jape. And with that last failed money-making enterprise the holiday is over.

The next morning Sean tries his diplomatic best to persuade Elgin a cunning heist is the only answer, but he fails miserably in doing so. Elgin is adamant he's going home. Sean on the other hand is moulded from a denser, different strata of clay - he's off to join the French Foreign Legion. Good luck with that then... the last item on Elgin's agenda was fighting Arabs in a bone-dry, parched desert.

They jumped trains to Cerbère, a French railway town just four kilometres north of the Spanish border, from there they shook hands, wished each other well and went their separate ways. Sean was heading for rough and tough Marseille and Elgin was taking the Lyon train back to a semblance of normality. But had Sean been a good luck mascot all along?... because events started happening for Elgin - and none of them were fortuitous.

Now he was on his lonesome, it was one pair of eyes fewer to spot the ever-encroaching *Monsieur Clippy,* the ticket demon and, sure enough, within half an hour, he sloppily let his guard down through sheer exhaustion and nodded off, only to be awakened by the ticket collector's stubby fat fingers prodding him in the chest. It was a fair cop and the first time on holiday he'd been rumbled, but here he was at his weakest. It was a pain in the butt, his journey for the time being was over. The procedure in France goes as follows; you are asked to fill in an ID form giving your name and current address, so they can bill you at a later date. Then you are unceremoniously thrown off at the next station en route, which in his case was Avignon. All this meant to Elgin was he had to wait for the next train to come along. Now, there was good news and bad news - the good; it was a direct line to Paris, the bad; the train wasn't pulling in for five hours.

   Avignon was another of those historic Southern French cities that went way back. It's one of the few places in France that still has its original medieval walls in great condition, but its main claim to fame, of which a lot of people are unaware, is that between 1309 and 1376 a succession of seven popes resided there instead of Rome because of the turbulent political climate at the time.
   Elgin had options; he could look around the stunning city or he could get his head down in situ. The second choice won in a canter as he was utterly cream-crackered. A five-hour snooze would bring his energy levels storming back up to prime time. That was the plan anyway. He slowly ambled over to a quieter platform and flopped down onto a bench and using his bag as a pillow. He could finally relax, lovely jubbly, job's a good 'un, tickety-boo. He soon fell fast asleep, but he wasn't at peace with the world very long.
   A vicious kick to his kidneys livened him up in a most unpleasant way, rapidly followed by a barrage of punches to his head and body. He was being attacked by four big lumps who were smashing him to pieces. They wanted his bag, they could have it, there was only soiled clothes in it. They got the bag and ran off. Chasing them wasn't an option even if the bag had contained jewellery and money as they had knocked the Paddy out of him. He was left sitting there, bereft of inspiration, in a pair of shorts, flip flops and a blood splattered t-shirt. He was a long way from home and his only saving grace was the passport he'd taken out his bag to show the ticket collector which he had then put securely in his shorts pocket.
   He'd had better days in France.

   Elgin jumped on the Paris train. He wasn't about to nod off again. He was bruised and aching all over. He couldn't give a toss at people giving him the once over when they spotted the state of him, he was just fully focused on getting home and out of this nightmare situation. He had murders attempting to get across Paris to the Station Gare de Nord from whence he could board a train to the channel ports, but he eventually got on the Calais train. Progress had been tortuously slow, but he was edging yard by yard back to his beloved England. The bulldog spirit was slowly beginning to course through his veins again. His ancestors had put the damned French to the sword at Agincourt and Crécy, so this was mere child's play in comparison. Elgin hopped off the train at Calais station. The weather had turned foul, "Jesus Christ, it's fucking freezing."

Shakespeare wouldn't have been too impressed with that would he?

So apart from having hypothermia, being *brassic lint* and his stomach thinking his throat had been cut, there was still the small matter of crossing twenty odd miles of water, a feat which had beaten both Hitler and Napoleon. There had been rumours of a third Antichrist but it was doubtful if he ever answered to the name of Elgin, although he had probably got too close to the Papacy when he was walloped in Avignon. Religious persecution was never going to stand up in court.

There was a plethora of people stranded at Calais harbour, most in the same predicament as Elgin. They were begging off British people getting on the ferry. He thought to himself, "I'm not lowering myself down to that level." Before remembering he'd been doing it every day for the last month. Beggars couldn't be choosers (get in). He was a past master, it would be all so *au naturale*.

He got chatting to two girls who looked liked they'd been dragged through a bramble hedge. They said they'd slept rough for the last five days solid. Bleeding hell, five days! *Think, Elgin think!* He called on high for divine inspiration and it came over in a blinding flash. He remembered that his mate Wiggy the legionnaire had once related that he never used to pay when he crossed the channel - he'd get a lorry driver to take him over as a co-driver. No cost to anyone.

The three of them went over to the nearby lorry park. Elgin did the negotiating. He was offering up three 'co-drivers' to these gifted, but sad lonely knights of the road. He had three within half an hour. Of course they all wanted the girls didn't they! (Randy gits) But Elgin insisted they all partake in pulling straws. The longest had first choice of the girls, the shortest would take him. Post pull we had two very happy drivers and another one who looked like his dog had just chewed his carpet slippers to bits. That's what you get when you gamble in human trafficking, but he turned out to be a diamond. Elgin and him got on famously. He had some great tales of being thirty years on the road and Elgin threw in a few of his own. It was a laugh a minute. After Dover Port was negotiated, Elgin thanked him profusely, then he was gone. A beautiful, fleeting friendship was over. He jumped a train to London and did likewise at Euston. The lad was back home on Friday afternoon, just in time for the weekend. The grass sometimes isn't greener elsewhere, but it never hurts to wander.

Katrina wasn't put out one iota about Elgin being away and never gave him any grief about it. The relationship had gone way past that - she was doing her own thing and so was he. The daft thing about it was they got on much better socially now. It's a strange phenomenon, love and marriage. They say they go together like a horse and carriage, but to keep it rhyming - over the years it gets worse with disparage. (Eat your heart out, Wordsworth!) No one knows the secret to a long and happy union. As a gay bachelor - the gay is literal by the way - I've always believed that if you do everything the wife tells you to, it can survive. It won't be much fun, but by God you'll chalk up the years. To be deadly serious though, it's not great to live with someone you underappreciate, dislike or at worst detest. Get away and go far away.

On the Monday evening after Elgin got back, someone came a knocking on the front door. He could just make out through the thick glass pane some dishevelled tramp crouched outside. Elgin started rattling round in his pockets for small change. It turned out to be Sean. That five-year stint in the Foreign Legion hadn't lasted five days.
"Can you pay the taxi fare mate?"
"Not from bloody Marseille I can't."
It turned out the cab was from Stafford station rank. And all would soon be revealed. Sean had applied to join the Legion, but had fallen at the first hurdle. They'd given him a drug test and found cannabis in his bloodstream, courtesy of the French girls on Lloret beach. So it was *au revoir, Beau Geste*. They gave him the equivalent of two quid, they didn't like throwing it around did the Legion, and politely told him to fuck off. They had their standards and being a thieving, drug-taking, alcoholic little twat wasn't one of them. Elgin wasn't convinced he'd actually gone there, but he took him out for a drink that night and they bumped into Wiggy. He cross-examined Sean about the camp and Sean knew things that couldn't be guessed. For a rare instance in his life he was telling the truth.

That was one of the last times Elgin ever saw him. He got 15 years for bank robbery not long after. His criminality star was rising, but so were the sentences. You live by the pen and die by the sword. The happy medium is somewhere between.

    All our lives are fated, we have choice, we all come to that fork in the road.

* * * *

CHAPTER NINE

Spaniard in the Works

The circle of life started all over again. Katrina had given Elgin free rein to do what ever he desired, namely sessions of drinking and gambling, even going out on the pull wasn't out of bounds. He had a pass, a golden ticket to the *anything goes club*. He wasn't particularly going overboard on any of the aforementioned extracurricular activities until a little bird whispered in his ear, "Will you do us all a favour and ask Pammy out? She's been driving us mad for a couple of months now, waiting for you to make a move on her." Well, well, well! He was staggered to hear that little gem of serendipity from Rennie, one of the fine upstanding cashier girl's at Rising Brook bookies. He had been totally oblivious to the fact that this Pammy had the hots for him. He thought she was just being extra friendly! It is one of life's mysteries that women will go round the houses for ages - years, even - putting out little signals, hints and clues that they fancy someone, but if they dislike you it comes through loud and clear in five minutes. It's a tough old journey this mating game.

Elgin informed Katrina straight away, but she really couldn't have cared less. *Ah, that's the spirit!* This was just what he wanted - good old apathy! He was right up for this next romantic interlude come hell or high water. Having the old trouble and strife onside meant a coordinated getaway where he could simplify all the semi-complicated loose marital ends that still needed tying into the little love knots of a civilized retreat. A woman scorned is a very dangerous animal. Elgin at that precise moment was dealing with a little fluffy kitten with ribbons, the last thing he needed was a pissed off feral Bengal Tiger trying to rip his boat race off.

It was as easy as asking her out for a drink. It might have been fun if she had said "no" - playing hard to get, but no such luck. It was all soon up and running. Elgin was 27 and Pammy had just turned 21, just about a tolerable age difference that would stop typical, nosy, middle-aged women congregating in the pub snug and declaring, "Ooh, have you seen so and so dating that little darling from down the road, he's nearly old enough to be her father. Mark my words, it'll never last. And no good will come of it, let me tell you. Oh, yes, another bottle of stout please Rita... and some cheese and onion crisps... You know, these sort of shenanigans would never have happened in our day."

Well, *quelle surprise*... after two months of courtship, all concerned thought it would be best if Elgin moved out from under Katrina's roof and into a mate's flat. All very amicable still, and a large raspberry to the snug gal's dire proclamations that things couldn't last ten minutes. Don't we all love it when a plan comes together. Pammy stayed at the flat most nights, so after three more months of being inseparable, they began house-hunting with aplomb. They ended up buying a house on the Stafford estate of Western Downs, just off the Newport Road that meanders into Shropshire, and also in close vicinity to the ruined Stafford Castle on the hill overlooking the golf course - you can actually see it off the M6 between junctions 13 and 14 if you don't blink - together with Izaak Walton the fisherman's cottage at the other end of town. This pair of historic locations must have brought in a least a dozen American tourists in the last hundred years. It's amazing how nobody knows anything about them, apart from the Staffordians of course. They are about as popular as a fire at an orphanage.

Elgin never did tedium. The relationship some days was up in the stratosphere, on others, lower than shark excrement. It was incredibly intense most of the time. He was going through the whole gamut of emotions - and then some. When it was good, it was fantastic, but when it was bad it was fucking unbearable. I liked a quiet life myself, middle of the road stuff, chill out and relax. I never fancied being an adrenaline junkie or a space-man or even a scaffolder 14 floors up on a very windy day. *Terra firma* was my motto, and *level terra firma* at that! We don't belong up there. Life is still dangerous whatever precautions you take, and so I'd rather be a boring old Bagpuss than a plunger. They say, *he who dares wins* - but I'd rather plump for a score draw. Elgin on the other hand, was a go-getter, a pioneer, a man who'd go to infinity and beyond. All I could do was stand back in awe and admiration and think, "You daft bugger."

They were in bed one afternoon (don't ask) when they had an enormous row over something trivial. Elgin jumped out of bed, got dressed quickly, left the house and jumped into his motor. He had only gone 200 yards when he looked in his rear view mirror to see Pammy running down the street totally naked chasing the car. It was like a scene from one of those 1960s avant-garde French films (which you couldn't understand). Pammy was a good runner, but it was doubtful whether she could have overtaken the car, still a few surprised white van men had more than an eyeful that afternoon. It was never mundane up Western Downs. God bless them both.

The money front was firing on all cylinders; Pammy was still going strong at the bookies and Elgin was making more than a nice few bob in his own damp proof business. But the times they were a-changing. Stirrings and movement were coming to the boil. It was the time when Elgin's mum and dad took stock, sold up and moved to Spain together. His father had quit his factory job quite a while back and gone into sales, where he had amassed a small fortune, but a serious heart attack had knocked him off course. The doctor assured him that he needed to give up his work. If he didn't, the stress would take him out. Elgin's mother took early retirement from her teaching career and they moved to their holiday home in Torrevieja on the Costa Blanca, which they had purchased a few years earlier as an investment for the future. They were going a decade earlier than they had planned though, but what was not to like?

Our happy couple went out to visit them and had a great time, but when they flew home, Elgin had that old yearning feeling that he was missing out on something good if he didn't go back to live there and try his luck again. The urge to return was with him every day, so off they went a few months later for a holiday, but combined with a recce to search for money-making ideas. Even though nothing concrete jumped out at them, Elgin was confident he could make a living out there and eventually prosper. A positive attitude and some hard graft would make all the difference. You can never beat the combination of inspiration and perspiration. They sold their house six months later and moved to Benidorm. They had, quite simply, burned their bridges and 'gone for it'. Fortune favours the brave, but sometimes it can take a while.

As any good bricklayer would tell you, Rome wasn't built in a day, but first impressions were favourable. They rented a bijou apartment near the Sunday market and Pammy easily walked into a job at the local bar. Elgin started setting about building a business, but this was easier said than done - the waiting time for a telephone was seven bloody years! Remember that the next time you're berating some poor sap on the other end of the line at BT. Mobile phones were only available on Star Trek. It was a very different world then, technology was only taking baby steps.

Elgin would have to adapt and go with the local flow. He had met some lads; brothers Nick and Pete, along with their mate Kevin, who had all been working for quite a while in Javea, a town half an hour away up the north eastern coastal road. They were sound fellas and obviously knew the score, making more than decent money, landscape gardening. There was plenty of work available, mainly for the colony of British ex-pats enjoying the Spanish sol and sangria. It would have been remiss of Elgin not to have offered his green-fingered expertise to the ongoing enterprise, and he was welcomed into the fold with open arms.

Things started falling into place - just like a life-sized Tetris - when a few weeks later, Steve and Glen, a couple of brickies over on a football trip decided they loved the area and lifestyle. They offered their services after quickly deciding they wanted to stay and experience a piece of the action. The six-strong crew could now offer general building work together with barbecues, swimming pools and everything else that affluent retirees wanted on their prized properties. After six weeks they had a work diary full to the gunwales, so much so that Elgin fed up of driving a combined distance of 74 miles each day wondered if moving to Javea was a sensible option. His mind was made up for him the next morning at 7am while he was stationary at traffic lights after just leaving for work. An imbecilic drunken youth staggered out of a nightclub, leapt on the bonnet, ran across the roof and used the boot as a springboard to jump off. Normally Elgin would have given chase and punched his head in, but he just sat there shaking his head and thinking, *I've got to get out this area pronto*. All he had to do on returning that evening was persuade Pammy as well.

When she got the news, Pammy wasn't exactly on cloud nine. She'd made plenty of new friends in Benidorm and was well settled there. Throw into the mix some domestic issues as well as it was clear that they weren't getting along that swimmingly at the time. Elgin was working long hours expanding the new business, and he himself admitted he was a nightmare to live with when he was empire-building as that would have been his main focus. So he had his work cut out trying to convince her to up sticks again. He told her Javea was like an 'upmarket Benidorm' and he finally got his own way after she bought that hook line and sinker. They rented a four bedroomed apartment in Javea Port. It was indeed an upgrade from Benidorm - as a dwelling place - but Pammy wasn't too impressed with Javea itself, it was much quieter than the party town itself. She seemed to lose interest in Spain.

She wasn't bothered at all about working to keep herself occupied when Elgin was away for long periods, and it seemed it would be only a matter of time before she decided to sling her hook.

They had one final row. Elgin told her to 'get her act together', and adding that she'd got lazy and was feeling sorry for herself when she had plenty to be thankful for. That was the clincher. Pammy was going back to England. This was a perverse sort of mutual consent - neither were happy, and it was probably all for the best. She'd only been in Javea two months and it obviously didn't suit her. You could smell burning martyr all the way to the airport. Then she was gone. But not forever... she would pop up again in the not so distant future, back on home turf.

Elgin started socialising with all the lads he worked with, they were his new surrogate family. He picked up some new pals in Javea as well; Little Mark together with brother and sister Trevor and Debbie. Lonely he wasn't. He loved everything about Javea; the weather, the food, the people he knew. Here he was in his late twenties earning excellent money, finishing work on a Friday dinnertime and holidaying until Monday morning. It was a tough gig for a single guy (not!). The crew used to get drunk twice on a Friday, just because they could. They'd down tools at midday, head for a restaurant and order a large paella with jugs of wine and beer. They'd be out of the game around 6pm, so a tactical withdrawal to the land of nod for four or five hours deep kip would set themselves up nicely to meet up again at 11pm for another lengthy session going deep into the early hours. *Ay caramba!*

One evening on a quiet uneventful social soiree in *The Leprechaun* drinking hole, two young lads staggered in battered and bruised and the worse for wear, complaining they'd been beaten up by a mob of Argentinians in a well-known South American bar on the beach front. With the Falklands War only half a decade previously and still a strong and relevant memory in the minds of most macho red-blooded males of both countries, this was an outrage that couldn't be ignored. The gauntlet had been thrown down, national pride was at stake, the boys had to defend England's honour. The builder-and landscaper-mobilized army went into a huddle for a military conclave. Field Marshal Steve took control of his troops with his operation, *Close the Argy bar*.

"These young, innocent lads are from your manor Elgin, so you go in and kick it all off, then we'll all pile in and properly smash the place up." It was a plan of tactical genius. Elgin had downed about six pints and he was right up for it. But the cold night air on the half-mile recce over to the enemy had tempered his patriotism a tad. So, he was glad when Little Mark offered to lead the charge with him. Another pair of fists might just come in handy (he wasn't wrong).

Elgin went up to the bar with Mark in tow, "Two pints of Belgrano." (*General Belgrano* was the name of the Argentinian battleship sunk by the submarine *HMS Conqueror* at the start of the conflict). The room went silent for a split second before a flurry of fists rained down upon our plucky pair. The locals obviously had no sense of humour! They were all-rounders as well, as many were now sticking the boot in. Elgin sensed they were going to die in that bar. He might get a posthumous medal at this rate. *But where the fuck were the Brits?* Steve thought it would be funny to wait half a minute before piling in. Now, he DID have a sense of humour, and the boys did crash in after the longest 30 seconds of Elgin's life and proceeded to smash up the bar... and its patrons. It was like an alcoholic Battle of Goose Green, but without the weaponry. Same result as well - surrender by the Argentinians.

Suddenly they were all on their toes. Down to the beach was the escape route where they could sneak back into town further up the shore before the police made an appearance. All to no avail though. They should have split up and gone home, but instead they went back to *The Leprechaun* for more beers and to share their tales of valour in action. They were all arrested at gunpoint and taken up the coast to the nick in Denia.

Even though police and arrested parties were all European, it was obvious that the feds would lean in favour of another Spanish-speaking country. The still-ongoing dispute over Gibraltar was hardly going to endear them to the court either. Three days in the cells gave them time to cool off and a morning in front of the beak didn't cheer them up in any way at all. They were fined and ordered to pay a stack of compo.

It didn't get any better when they finally emerged from the courts. They were herded into police Land Rovers and taken back to a police station in Javea. They were all 'illegal', because at that period of time you needed to possess a residency card to work in Spain. They were all concerned that the next step was an escort to the airport. The police put them in a big room for an hour to let them stew, and then a high-ranking officer came in and warned them, "Anymore violence and you'll be off to *El Altet*." This was the name of the Alicante airport - and they knew it wasn't a thinly-veiled threat. Elgin tried to blag him, insisting that they were all holiday makers, but he knew the time of day, he even knew what jobs they were working on. He finished off by saying, "No more drunkenness in public, and absolutely no more violence and have the respect to pay your fines."

All had thought that they were proper Jack the Lads working without permits and the police were daft, but the upshot was they were the idiots for underestimating the intelligence of the authorities, and of course all the fines were duly paid off that week.

It had been a serious wake-up call. They had been hit in the pocket and lost precious work days and they vowed not to go down that path again. From then on they would work hard and play hard but, if confrontation arose, they would walk away from it. You couldn't fault the logic.

They got straight back into work mode and carried on regardless. Having an excellent reputation for top quality materials and workmanship gave them a surfeit of bookings and a growing standing all over town. There are thousands of British builders over on the Costas these days, but back then in 1988 they were few and far between. The ex-pats were wary of Spanish construction people who had a reputation of being unreliable. Whether that was true or not was inconsequential as the boys had a massive file of photos and plans which could all be backed up with recommendations from happy previous clients. There were a few other British builders out there who were cheaper - *some might say cowboys* - but it is always better to pay a bit more and get the job done right and to the correct specifications the first time. We all know someone who has paid a bit less to a shoddy builder and lived to regret the £500 difference they thought they were saving instead of hiring someone more reputable. Elgin caught a crab later on in his life by having top people working for him with the best equipment and materials and charging the customer accordingly, but in Spain that mantra was a winner and a full appointment book with a three week waiting list was proof of that.

Now that Pammy had returned to Blighty, he could rent out the spare three bedrooms to workmates and pals. This more than covered the rent, so no worries there, but the fly in the ointment was the owner's family came down from Madrid in July and August for their holidays, so a mass vacate of the premises was needed before they arrived. Typically, with four young guys, it was left to the last week of June before anyone worried about the transfer, then the last two days... panic set in! The old saying, *The changes of no consequence will pick up the reins to nowhere,* were never so apt. Panic turned into a last minute frantic evacuation to the only place available - the already-full studio apartment (bedsit) of Kevin. There were now twelve sweaty males living like sardines together. Elgin and half a dozen others slept on the outside terrace. It was no big deal, the inside was like the centre of the sun and after a week stunk like a diseased abattoir for polecats. Thank God, brothers Nick and Pete came good with an offer to stay at their parents' huge luxury villa.

Their mum and dad had been visiting friends and family in the UK when the father suffered a heart attack, so they were going to be away for some time. The motley half-dozen on terrace sleep duty made the magic pilgrimage to the huge villa. It was a beauty, and Elgin even got his own bedroom again. Cowabunga! Life was great again, and they were all set up for the summer. It was madness some mornings: Elgin would be getting ready for work when Nick would burst through the front door with half a dozen slappers he'd picked up in a club, ready for another party. Talk about the Spanish being unreliable, well, it was Summer, and it was Nick's gaff in a way, but the work kept piling in and so did the money. They were all living the good life, and there was nothing on the horizon to spoil it...

Oh, wasn't there?

It was a fabulous villa; beautifully decorated and adorned with expensive antiques and curios, but slowly and incrementally it was getting wrecked. Works of art got broken or purloined and the general state of the place was filthy. Eight guys and numerous drunken female guests weren't the best fit for conscientious housekeepers. One morning in late August, Nick answered the phone; it was his worst nightmare. His mum was on the other end. They were at Gatwick Airport and returning home. He put the phone down, and white as a ghost, he whispered, "Lads, we've got about six hours to get the place cleaned up."

Mission Impossible had nothing on this one. There was a large Persian Carpet in the lounge that must have cost thousands, and it now reeked of every type of human body fluid available: excrement, sick, blood and urine were just a few of the curious and unusual, multi-coloured stains on it. Someone with a warped sense of humour offered up the stunning ploy of chucking it in the outdoor swimming pool to somehow clean it. Brilliant! That plan was approved by all. The pool instantly turned green... and it wasn't *crème de menthe*. The chemicals in the water immediately reacted with all the shite on this alien object and it probably wasn't doing the carpet a power of good either. They all did their best before the parents got back, but you can't put lipstick on a pig. Hopefully the brothers' dad didn't have another coronary when he saw the state of the villa. Stop Press: Nick and Pete were not seen at all for two weeks!

Wouldn't you have liked to have been a fly on the wall just as the parents walked in the villa?

Although Elgin was happy in Spain, his paternal pangs kicked in. He was missing the children terribly. He'd had a terrific 18 months in Spain, and Katrina had brought them out a couple of times on holiday, but it wasn't the same as seeing them more often and when it was convenient to do so. When they came out to Spain they had stayed at Elgin's parents, but on one occasion, he'd had a massive bust up with his dad over the way he was treating them, so he put them in his car and drove off. Sadly he never spoke to his dad for years after that.

Steve and Glen, the brickies, had also decided to return to England, and they offered Elgin a lift back with them in their motor, which he happily accepted. The night before they left the whole gang had a good old knees-up and said their goodbyes to all that were staying on.

It would be nice to finish on a happy note, but life is not always like the end of a Disney movie. Two weeks after the threesome got home, four of their pals, Kevin and his girlfriend, Debbie, Trevor's sister who Elgin had dated for a short time and Little Mark had gone for a night out in Benidorm.

On returning home, the car went over a cliff, Little Mark and Kevin's girlfriend were killed outright, Kevin lost a leg and Debbie's injuries were that bad she now needs full time care.

There but for the grace of God go any of us. We know not what is around the corner. Live every day to the limit, regret nothing and try every thing in life at least once...

...except incest and clog dancing.

* * * *

CHAPTER TEN

Need for Wheels, Before Deals

It was the glorious late Autumn of 1988, the year of more Hounds vs o'Rourke coincidences. I'd been away myself down sunny Lymington in Hampshire - the posh, yachty town on the Solent. I'd gone down in my MGB GT with my best pal at the time, Kerry, the giant apricot Standard Poodle, for a long break away from the trials and tribulations of being a Staffordian. I'd been burgled by two blokes I knew: one a real scumbag, who is dead now (if there's a Heaven and Hell, I hope he's down there lying on the hottest piece of sulphur in the universe), the other a so-called mate who I'd worked with over the years. You know which one disappointed me the most - he has to live with the stigma.

I'd been invited down there by the Janet and Mick Maguire. Janet was one of the twelve Woodman children who were a terrific family (if you could remember all the names) from the North End of Stafford. Fred and the absolutely wonderful Margaret Woodman were the proud parents.

Mrs Woodman treated me like one of the family as I was best friends with her son Mark and also very close to his older sister Dawn. These people were the salt of the earth.

No word of a lie, you could see The Needles quite clearly on The Isle of Wight from my bedroom. I traded the MGB GT in for a mobile burger/chip van as I had spotted an opening in the market. Lymington High Street used to close right down around 9pm, and there were no takeaways or chip shops... this was Tory heaven. Mick Maguire, myself and his daughter Janet, used to have a queue outside every night stretching back to Portsmouth (a slight exaggeration - but you know what I mean). After wages and overheads this covered my rent and outgoings.

At the end of the holiday season I was ready and fresh enough to come back home to Stafford. I'd gone down there with eight grand and I returned with eight grand, so a free holiday with plenty of romps on the nearby beaches for Kerry Poodle - everyone a winner.

I have to mention a sad postscript to this though: in 2021 Max Maguire, a young grandson of Mick and Janet, was stabbed to death outside the British Legion Club in Lymington. One of the assailants was only 14. Until the government get serious on knife crime these tragic events will keep coming back to haunt families. If you are caught carrying a blade it should result in a mandatory 5 years behind bars. If this can happen in prosperous Lymington then no area is out of bounds. The woke Left make me grieve for this once great country.

RIP
MAX MAGUIRE
2021

I was back in Stafford and fancying a bit of empire-building myself. I traded the burger van for a silver, seven-seater Peugeot 505 and set up *Bee-Line Taxis* with my ex-brother-in-law Paul Noddles. If he was tough enough to live with my sister Pauline for five years, he'd do for me if the going got rough. We worked 20-hour days at the start, I kid you not, but we quickly expanded from two cars to four, and taking on Jim from the South End and Gerry a Northern Irish guy from nearby Stone. This is the exact period I bumped into Elgin back from Javea. We'd both had a break from Stafford and fate brought us together. He needed some wonga quickly and I offered him accommodation if he needed a roof over his head. Well, that's what friends are for (there's a hit record there!). I told him he wouldn't get rich in the ratio to hours worked, but it was cash in hand. That would do him nicely until he got back on his feet. Gerry used to drive days and he was well made up when I told him that I had a new driver for his car at nights.

Elgin was in his element. He was getting plenty of tips and attention from the *ladieees*. I knew he would of course. I was getting my leg over with a different one every week and I wasn't even looking for it. He had six on the go at one stage! Forget about lonely hearts ads, taxi driving is better than a disco for meeting up with the opposite sex... that, and owning a pub or club. I had attractive women and not so attractive ones throwing themselves at me when I had those establishments, must be the combination of alcohol, after-shave and good looks! *Ha ha!*

We'd just moved into our new second floor office in a big building in Rowley Street when Elgin had a slight problem. He'd clumped the back wheel arch on Gerry's motor, and he came in asking what I thought. I'd mistaken Gerry's soft spoken lilt for weakness, notwithstanding that he was a big lump with a large scar on one cheek, "He's a pussy cat, Elgin. Tell him to pay for it himself."

Gerry met up with Elgin on the next shift change in the office, "I'm not paying for the repair Gerry."

That didn't go down well. First, Gerry's face went red, then it went purple - he was like a human chameleon. He never said a word, then turned on his heel and walked out. "Told you, he's bottled it." I proclaimed.

Elgin thought he was going to tear him in two - he was right and I was wrong. Someone told us later that Gerry was the real deal in Northern Ireland and he was on license with the authorities, and that if he did anything seriously wrong he would be recalled to prison. As close to death as Elgin was, he got me back good style a few months later. But first, one more tale about Gerry who was the most wonderful man. He had more wit and charisma than a room full of comedians. His face used to light up if you made him laugh, but woe betide if you upset him.

I gave him a job to the station one day. We could drop off as private hire cars, but we couldn't pick up at the station itself as this was the remit of hackney carriage licences. At that time the subtle difference was private hire could only supposedly pick up phone bookings, but it was a common practice for one to be approached in the street and the driver would call the job in to the office over the intercom. This was still illegal, but seldom prosecuted as it was nigh impossible to prove in court, much to the chagrin of the hackney carriage taxis.

Gerry drops off and hangs about waiting for his next booking, and over comes Bernard Infante, a small Egyptian guy from Doxey, a man who I got on well with. If the intercom radios broke down he would fix them. Bernard, who was chairman of the Stafford Taxi Association as well, taps Gerry's window and said, "You need to go now."

Gerry says "I'll go when I'm ready."

Of course it gets out of hand. Bernard is quite fiery, but has no chance of beating Gerry in a straightener, and gets two gentle slaps for his trouble, nothing that would hurt, but Bernard keeps coming forward aggressively, so Gerry simply gets him down on the ground and throws his hush puppies onto the busy road in front of the taxi rank. People who witnessed this told me it was hilarious... and the shoes never recovered either. Gerry makes himself scarce, but the police were called and it went to Stafford Magistrates Court. Gerry was fined £150 for disorderly conduct. The chief magistrate asked Gerry if he had anything to say in mitigation, "Yes your honour Mike Tyson doesn't earn £150 for throwing two punches!" That cracked the courtroom up: Gerry left them laughing.

Bee-Line was growing rapidly. We had about ten motors a few months in. Pammy, his old flame, would ring late at night asking for Elgin to pick her up. I always made it his last job because for some strange reason you couldn't contact him after that. God knows what he was getting up to. We had a contract with a hairdressing group, taking their staff to and fro, and this is where Elgin met Lucy, the mother of his two youngest daughters. So I had a small part in those two getting together. Lucy was 20 years old and Elgin was coming up to 30. Disgusting really. I was dating the new girl on the base radio Marion (Maz) who was 19 years old and I was 33. However, that was quite acceptable... *because I have authors privilege dontcha know.*

They were only together six months when Lucy announced she was pregnant. It was a big shock to Elgin's system, but it was the moment he realised he had to get his act together a bit smartish. He was too good for the cabs. We've all seen most private hire drivers - you struggle to get a grunt out of them. While he and myself were together at Bee-Line, we doubled the IQ ourselves - and there was another 20 blokes working there. He went back into sales and got a job as a salesman with a big outfit called *Stormseal* - a top double glazing company. He excelled there and was quickly promoted into management.

Elgin and Lucy had now started living together at her mother's house. Edwina, who was a really nice lady, was divorced and so not used to young men and their drinking habits, so I don't suppose Elgin's antics that first night endeared him to the matriarch of the family. He was due to go to Lanzarote the next day to do a favour for a mate who lived there; he was being picked up early doors - jobs a good 'un - but two of his best mates, Geoff Brundrett and Big Colin (the doorman from the Reynolds bar), invited him out to the nightclub. Lucy, who was going to the airport with him said, "Don't come back late either!"

As if he would.

Yet some strange magnetic force kept him close to that bar until 2am. He'd had enough beer to sink the Queen Mary. He gets back to the house at about half past two. He somehow gets upstairs but his bearings have gone completely. He doesn't know if he's in Lucy's bedroom... or the bathroom. Unluckily, he was in neither. The light goes on and he's in Edwina's room, todger in hand trying to piss in the wardrobe.

Well, we've all done it.

Edwina was fine about it though - what a great mother-in-law she was.

Two months later they bought a bungalow - No 2, Berry Road, up the posh part of North Stafford. And guess who lived in a bungalow at number 12?

Yep! Got it in one! So now I have stalkers.

I introduced them to *Standard Poodle Mk 2, black 'Bismarck'*. We actually reduced the average age of people in Berry Road as most people up there were in their seventies and eighties. We started going out as a 'fab foursome' - Elgin and Lucy, with Micky and Maz. Even though we were both making top money, we weren't pretentious. We'd take the girls to pubs most guys wouldn't, *The Queen Vic, The Four Crosses* and the not always salubrious, *Hop Pole*. It was always a treat for the older patrons in these inns to see some top totty. They loved a bit of eye candy. They couldn't have cared less about me and Elgin though... don't you ladies see what *oomp* you hold over us mere mortal males? It was *petticoat power* all the way.

One night in the *Hop Pole,* Elgin and I are having a few frames of pool, and the girls are chatting at the bar, when Liam walks in via the back door. A quick resume (as they say in America) on Liam, another Northern Irish man, but this one is loud and quite volatile. His attractive wife has just left him over his drinking. He must have been a nightmare to live with. He is the double of 'Yosser Hughes' in the classic TV series, *Boys From The Black Stuff,* but bald on top. He then resided in the *Hop Pole* beer cellar with his Alsation dog, 'Sin'.

In he struts confidently with his un-ironed shirt and trousers covered in dog hairs - never a good look that - and asks the girls if they want a drink. "No, we're with them."

He comes out with the greatest statement ever in his strong Northern Irish accent, "What are you doing with those pair of losers?"

Elgin was just about to take a shot, but miscues and collapses with laughter. I've got tears running down my face with laughing so much! Never to be forgotten that. I used to wind him up and call his dog 'Cindy'. He'd shout back, "It's fecking 'Sin'... the dog's name is fecking 'SIN'!"

I knew he was from Derry so I'd say, "You're from Londonderry aren't you Liam?"

He'd scream back, "I'm from fecking Derry, you know that!"

Happy days indeed. We'd all been out for a drink again on another occasion. I'd had a big row with Maz, a real humdinger, but over what,

I don't recall, but she was not a happy bunny. We stopped outside her second floor flat. She stormed out of the taxi, slamming the door. Every time we all went out I'd always stay at hers overnight. This is when Elgin got his revenge for my opinion on Gerry. I said, "It doesn't look like I'm staying with her tonight."

Elgin replied blandly, "She's fine. Just go up and apologise."

"Are you sure, she looks really pissed off?"

"Sure, I'm sure. We'll wait five minutes for you to sort it out, just give us the thumbs up."

I climbed the stairs and rang the bell, and out rushed this mad banshee with a kitchen knife and lunged at me viciously. I'm sure I unduly panicked as she seriously missed skewering my liver by half an inch, "Fuck off, now!"

I didn't need telling twice. I ran back to the taxi, even the driver was laughing as I said, "You fucking rotten bastards, I nearly got killed up there! I'm attached to my vital organs!"

That only made them laugh more. What could you do?

There was more than a sense of panic whilst Lucy was pregnant. A silly little mishap like cutting her finger while peeling potatoes nearly resulted in dire consequences. She caught the sometimes-deadly tetanus, which is often called lockjaw, which must be a bit of a misnomer really because she wouldn't stop talking about it when she found out. She was taken to an isolation hospital in Stoke for an injection. If you don't treat tetanus, death is not out the question. It's an extremely rare condition, only 5-10 people contract it each year in the UK. The vaccine had never been tried out on a pregnant woman before so the doctors couldn't say one way or the other what effect it would have on the baby. It was an agonising few months wait until Lucy gave birth to Elgin's second daughter, Lotte. If the vaccine had any affect at all, it was to make her extremely beautiful. She was a little stunner.

The trio had only been at the new bungalow for a few weeks when disaster struck. *Stormseal* went bust... tits up, kaput, down shit creek, they were an ex-window company... and it couldn't have come at a worse time. They had spent all of their savings on the deposit for the new bungalow, furnishings and baby clothes and accessories. As is everything in life, timing is crucial. What a cruel blow.

Elgin decided the only thing he could do was start a new business of his own, so he contacted his mate Tommy Rowlands. Tom had been in charge of the canvassers at *Stormseal*, whilst Elgin had been in charge of the salesmen. He reckoned that their combined expertise could produce a lean, mean, selling machine. They arranged a meeting in a Wolverhampton hotel to discuss their plans for going forward. Elgin had his mind set on carrying on in the double glazing business, but Tom wasn't that keen and suggested that 'garage doors' was the way forward. Elgin got on his high horse and was about to make a declaration that he has never been able to live down, "There's no money in garage doors, Tom. You're losing the fucking plot!"

He had dismissed the suggestion out of hand. At that particular juncture Tommy went back home up North and Elgin started his own window company.

Chronological announcement: time machine mode... We are now doing a Quentin Tarantino-type *Reservoir Dogs/Pulp Fiction* fast-forward five years into the future for a few pages. You'll understand exactly why when we rewind back to where we have just left off. (Warning to any young children reading this, we haven't really got a time machine, it's all done with smoke and mirrors.)

We have now returned to Spain half a decade after the meeting in Wolverhampton. Believe it or not, Elgin is back in the damp game. It's Monday morning, and hopefully it will be a big week. The lovely Lucy is answering the company telephone, and nobody has the slightest idea what is about to unfold. But events developed very quickly into something extraordinary and historic.

It hadn't started well...

Lucy called Elgin on the road with a lead - described in her own words as 'an absolute raver'. He'd normally be right up for that, but he was pissed off with her. All he'd had all morning was shite, garbage and time-wasters. It was a boiling hot day and he was sweating all the weekend booze out of his system. Unusually for him, he wasn't his normal positive self. Look, the man was only human. We all have our off days.

It was part of Lucy's job to rate the people who rang up responding to their advertisement in the newspaper, thereby sending Elgin the 'live' prospects. This clearly hadn't been happening, so in his mind this next raver was no doubt another waste of space. He asked her for the details and reluctantly wrote them all down before ringing the fella for directions. It went exactly like this, *verbatim*.

Punter: "Where are you now?"

Elgin: "I'm in Nueva. Andalucia, opposite Puerto Banus."

"Do you know the Golden Mile on the way back to Marbella?"

"Yeah, sure do!"

"Well, do you know where Sean Connery's house is?"

"Oh yes!"

"Do you know where the house of Antonio Banderas is?"

"I do."

"Well, mine is the really big one in between those - the one with the marble drive."

Suddenly Elgin is ever so slightly interested and turns into Fangio - the run to the Golden Mile is over in a flash. The proportions of the house were staggering. It had servants' quarters on either side of the gates, both bigger than Elgin's house. The owner, a guy in his forties called Nick, shows him around. Not only has he got a marble drive but - just for luck - he has a marble roof too. The huge, ornate dinner table was set for forty people. He obviously liked entertaining. There was also an indoor swimming pool which connected to an outdoor pool, divided with a retractable solid perspex wall, so in the winter it came down and the indoor pool could be heated and in the summer it went up and you could swim in the sun or the shade. Absolutely unbelievable.

It turned out that Nick had bought the prime property for fifteen million pounds cash. It was advertised for a quick sale at a bargain price. The previous owner was a Russian Mafia boss who came home unexpected one day and found his wife in bed with his accountant. The bean counter was a wizard with figures, but examining the wife's vital statistics was going way past the call of duty.

The boss seemed a reasonable guy - he only shot them both twenty times with his Uzi 9mm sub-machine gun. They definitely wouldn't be coming back. He got a double life sentence - fair really, but the poor sod had been provoked. It was just another of those lazy, hazy, crazy days on the hedonistic, money mad, anything goes, Andalusian coast.

Nick was a man who wasn't shy at coming forward about his wealth, so there was no need for Elgin to go through a long sales pitch and presentation. All that Nick wanted was a top notch job for a good price. Elgin measured up the massive building and servants quarters. He didn't need to inflate anything or add any extras. He really wanted this job. Coming back with a very fair price of six and a half million pesetas - which sounds like a fortune - but was in reality just over £32,000. That was still a lot for the average man in the street, but for Nick, it was chicken feed.

Elgin oversaw the job himself. He put his best men on the gargantuan task and soon became good friends with Nick, popping over every day. He had noticed that the house - as magnificent as it was - had plenty of missing, chipped and shabby, weather-worn painted areas. He mentioned to Nick in passing that he also sold and applied an innovative new product on the market, which had been laboratory developed, 'Long life paint', which had a lengthy guarantee to boot. Nick simply said to Elgin, "Yes, I thought the old girl was looking a trifle sad, bring her back to life, Elgin. She probably hasn't had a paint job since she was built, poor thing."

If only all jobs were as good as this one. Elgin doesn't recall the final figure, but it was nothing short of astronomical and he had to have the cheques in part payments of a million pesetas, just to be able to cash them in the bank. Happy days!

Nick was not only rich, but a lovely guy as well. He'd talk to Elgin for ages when he came round for another part payment. On one such occasion Elgin found Nick looking really perplexed, so he asked him what was the matter, "I'm having a bad day, Elgin."

"Why, what's up mate?"

"I can't get my new Ferrari into the underground garage, the slope's too steep and the car's too low."

Jesus, ain't life just a real bitch when it won't go your way? Elgin mused. *Come and live in my world!* You think you are doing well yourself until you meet an uber-successful guy like Nick. When Elgin went round for the final payment, Nick had obviously been impressed with Elgin's professionalism and offered him a top job out of the blue; the task of training all his new salesmen. "What do you actually do, Nick?" Elgin enquired. In the months he had got to know Nick, he had never broached that question before.

"Garage doors, my boy, I sell garage doors," came the unexpected response from Nick.

This is the *eureka moment* for which we've gone forward five years. Remember that grandiose declaration by the infallible Mr Hounds? *There's no money in garage doors, Tom!* Whoops! Maybe there was! It was years later that Elgin recounted to Tom the tale of his garage door saga. Well, you can't win them all. As for working for Nick, Elgin thought long and hard about it, but the big downside was the position was in England and he was making a good living in Spain as his own boss, so he reluctantly turned down his kind offer. But they kept in touch and are still good mates and lastly and importantly, the big house still looks as good as the day it was painted.

Anyway, rewind, dear reader. We now return to the present woes and travails. Tommy has fucked off to the North - fat lot of good that plan with the garage doors was. Elgin was utterly skint and had only one option (no, not cut his throat...), he had to raise capital. Easier said than done in a tight corner. The only thing available - and it was a long shot - was getting 'Pitch and Misses' off salesmen that he knew who worked for other window companies. He called in a few favours and then collected a batch of leads for addresses that had already been visited by salesmen, but hadn't produced any sales.

He really was up against it, but try he must.

Elgin got Lucy to telephone canvass the leads and make all the appointments for him, then all he had to do was the hard bit, sell the windows at a higher price than the previous salesman had failed to get, which was obviously at rock bottom after they had started high. Miraculously, he sold in the first three houses he went into and more importantly, got three decent deposits as well to pay for sample windows, a batch of printing and money to pay for advertising. Even then he wasn't out of the woods. He'd put himself in a precarious position - not only did he have to sell more to feed the family, he also had to sell more leads just to pay for the windows on which he had already spent the initial deposits. If he couldn't keep up this momentum, he'd probably be going to jail. You have to wonder what percentage of people would have had the balls even to attempt it.

One thing that has become crystal clear over the years, is that Elgin is at is very best when all seems lost and the pressure is unbearable. But you know the saying, 'When the going gets tough, the tough get going' - this is as true today as it has been throughout history - it's the indomitable spirit, the bulldog breed, the difference between leaders and followers, not many have it, but it's a great trait to possess. Apart from that quality, you must also be able to close the deal. It's no good having a fantastic presentation if you can't close. You can't be a great football centre forward if you don't score goals. Closers are born - I don't think you can teach it, you've either got it or you ain't. It's the most important aspect about selling. It's a salesman's daily mantra - *Always Be Closing* (ABC). Elgin had it in spades. There is a very good 1992 film called *Glengarry Glen Ross* featuring a very strong cast including Alec Baldwin, Al Pacino and Jack Lemmon - It is about the cut-throat world of sales, and it's a film synonymous with the term *always be closing*.

Elgin had already put the heavy spade work in, so he felt he had thoroughly deserved it when he walked onto a real live one. He sold a lead for four and a half grand and they paid for the whole job up front. This gave him enough dough to install the three earlier jobs and bank the larger balances that were still owing after the deposits. He gave the salesmen who had fed him leads a bloody good drink as well. They were delighted and gave him a load more. He wasn't king of the castle yet, but he'd climbed up four or five rungs of the ladder.

Life was looking brighter.

Even though Elgin was on a roll, there were still hurdles to leap. For installations he'd been using the lads who worked at the factory where he bought the windows from. They would come out and install the jobs, but it was only a short term measure and so he really needed his own installers. Without his own reliable fitters, expansion was out of the question, but out of the blue he got a phone call that could solve all of his problems and then some. It was a guy named Nigel Hobley who had worked with him at *Stormseal*. He was a joiner by trade and had done moderately well at selling windows. He'd heard on the grapevine that Elgin had started out on his own and was doing well. He only wanted to buy into the company didn't he? His father had recently been made redundant after working many years at the same company, coming out with a massive wedge of wonga. Nigel wasn't slow in coming forward with multiple mentions of being awash with money..

On the programme Watchdog, our eponymous hero is known as Elgin 'Lucky' Hounds... that televisual treat is yet to come in our story, but for all the talent, skill, graft and ability one has, surely the greatest gift in life is good luck. We all need it, we crave it, sometimes it disappears for long periods, but it's a great thing to have on your side - the extremely attractive Lady Luck.

Elgin was looking for help with the business, and it fell right onto his lap; ten large. Hobley wasn't a guy Elgin had ever warmed to in the past, but the handover of a chunk of cash would send the mercury in his thermometer racing up a few degrees (ooh matron!). However, it remained to be seen if it all stayed temperate. The only truism at that moment was Elgin was lucky *and ten grand richer*.

Elgin didn't like socialising with Hobley because he always thought he was something of a pervert, but it was inevitable sometimes - for example, as after the christening of his daughter Lotte, Hobley made some extremely inappropriate, crude alcohol-induced remarks to Lucy's cousin, Sue. Elgin had his work cut out trying to prevent her husband Shifty getting past him and smashing Hobley to pieces. In all the time he saw him, he never saw him with a woman. There was definitely a dark side to him. They were never going to be mates... who knew?

The main thing was that Elgin was staying ahead of the game. He had to carry Hobley half the time, but good money was being made. He even got his dad - who was just as obnoxious as his son - (it must have run in the family) to invest more dosh into the business. He was delighted to do so. Anything to help 'me babby', as he called him. *(Could you pass the sick bag please?)*

Elgin was regularly working 14 hour days and Hobley and his dad were giving him the incessant hump. He was getting home each night cream-crackered and then falling asleep on the sofa. Lucy had warned him at least a dozen times that he looked washed out and was heading for a heart attack. They were still making really good money, but was all the stress worth it? He was living to work instead of it being the other way round. He had a long discussion with Lucy and they both decided it was time to bale out and to cut ties with the horrible Hobley's. Elgin wanted to get the maximum leverage on Pinky and Perky for a big payday. He'd built up the company, put in blood, sweat and tears, he needed adequate compensation.

He came up with a cunning plan. First, he asked dad and son if they wanted to 'buy him out'. What? They were all over it like a rash! Then, after he had talked up the business for a couple of weeks he had them salivating like two hungry Alsations with ten inch tongues at the pub meat raffle. And then he came in with the *coup de grâce* - he feigned a heart attack.

If Lucy was indeed right that he looked like shit and was heading for a coronary, he could probably pull it off. This ploy had been done on the classic sitcom, *Only Fools and Horses*. In another weird coincidence, these two fake heart attacks both happened simultaneously - in 1989. Elgin swears to this day that he has never seen the episode, so we are suing the BBC for plagiarism. It's only fair after all - they took my 107 year old gran to court for not having a bleeding TV license!

Hobley turns up at Elgin's gaff as per usual Monday morning to find a man prone on the settee complaining of chest pains. Elgin has already booked an appointment with the new student doctor down the surgery, so he gets Hobley to drive him down there. It really was an Oscar-winning performance. He's really laying it on thick. He gets in to see the student doctor and demands an ECG up at the hospital. He tells him there are terrible pains in his chest and down his left arm to go with a long history of heart problems in the family. The young guy craps his pants and hands him a form for the procedure. Elgin staggers back into the waiting room, tells Hobley the doctor thinks he's had cardiac arrest and that he was going to phone for an ambulance. But Elgin told him it would be quicker - as his mate is with him - to drive him up there. Hobley gets up there faster than Ayrton Senna. All the while Elgin is giving it the old dying fly. "I'll wait for you then take you home," says Hobley.

"No mate, I could be hours or even kept in, you've got to look after the business, that's the most important thing." Hobley didn't disagree and fucked off. As soon as he was gone Elgin was on the phone for a taxi, laughing his socks off.

The next morning Elgin is on the dog and bone, "Come round mate, I've got things to tell you." Hobley is there before the phone's put down. He's keen as mustard. Elgin shows him one of Lucy's diet sheets, informing him the consultant has told him he must follow the rabbit food plan for the rest of his life in conjunction with packing in all stressful activity and labour. Hobley's eyes light up like crazy emeralds, the sly smirk on his face give away his protestations of solace and regret. The filthy twat was deserving of everything that was coming his way. He kept asking, "What's going to happen now?"

Elgin kept him walking on eggshells, "I don't know, I'll ring you again in a few days." Hobley walked out beaming from ear to ear, followed ten minutes later by Elgin and Lucy going out for a slap up meal and just a few drinks. The trap was set, and so far it had been a textbook operation. He was gagging for it.

A sale is not simply a sale. You can get a good deal or you can get a turkey. Every extra ten pounds you can get off a buyer is money in your pocket and less in his. Most transactions are to the satisfaction of both parties and a handshake will seal it. The best negotiators are always aware of leaving some meat on the bone for the next guy, but there is always a chance with a durable, tough negotiator so long as he is not taking the piss. As in life, there are winners and losers. In the 'changing of the guard' in this window company, one man held a prial of aces and the other held ragged seven high. There was a lot to be said for folding, but when you covet possession at any cost and this is your overwhelming desire, then sometimes... just sometimes, you might just be buying a pig in a poke.

Hobley was on the phone two days running. Elgin could hear the compulsion through the timbre and tone of his speech. He decided to strike while the iron was hot. As a master salesman, he knew that it mattered not whether something was worthless or priceless. The main attribute to any deal is the buyer's avarice. The Eiffel Tower was sold to a Parisienne scrap merchant in 1925 - all seven thousand tons of it - by a con man masquerading as a government official. This was pure and simple greed at work. And, if you've been to Paris recently, you can't but help notice this large 300-metre-high metal structure still standing there... *Sacre Bleu*!

The buyer, by the way, never pressed charges in court, he was too embarrassed.

Elgin had long reasoned that Hobley couldn't have given a fuck whether he lived or died, all he was focused on was the prize. In his eyes, a thriving business. Elgin was apathetic to Hobley's indifference, it didn't come into his calculations. He'd seen peoples' worst sides all through his life. He simply wanted the best price he could for the business as it stood, because Hobley had badly miscalculated. With Elgin gone, the window company was losing its best and main asset. He was the power and driving force. If a Grand Prix champion racer is taken out of one of the faster cars and put in one of the slower cars, he won't get on the podium. The *quid pro quo* here was pre- and post-Hounds. It was a massive difference. The company was doing well, but could it sustain the momentum afterwards without him? What did Elgin care... he would be well away with his pockets hopefully full of holding folding.

There was one more tactic to possibly eke out some more money on the deal. Elgin decided to implement something called a *negative sale* - that was to get Hobley to inflate the price he was going to pay himself by his own actions. You may all be wondering, how the fuck are you going to do that? Well, it's a simple technique of making the buyer do something by putting the germ of an idea into his head, for example by convincing him that he is saving money by doing what he is doing, but it actually has the opposite effect by costing him more. Are you all clear now? I told you it was dead simple.

The big day was here. Hobley comes round to the bungalow bang on time. Punctuality is always a virtue when you're carrying a large brief case full of high denomination banknotes. Elgin comes out with the old sob story that he was dejected over the fact that it would be a tragedy for himself and his young family to completely forsake the business he built, which was so obviously going to become a hugely successful company and not keep a small percentage, thereby having an income from it. That was the last thing Hobley wanted to hear, having to pay out a wage... and in his mind, maybe for decades to come. When Elgin told him he wanted a lump sum and a monthly wage, all the blood drained out of his face. He did a marvellous albino impression. He just hadn't seen it coming - a bit like Stevie Wonder walking along some tram tracks.

Now, Elgin knew quite candidly that once he left, that the company could possibly go to the wall at some early point. He certainly wasn't a modern day Nostradamus of course, and it could have also grown and prospered, instead. But his money was on it *going south*... rapidly. The last thing Elgin was interested in was a short term wage, but if the notion of that influenced Hobley to be kinder on the lump sum, he was all ears. They sat down at the table: two poker players vying for the pot. As predicted, Hobley started to beat Elgin down on the percentage of the wages, thereby raising up the cash lump sum. Elgin kept putting forward his argument about starting the company and Hobley kept trying to justify his end by raising the lump sum and reducing the monthly income. Hobley eventually got the wages down to nothing by compensating the payoff. In his eyes he'd played a belter, but it was a total pyrrhic victory... there was only one winner, and he wasn't called 'me babby'.

Lucy had left the room because she couldn't keep her face straight. But it must have been woman's intuition, because as soon as Hobley started counting out the money she was right back in amongst them. He was covering the table with thick wads of twenty pound notes. Cash is king, as you all know, but it's strange how royalty never carry any about with them, tight bastards. About halfway through the count, Shifty walked in, his face was a book that said, "What have you got this pervy idiot doing now?" He still hadn't warmed to Hobley. He'd calmed right down since the christening though - he now only wanted to break one of his legs instead of both - but it probably wouldn't have been an opportune moment. Nobody wanted a recount. It must have been a right good result as it took ages to count and guess what? Hobley was a bag of sand short. So he said to Elgin, "I'll get that grand round to you tomorrow morning, Elgin, if that is OK?"

"No problem mate, whenever you want," came the nonchalant reply. It was all signed, sealed and delivered. Elgin felt like a huge millstone had been lifted from his shoulders. It was onwards and upwards from here.

First article on the agenda; book a holiday. Just a cheap package tour to Benidorm. It would be just the ticket after his 'heart scare'! It was two year old Lotte's debut abroad and she loved it - a chip off the old block. While they were over there Lucy persuaded Elgin to hire a car and drive an hour and a half to the south to his parent's house in Torrevieja. It had been nearly five years since he'd seen them after the bust-up with his dad. They had never met Lucy and Lotte, and Elgin was a tad apprehensive when they pulled up, but they were all made extremely welcome. Elgin and his dad had an alpha male hug and all was well again in the world.

They had had quite enough of Stafford for the time being, so they put their bungalow up for sale. Five bungalows up the road, I was sad to see them go, but we all have our lives to live. It would only be a few months more before I would sell my taxi company and go to work for Elgin. Whilst the property was being sold they had a short stay in Tenerife where Elgin was part of the team that broke the world record for selling timeshares.

There was only one place in the universe to go after that great success!

That's right... they travelled from Stafford the 35 miles down the A50 to the grand old City of Derby.

* * * *

CHAPTER ELEVEN

Derby Delight... and Doldrums

They rented a house in Mickleover a large village in the West suburbs of Derby. I visited them there a few times. The only reason I had ever heard of Mickleover was because of the infamous lunatic asylum, so they were in real good company at the time. I think it was shut down in the mid-nineties, but half those people are probably still walking out and about these days. (about par for the course with Derby) It was a lovely three-bedroomed accommodation, but danger laid in wait just yards away. The house next door was inhabited by a copper... and a right horrible bastard he turned out to be as well. There is no point applying stereotypes here, the police are a mixed unit of quite a few (maybe more) bad eggs with a majority of decent types. It's true that they are never off-duty though, so watch what you say in their company. But my brother-in-law is ex-plod and you won't find a nicer bloke in the Midlands.

Elgin, a man in his early thirties, miraculously hadn't yet come into any serious contact with the Old Bill, so had no reason at all to dislike or mistrust the police. Both families got on well, they had a daughter the same age as Lotte and two older kids roughly the same age as Elgin's two eldest. The wife was an ex-copper, but a really lovely woman. Dave, the serving copper, was a racist bully with a split personality - a real *Jekyll and Hyde* character, but unlike the novel by Robert Louis Stevenson where the main protagonist changes from good to bad, Dave was bad... *and extremely bad*. Even his mates in the police used to say, "Have you met Dave's alter-ego yet, Elgin?" and laugh. His darker side always came out when he'd imbibed copious amounts of alcohol - and he wasn't a fun drinker either - he'd drink so much that he'd struggle to get out his car or even climb a flight of stairs.

They decided to move to Derby. The reason being that Elgin had previously worked there in the damp course business and it was where he had always done remarkably well. Derbyshire itself, with its many ex-mining communities in the towns and villages in and around the hills north of Derby, was now a veritable gold mine in terms of profit in this line of work. Lucy was not keen on him going back into damp proofing, but it was becoming harder and harder to make a living in the double glazing business without self-manufacturing as well, so his mind was made up.

The damp boys were back in action.

He rented a suite of offices and began to recruit staff. The first person he took on was a 22-year-old divorcee with a single child, Michelle Croxford. He wasn't sure if he'd made the right decision, but after a few weeks she turned out to be brilliant at her job, organising both the admin as well as the burgeoning office staff expertly. Elgin took on a large team of door-to-door canvassers to book vital appointments for all the salesmen of which there were about eight or ten at any one time. This was all flowing successfully... until he had a brainwave. He advertised in the local papers offering a FREE DAMP SURVEY. That next week they were knocked over with the response. The dam had burst and it was all hands on deck.

That week I got a phone call off Elgin. It was another strange coincidence; I had just sold my half share in Bee-Line taxis to my partner Paul Flello and his dad (both who I liked by the way). Paul had bought in two years earlier for eighteen grand, so I banked that and teamed up, but as many of you know to your cost, partnerships rarely work. He was seriously overweight and didn't move off his chair very often. I thought to myself, *I know who is going to be doing most of the spadework here!* And it was a big operation. I had built it up to 40 cars including three London Hackney Cabs and was now renting *The Reynolds MOT Centre* at the side of the nearby night club as well. The place had four ramps and three mechanics. Yet my accountant informed me that we'd made less money with 40 cars than the previous year when we had 20, and we were working like a Chinese laundry on heat. We never stopped.

On top of that, I had a 20-year-old, six-foot brunette called Amanda back at Berry Road demanding sex five times a day. I looked up the definition of nymphomaniac in the Chambers Dictionary and there was a picture of her by it. She had a large suitcase full of sex toys and attachments; dildos, vibrators all that nonsense. I was right out my depth. She said to me one day, "What's your best sexual fantasy?"

I didn't have one. But I told her, "To have a week away from you!" That didn't go down well, but it was seriously making me ill. I didn't want to go to work or be home either. It was like a pincer movement 24 hours a day. I had hooked up with her after she used to come to the quiz league matches if I was playing. She was going out with another taxi bloke at the time, and I said to her one night, "You like your quizzes, Amanda?"

She replied, "I don't like quizzes, I like you." And like the bloody fool I was, I fell for it. She'd been at Berry Road about six months and I was fatigued. I ended up watching any old shit on late night television, synchronised swimming, potholing, yoga, open university, anything rather than go to bed. It had been a dream for the first week, as I just thought she was being exuberant. It soon became monotonous. I could fathom it say, if your girlfriend or wife was repulsive, but she was gorgeous. But I suppose it was all too much of a good thing. Apparently Bjorn Borg got divorced because his wife was a sexual maniac. He has my deepest sympathies. He was losing too many long rallies at tennis.

Where were we...? Ah yes! Elgin's phone call. He knew I had just sold Bee-Line and wasn't working and so asked, "Would you like some repping work, Micky ?"

"Not particularly."

He could tell I was keen. "Come on mate, I'm snowed under over here! Give us a hand. It will get you away from that mad bird of yours. You can even stay over in Derby some nights."

That was the clincher. "I'll be over tomorrow." I told Amanda I'd be away most nights. She was a month away from going to the famous UMIST (University of Manchester Institute of Science and Technology). God only knows why... I'd told her a million times that I wouldn't be going up there to visit her, and so she finally got the message and went back home to her very wealthy parents in Penkridge.

The last I heard of her was a couple of months later. Out of the blue the phone rang. She came on, she'd found a new boyfriend - a South African. I thought, *thank fuck for that, the poor bugger!* But I still had a nice chat with the two of them. It's always best to go amicably when you go your separate ways. On looking back you can get quite nostalgic for the heady days of the past. In fact though, times have certainly changed these days... I've just christened my new water bed, *The Dead Sea.*

I had freed myself from two bonds: Bee-Line had been part of my life for five glorious years, but I was now 38 and on my way to Derby. Unlike Elgin I didn't get as much out of the Flellos as I could have done.

My main concern was just getting away - notwithstanding the cash settlement. I was proud of what I built up from scratch; the biggest taxi company Stafford has ever seen to this day and a million pound turnover in the first six months. However, I quickly learnt afterwards that *turnover was vanity, profit was sanity.* Wise words for anyone starting up in business.

I picked up various famous people in my cab, amongst them were; Nasty Nick (John Altman - very posh), Gail Platt (Helen Worth - even posher), actor Robert Hardy, some famous bloke from *Neighbours* whose name escapes me and - Elgin will like this - Steve Bull, centre forward from Wolverhampton Wanderers Football Club. Years later on the rails at Wolverhampton Races, I was the only bookie Steve would ever bet with. I'd give him better odds than the others. His bet was always £60 and - he won't mind me saying this - he was better at goalscoring than picking winners.

My meeting with the Flellos had me taking away six grand and a Nissan Bluebird worth about four grand. I'd already had that other eighteen grand two years earlier, and the last few years I'd been taking home £700 a week - not bad for the early 90s. I'd had a good run and, like Elgin, I was the major asset there. I'm not boasting here but I knew the shift I was putting in. After the accountant let me know we were becoming busy fools, it was time to go. The writing was on the wall and six months later Bee-line was gone. I wished they could have saved it, but it was not to be. The Flellos are both dead now, sad really, but lots of Stafford people fondly remember Bee-Line.

Elgin won't mind me mentioning one last amusing taxi story as it involves our great mate - the one and only Geoff Brundrett - but only in a small way. It predates Bee-Line by a few years at Yellow Cars Taxis on the Newport Road by the *Top of the World*, owned and run by Geoff. All the motors had to be painted bright yellow in the New York City taxi style. I had a mark III Ford Cortina - the one with the huge bonnet. Elgin is a Wolves fan as you know. I'm a Chelsea man - my dad and grandad were both cockneys and I was living in *The Smoke* when I was young and that is when I saw my first match at Stamford Bridge with Chelsea beating West Ham 6-2. Elgin has actually been to matches with me and stood in the infamous Shed End. Anyhow, I'm digressing! (Again) Chelsea had just signed a striker - Kerry Dixon - who was knocking goals in for fun so, after naming my standard poodle Kerry, it was time to get some big black lettering to put on the driver's side wing. I carefully patted on the sticky letters *KERRY DIXON*. I thought it looked the dog's bollocks. Punters would often get in the taxi and call me Kerry. The best tale was a really posh guy who seriously thought I was Kerry

Dixon himself and asked me why I was in Stafford. I told him that if Chelsea didn't have a midweek game, I'd come up to Stafford and moonlight as a taxi driver for some extra wonga (Dixon was playing for England at the time). He got out at Brocton, gave me the fare and a tip and asked me who Chelsea were playing on Saturday. I couldn't remember and told him Spurs, I'm still dining out on that story. I used to go Chelsea every home match and once met Kerry Dixon at Scratchwood Services after they beat Stoke, I told him I'd named my dog and car after him...

He couldn't get away quickly enough.

Elgin got me a Rover Stirling for repping. The best car I'd ever had, soft top and all computerised. I'd had my hair cut, and was wearing black slacks, white shirt and black tie. I had a two-hour course and sent out to conquer the world. Being the mate of the boss was handy because he knew all the answers. If I went through my pitch with him, he'd improve it. I wasn't top earner amongst the reps but I wasn't bottom either. If you sold damp proofing to a big house you had a week's money just from that. It was all enjoyable and a nice break from Stafford.

They were a good set of blokes there as well, until Elgin said, "Tell them about your bird, Mick." We used to have them with tears rolling down their faces with some of her exploits, none of which are printable on here unless I want to wear a real set of handcuffs. There was a fat rep always mooching about the office - I can't remember his name - he always used to wear the same crap anorak, making me look somewhat debonair in comparison. I christened him *The Slug,* a name that suited him down to the ground. Elgin was talking to me one day saying he'd been out to a great restaurant the previous evening, so The Slug slouches over in his anorak, uninvited and says, "I never, ever tip less than £50 in a restaurant." and walks out of the room. I said, "Can you believe that shit Elgin," he says "he doesn't earn that much some weeks!"

We both burst out laughing. I think I stayed three or four months. He had plenty of salesmen by then and I didn't need to work at the time as I was quite flush, but I learnt a lot of useful things about selling. Elgin used to say that I had 'a unique way of selling'. I used to make them laugh. If you can get them to trust and like you, it's easier when they come to sign on the dotted line time... as you know, *Always Be Closing.*

There was good news as I was making my retreat, Lucy declared herself pregnant again with Elgin's youngest daughter Sylvia. He was to be a father for the fourth time and none of the offspring were really planned... well, not by him anyway. He'd been there at the conception of course. How many different hats did he want to wear? He was blessed. It's all called SERENDIPITY, the greatest gift in the universe.

After twelve months he was cooking on gas. He had opened offices in Northampton, Cardiff, Sheffield, Reading and Rochdale. That covered large swathes of the country. The money was rolling in, much to the bitter disappointment of flatfoot next door. He had banned his wife from coming across to visit if Elgin's car was parked on the driveway. He truly thought that she fancied him. She didn't - it was all in his tiny addled brain, along with his paranoid insecurities and inadequacies.

They were living a great life as the money poured in. Of course money doesn't always bring happiness, but whatever state of health you're in or how many problems you have, a big lump in the bank is far more preferable than having to watch the pennies. This was a period when nothing was out of reach. Holidays, quality cars, expensive clothes and the best food and drink were all on tap whenever, or wherever, Lucy and the kids wanted anything. Elgin would earn big, then spend big. It's a mystery why a lot people, both rich ones and the comfortably off, would never treat themselves in the short time they are around. It's not uncommon to read in the local obituaries about someone you knew well, leave a million quid in their will, but you remember them saving elastic bands and making a ball of them and wearing clothes and shoes with holes in. There's you thinking they didn't have a pot to piss in. Let me tell you, these people have no friends. There's careful, and then there's mean. People gravitate towards fun folk who enjoy their life and spend their money, not the ones who get involved in five rounds of drinks in the pub, but when it's their shout, disappear. As you're reading this you're thinking I know that guy; *Billy no mates*.

Speaking of beer, Elgin became a regular imbiber in the pub across the road from his office - the *Buck in the Park*. Steve Hughes and his wife, Jackie, ran it. Steve was a larger than life character who didn't give a flying fuck about anything. It was all water off a duck's back to him, including coping with some family tragedies over the years. Elgin got on with him from day one. All Steve's boyhood mates drank there and they were all Derby County fans - *The Rams*. Even they quickly accepted him (he must have been a wolf in sheep's clothing). Roll call here: Elgin has yet to meet a better set of lads than Nipper, Watto, Carl, Ally Chen, Charlsey, Rhino and Jules, not forgetting the rest of the Alvaston mob. Geoff Brundrette and Big Col used to come over from Stafford at the weekends for some fucking mad times. It's always a good catalyst that, to have two more like-minded souls in tow.

Elgin and Steve went over to America to watch the 1994 World Cup Finals. England hadn't even qualified but they were football mad those two. It was a boys only vacation to Florida. It was like a busman's holiday for Steve - you couldn't get him out of any of the many bars of Tampa Bay. It soon became clear to Elgin that he wasn't going to see any games. On top of that, they were close to Cape Canaveral which was holding a massive 25th anniversary of the first moon landing, with a carnival and events. They had even been invited to go to a speech by Neil Armstrong, but Hughsey - always the culture vulture - said, "Fuck that moonman shit, Elgin, it's a load of bollocks, get the beers in!"

If only Britain had still ruled the USA, they would have erected that fitting tribute on a polished brass plaque at the entrance to NASA. It would have been in homage to Steve. On the day they were supposed to come back there was another problem. He drops this on Elgin, "Errrr, I'm staying here mate."

Elgin thought he was winding him right up, but he'd met a local geezer in the bar on their last night, way after Elgin had gone off for an early night. Apparently he had offered Steve a job. "I'm gonna be a lifeguard."

Elgin roared out laughing, "Who do you think you are, the Derbyshire David Hasselhoff?"

He was more than deadly serious though. Elgin put his cards on the table, "If I go back alone, Jackie will stab me through the heart. I don't care if you return here next week, but I'm not being held responsible for this ongoing fiasco."

He eventually managed to bundle Steve into the car after two hours of begging and manhandling and off they sped to the airport.

Elgin decided to open up another office in Torrevieja, selling wall coatings to ex-pats. He had previously invested in a villa out there on the other side of the town from his parents. That way, the whole family of four could relax in Iberian comfort before visiting his mum and dad. They weren't getting any younger, so it made sense as Elgin wanted to see more of them in their Autumn years and, of course, it was great fun for them to see their grandchildren growing up. The legend Tommy Rowlands had been recruited as canvassing manager along with old mates, Sugar and Mark Bradbury from Stafford as salesmen. Tommy was a man Elgin trusted through good times or droughts, and soon the old slick combo were back in business.

Everything was great, then in a split second, it all turned to darkness and despair. Elgin had decided to be in Spain for the grand opening of the new company. He had driven down solo to Portsmouth to catch the ferry to Santander in Northern Spain, and from there he stopped off in Madrid for a day, before completing the third part of the journey to Torrevieja. He took his mum and dad out for lunch that Friday. The conversation was lively; his dad had previously asked him to lend his brother Ivan some money for a short period a month earlier, but Elgin had refused saying that Ivan already owed him thousands, but finally agreed after his father guaranteed the money. "Has Ivan paid you that five grand back yet?"

"No, you know his track record."

"Right! I'll get my cheque book and straighten it out." He went and came back into the room, but Elgin in his heart couldn't accept it and told his dad he'd get Ivan to pay by having him work it off installing damp proofing.

They had an excellent repast and Elgin went back to his villa only to find he'd mislaid his phone somewhere. He was still waiting for a phone to be installed at the villa, so he went out to a payphone to check on all the sales figures from England. He couldn't get through to anyone. All the office numbers were engaged. *What the fuck was going on?* Friday afternoon was a quiet part of the week for damp enquiries. He was starting to lose his rag. He eventually got through to a crying Michelle, who told him to ring Lucy urgently. Elgin rang home, Lucy through floods of tears told him that his mum had taken the dogs out for their daily walk. When she got back, she discovered his dad had died from a heart attack. He was only 62.

Elgin was utterly devastated. He was all over the place. He couldn't function to work. Tommy went in and set the new business up, but Elgin had gone AWOL in his own mind. He woke up the next day with all his face covered in bruises, looking like he'd gone 12 rounds with Frank Bruno. He couldn't remember how it happened, but apparently he'd been punching himself in the face. Elgin had obviously taken the loss very badly. He remembers clearly Steve Hughes ringing him up at night saying, "So sorry about your dad mate, it's shit for two weeks." He also remembers telling Steve two years after that call, "This is a long two weeks Hughsey."

The only blessing for Elgin was that he had been with his dad on the day he died. There was a lot to be said for that. He rang his brother Ivan, in Antrim, Northern Ireland (he'd married a local girl called Patricia) arranging for him to get over to Spain via his office in England. He turned up with a lilo under his arm after booking a two week return flight. He was taking the piss as per usual. Elgin had to get him cheap hotel accommodation as well.

It didn't help Elgin on the day of the funeral when his mum told him that his dad had been stressed recently by a next door neighbour from Hell. Now he had someone to castigate other than himself. The guy next door was a Hungarian headcase and was driving Dennis mad with his behaviour. He had chased him up the road a few times trying to grab hold of him. After the funeral Elgin was rat-arsed and phoned up the Magyar giving him dog's abuse, calling him every name under the sun. He actually felt a lot better after the phone call as all the 'guilt demons' had been passed over to the Hungarian. They were now his to cope with.

A short while after the funeral, Geoff Brundrette came out to 'look after him'. Tommy had called Geoff telling him about Elgin driving through a Guardia Civil (Spanish Police) roadblock whilst pissed up to high Heaven at 90mph. *Look after him*. That was a euphemism for sitting in the pub every day and night. After the first day, Elgin hardly saw him again the entire month he was in Spain.

One of the England office girls with a warped sense of humour booked Elgin on the same flight out to Spain with a guy called Terry Boylan, who was going to be one of the team leaders for Tommy. They ended up travelling together and were waiting in the airport bar before the flight. In strides George Best - as if it's an everyday occurrence. He comes up to the bar and stands next to them. Elgin had just finished reading his autobiography, so that gives him a nice opening gambit for a chat. Best is wearing a leather jacket with the word LEGEND in big letters emblazoned on the back. Elgin says he has a dog and a car named after him (No, he didn't). He informs him that, "Not many people in the world could justify wearing that jacket, but you sure can."

What a smoothie eh?

He tells Elgin his favourite story from the autobiography. It's been well documented, but it's worth another airing because it's funny. And hey, some of you might not know it!

He's missed training again with Manchester United to go out on the lash with an ex-Miss World. They've had dinner a good drink and finish off the night with a few bets at the casino. Best has won big and they return to their hotel in the very early hours. George orders a night cap - a magnum of champagne. Ten minutes later there's a knock on the door. It's room service in the shape of a small elderly Irishman. He comes in with the champers on a tray with two morning papers which he's read in which there is news coming up about Best copping off from United and also on the tray... wait for it, three glasses. Best passes him a glass back and says. "Not tonight, Paddy." The Irishman then takes a look to his left where a half-naked Miss World is lying seductively on the double bed with wads of £50 notes scattered all around her...

He turns to Best and says, "George, where did it all go wrong ?"

Best swears that's a true story, and I for one believe him.

By this time Terry has sunk far too much alcohol and is starting to misbehave. He starts slagging Best off for no particular reason. It gets worse, so Best shakes his head and does one (You couldn't blame him). Elgin is incredibly pissed off and on the verge of sacking him before they fly, but it wouldn't have been fair to Tommy over in Spain. Elgin just hoped that Tom knew what he was letting himself in for.

The 'trolley dollies' wouldn't serve him any drinks on the plane, so half an hour later he's sobered up a little and asking Elgin about the night life in Torrevieja. Elgin still has the raving hump with him, but speaks kindly. He has decided to set him up for a fall when they get to Spain and show him right up for the ignorant prick he obviously is. He tells Terry, who's probably never been out of Derby before, that all the top faces at work go out every Saturday to this club/bar where all the girls are gorgeous, wearing scantily risqué clothes and love all the English blokes. This was all bollocks of course... as it was a 'knocking shop', and that was where Terry was going tomorrow night to be humiliated

It was Saturday night, Tommy and a few of the lads had been given the 'SP' on what was going to unfold. Sure enough, they had Terry tanked up before they made their grand entrance into the *If Heineken did night clubs it would look like this brothel.* Terry's eyes popped out of his head when he clocked all the totty milling about. He was coerced to go up to the bar as Elgin found a suitable young lady to nibble his ear. It was the best hundred quid he'd ever spent. She could only speak limited English, but understood that she was picking him up.

The brass walks over - everyone is pointing to Terry - she didn't wait for an introduction and she grabs him and puts her tongue down his throat. He had a face like someone who had got six numbers up on the lottery. Everyone is pissing themselves laughing. Only an imbecile would believe it was all kosher. Elgin tells him to buy her a glass of champagne - because she obviously likes him. That is the clincher. She's practically mounted him on the settee. They mooch off upstairs for half an hour. He comes back down and says, "Fucking hell, Elgin, it's much better here than the Pink Coconut! (the top nightclub in Derby)... I'll be coming back every Saturday!"

They move on to their local bar, *Delboy's*. Terry has told every man and his dog in there about his sexual exploits. He was starting to bore the pants of everyone - including the barman, so Tommy decided to tell him the truth about what had just happened. But the deluded moron wouldn't have it at any price. He was returning there next week. Fair enough of course, but it would cost him a cool ton though

.

Back in Derby, Lucy and the psychotic copper's wife were plotting a foul and heinous holiday, ie, all going away to Majorca together. It was stated by Elgin that he'd rather go with Rasputin and Typhoid Mary - *What the fuck was she playing at?*

Lucy had invested in a bargaining chip; namely two tickets for the big Lennox Lewis v Frank Bruno punch up in Cardiff, where the men could bond together, show some fraternal *bonhomie* and return to Derby the best of pals. It was a bit of a long shot really. Elgin detested him with a passion and safe to say the feeling was mutual, but it looked a good fight so reluctantly he agreed to swallow it.

Elgin drove down to Cardiff with Bad Dave as his front seat wingman on the day of the fight. They had booked into The Marriot Hotel, a four star establishment in the city centre. Against Elgin's better judgement they went to the hotel bar early doors. It was full of Bruno's family and the atmosphere was electric. He knew *Very Bad Dave* would appear in a couple of hours time at any given moment - once he'd downed about half a gallon of ale, but hopefully he may upset some large geezer who would then proceed to knock him out and put him in hospital. They had been there two hours when Elgin went up the bar for more drinks. Bad Dave hadn't yet morphed into his evil alter ego. He got in amongst a group of people from *The Sun* newspaper that included a couple of really attractive young ladies - they turned out to be 'page three girls' who were going to be the round girls for the big fight.

He got talking to one of them who gave him an invite for Lennox Lewis's post-fight party at *Browns Night Club*. "Have you got two? I'm with a mate."

"No problem!"

But there *was* going to be a problem. *Very Bad Dave* had finally shown up at the bar wondering where his drink was. So what did the cretin do when Elgin told him they had golden tickets to the hottest party in the city and formally introduced him to the girl? He only started pawing her that's what... on top of telling her that she looks really tarty. He then spills some beer over her top as he staggers from one side to the other. It was *bye-bye night club*. She says, "I'm sorry" to Elgin before walking off utterly disgusted. There wasn't that much dialogue between the blokes after that at the fight or the long drive home.

The fight went into pugilistic history as the first heavyweight title match between two Britons. There was very little love lost between Lewis and Bruno - in fact they despised each other - so that made it a rare needle match that everyone wanted to see. It was shown in America and the UK on pay-for-view television and 25,000 saw it live at the old Cardiff Arms Park stadium. Dubbed the "Battle of Britain", it was a close fight for five or six rounds until the class of Lewis came to the surface. Bruno was a stiff fighter. If he tired, he was as easy to hit as a cow's arse with a banjo. Lewis caught him with a tremendous punch in the 7th that stunned him. Bruno was unusual as a fighter because he hardly ever went down from big shots. He would stand there dazed and helpless like a rabbit in the headlights. He had previously done the same in another title fight against Tim Witherspoon and this time the referee had to jump in to save him from serious injury.

It was the only high point of Elgin's trip to Wales.

Just for a quiet life, he let Lucy have her own way and they all went to Majorca on one condition; that the two families stayed at different hotels. This ultimatum was non-negotiable, as the further he could get away from shit-for-brains the better. Thankfully, *Very Bad Dave* seldom made an appearance on the holiday, but if Elgin thought the man had turned over a brand new leaf he was very much mistaken. The next time he would be in close proximity to him, his actions would make the Battle of Rorke's Drift resemble the vicar's garden party.

That nonsense would come later. At the time Elgin was still grieving for his dad and was spending more and more time in Spain where he felt closer to him. This escalated to a point where he told Lucy that he planned to close most of the offices in England and concentrate on the business in Spain. He persuaded her to bring the kids out there for a six month holiday in the hope that they could all settle in sunny *Espagne*.

A dozen or so staff in England came over to work too; salesmen, canvassers and, of course, office supremo Michelle Croxford. They all kicked in like Flynn after adjusting to the different routines and climate, earning very decent dosh on top of experiencing a great life in the Spanish sunshine. Elgin was still earning a substantial amount of income from previous transactions that were still being paid into his account back in Blighty in the form of part payments. A lot of folk preferred to pay piece-meal on a monthly basis rather than dish out a lump sum, so he always had a more than adequate buffer if anything untoward ever occurred. He had another idea for a business, so he sent Michelle back over to England to open up another account, transferring all the direct debits into the new one. Now, in a perfect world that's not a lot to ask is it? But this old adage still holds water today; "If the cat's away the mice will play."

Well, this rodentia trustee wasn't just after the odd slice of Camembert cheese either... she was planning on pulling off an 'enormouse' coup. Elgin at the time thought all was harmonious in his cosmos of fluxing variability, he was sadly mistaken. He was about to enter the black hole phase, but first he had to navigate his way through two hot seasons with mucho wonga, wine and top cuisine.

Most of Elgin's Spanish working days went like this; in the office for 8am in the morning, finish around 2-ish, pick up mother, Lucy and the kids, head off to a restaurant on the beach to meet up with other members of staff. They'd sit around for a couple of hours, eating paella and drinking sangria, then it was off to have some bets on the late afternoon horse racing on TV at their local bar, *Delboys*. Elgin would get home about half-six, pick Lucy and the kids up again to go out for dinner, then round the night off at *Delboys* with Tommy, Sugar - and not forgetting his golf partner - Mark Bradbury. Now if this seems like it was the *Magic Roundabout*, it was even better than that, because Zebedee never once turned up and proclaimed that it was, 'Time for bed.'

Does everyone remember Frank Duffy who years earlier got the sack from Venables Timber Yard in Stafford when Elgin worked there as a young man? Well, it's irrelevant if you do or don't, but Tim, his brother, was over with his family working for Elgin. They were great company for Lucy and the girls when he was busy. Some weekends they would all drive up to Benidorm for a fun-filled fiesta. If not, it was down to the beach, rounds of golf and watching Premier League football down at *Delboys*. You could get into a rut taking all that punishment week in week out, but Elgin's company were representing England. The locals wouldn't respect modesty.

And so the days turned into weeks... and the weeks into months... until two sizzling seasons had come and gone. Lucy then declared she wanted to return to England to get back to a semblance of normality. Elgin averred that surely this was a normal mode of living, but his pocket and aching liver were starting to disagree, so he reluctantly waved the white flag. Winter was approaching - the best time of the year to earn mega dough back home on the damp, so everyone agreed it would be a grand exodus. The glorious God-given, gleeful sojourn had been a wonderful experience. The local bars, bodegas and restaurants would miss them all badly, but it was time to bade farewell.

For the time being, the carnival was over.

* * * *

CHAPTER TWELVE

Done Up Like a Kipper

After arriving back in England, they rented a gorgeous 1960s split-level house in the hills of Hopton, a smallish village north east of Stafford, just faraway enough from the madding crowd. There had been an English Civil War battle less than a mile away in 1643 on Hopton Heath, with a big win for the Royalists (aka *The Cavaliers*). They cut down 500 Parliamentarian troops (aka *The Roundheads*) ensuring that they would never take the prized county town of Stafford. All had been calm since, apart from 1936 when the pissed-up local butcher driving home from the pub went through a farm hedge at speed, nearly decapitating a few cows. (He was obviously trying to cut out the middle man).

Elgin was setting up another damp company. What's the old saying, *If it ain't broke don't fix it.* He now knew the game inside out, therefore it would be as easy as apple pie with a great big morello cherry on the top. (Well, only maybe baby) He couldn't contact Michelle the office whizz. She'd come back from Spain early to set it all up before the emperor returned. This flashed up several warning signs and, on checking the bank account which should have been teeming with wonga, he discovered it was bereft of any sum worth drawing. The emperor's new clothes were now gone. Crikey! Who could have taken that out then?

It wasn't going to need Columbo with a late twist.

Elgin eventually got hold of her dad, who had also worked for him in Derby. The bottom line was she felt underappreciated, underpaid and overworked, so had taken out her own mandatory unofficial bonus, which would have delighted any National Lottery winner getting five numbers up. By the time he caught up with her most of that stipend was gone, but she agreed to give back the little that remained. Elgin only had one stipulation: never contact him again.

It wasn't to end there though, machinations were at work behind the scenes.

Shortly after that debacle, Elgin was over in Derby sampling a few jars in *The Buck in the Park*. He can't remember what the occasion was, but any reason was juice for the goose. All the regular lads were there including a few young Crown Prosecution Service guys who were on the periphery of their drinking firm and a nice bunch of blokes to boot (not literally). The party was in full swing when in bursts Derbyshire's Dirty Dibble himself, *Dastardly Dave,* accompanied by wifey - both as pissed as soused newts. He'd been having a private drink up the road at another tavern in celebration of being promoted to inspector. Yeah, that's right, *inspector*.

Now, everything mentioned in this luminous saga is gospel including this sordid occurrence. Next time you wonder why crime has spiralled out of control and prosecutions are at an all time low, it can all be explained by men of this pitiful, knuckle-dragging calibre rising to the top. He had about the same languid dynamism as another inspector; Blakey from the 70s TV comedy series, *On The Buses*. But wait, we might be doing Butler's mate a disservice here.

He was as tanked up as Oliver Reed, Lee Marvin and Richard Harris combined. It was about to get very interesting. The rumour going around was that Dave had read the best-selling positivity book, *How To Win Friends And Influence People,* but he'd obviously forgotten every thing in it. He kicked off at the CPS men, "What the fuck are you doing in here drinking with these scumbags when you were invited to my do?"

Scraping of chairs, empty glasses banged down on the table - they all scarpered out of there in good style. It was a wise decision too. Dave was just warming up though... he politely requested of Steve the landlord to, "Get that slag of a wife of yours to bring me over a drink."

Steve, who was twice Dave's size had to be restrained by three blokes with the urgent caveat, "Think of your licence mate... it ain't worth it."

Steve calmed down, vowing that the wayward copper would be leaving the premises after he'd finished his drink. But Dave was intent on more mayhem. Next in line was Elgin's brother, Ivan, who was sitting quietly at a table on his own enjoying a Margherita pizza. "Give me a slice fat boy!" That probably wouldn't clinch it, Ivan despised any creature in police colours including the good bobbies.

"I know you're Old Bill, but I don't give a fuck, behave yourself or I'll make a mess of you."

Now, he may have been bluffing, but would you risk getting your head kicked in for some cheese and tomato puree? "I'll help myself then." He lurched over and pawed at the pizza. In a split second he was prone on the floor, holding his face. Ivan leaned down and half lifted him up by his upper shirt buttons, "No pizza for you, if you try that again you'll have no front teeth to munch the next one."

It was droll watching wifey up at the bar, purposely oblivious to her better half getting a good hiding down and out amongst the slops, all she was interested in was her next tipple. So there it was, just another normal day at *The Buck in the Park*. *The Queen Vic* and *The Rovers Return* could learn a few tricks from the dear old Buck, but the late night watershed on TV might have to be raised to midnight or two in the morning because of all the shenanigans. Dirty Den eat your heart out.

A few months later Elgin was about to get another arrow in the back and this baby was straight between the shoulder blades. He'd taken on a salesman called Ian Wright (No, not the Arsenal forward attempting to do a Kerry Dixon-style moonlighting stint selling damp course in Derby!) who had been very good at his job until he announced out of the blue he was leaving. Elgin was disappointed, Ian had picked up all the salient details of working the damp course selling structure in double quick time, he was confident, self-assured and had a touch of hubris. A little birdie whispered in Elgin's ear a few weeks later that Ian had set up a rival company. So what? It was a free country. He had clearly learned from the master, he could do whatever he wanted. That was until he started poaching Elgin's office staff, fitters, canvassers and salesmen. This pissed Elgin off, but he would grin and bear it. That was until replica adverts of Ian's began appearing alongside his own in all the relevant papers. He was taking Elgin for a pussy, and not only that, he was stealthily destroying him from within.

Elgin wanted to rip his head off, but decided it could all be settled amicably. He tried through intermediaries to get him to come to the table. Nothing worked, until one night in the *Buck in the Park* after he had downed more than one or two bevvies, he got a message that his best salesman had gone over to the other side. He immediately rang his ex-main man and got Ian's phone number from him, with assurances that he wouldn't mention who had given him that information. Now, you should never go on the dog and bone to confront somebody if you are raging mad drunk, angry and aggressive as there is a tendency to bellow out more than you were intending to do in most instances, but there are the odd encounters where the person on the other end means every word they say. In my opinion this is rare - the hard cases I have known in my life will not give someone a warning, they will just go ahead and do the deed. Another slant on this is that some people who menace over the phone with absolutely no intention of committing any violence, but the person subject to the threat believes that danger is coming their way, if not today then possibly tomorrow. They constantly have to look over their shoulders. The stressful scenario is forever ongoing, mentally and psychologically, and in some ways it's a lot worse than actually getting clumped.

Well Elgin gave the guy a month's worth of pent up vitriol, condemnation and chastisement. He was going to get what was coming to him and a bit more for the hell of it. The trouble was, Ian Wright was taping the conversation over on his side and guess who he thought might be interested in hearing it played back?

The police paid Elgin a visit a week later and arrested him. If anyone simply says, "I'll kill you" over the phone they can be charged with conspiracy to murder or threats to kill - both very grave charges which the Old Bill, the CPS and the courts take seriously. I know about this personally. That said, I only told the guy that I'd break his legs - another taxi company owner actually - he'd phoned up the work and pensions offices in Stafford and told the enforcement officer outrageous lies and fabrications about me fiddling VAT, tax returns, etc. - real slimeball filth. Unbeknownst to him, he was talking to one of my best mates who I went to watch Chelsea with. He asked me what I'd ever done to this guy. "Fuck all", was the answer. He was obviously jealous of what I was building. A great moral here is to never do anyone a bad turn. Karma will always come back to bite you like a crocodile.

Of course I had to ring my accuser ten seconds after hearing about it - mad as a march hare on steroids, instead of letting it all wash over. It's still one of my pet aversions, some nimrod lying behind my back, but as sociobiologist Desmond Morris once said, "We are all killer apes."

We have the propensity to cave someone's head in for queue-jumping. (Probably not the best example that, but I know you know what I'm saying) Half hour after I'd given the bloke a piece of my mind, a young policeman and policewoman turned up at my business - both smiling and laughing by the way - "Mick, you can't say that over the phone."

I apologised and they were gone. Elgin wasn't going to be as lucky.

It seems an innocuous crime, but it's reported thousands of times to the police each year. There doesn't have to be a recording of the threat either. It will still go to court in certain cases - being simply one person's word against another. The police had a term for it from 1988; an 'Osman' - Named after the occasion when a guy - Ali Osman - was killed by a deranged schoolteacher. A case too complicated to go into here, but simply put, if the authorities garner information about a threat to someone they don't think knows about it, they are obliged to send a letter out known as a warning. Today with the internet at full throttle there are thousands of keyboard warriors as well as tough guy phone callers... so be careful what you say in these woke times of ours because Big Brother is omnipresent. It never sleeps.

Say your worst and expect the worst.

Back to beleaguered Elgin...
This was the first time he'd been in serious trouble: not bad for a man in his thirties, but hardly likely to score him double bonus brownie points with *The Beak*. Seldom was Elgin naive in his life, but he expected the police to play with a straight bat. However, that was like asking Fred Dibnah not to climb a chimney stack. He was visited in his cell at the police station shortly afterwards by the duty solicitor who he assumed was on his side. He went through the whole case and background data with him, only for the wanker to freely cough up some missing information the police needed. At the magistrates court bail hearing the police then fed the prosecutor a load of flannel. He sternly demanded that Elgin be remanded in custody as they all regarded him as a flight risk back over to Spain.

Elgin had told the duty solicitor he'd had a few minor run-ins with the Spanish police, but surely he wouldn't bring that up would he?... you know, being in Elgin's corner and all that. His champion advocate's learned response to him attempting a moonlight flit was, "Mr Hounds won't go back to Spain, *(yes, very good keep it up)* because the Spanish Serious Crime Squad are after him." *(You lying bastard, thanks a bunch)*

There was more chance after that of John Dillinger Public Enemy Number One getting bail than Elgin. It was a stone-cold formality for the magistrates to send him off to Leicester nick on remand. Our law courts go right back to the Magna Carta in 1215: and, as a betting man, I'd like to suggest there have been many more falsehoods uttered by the prosecutorial powers than the defence since that time. God only knows about despotic countries like Russia, China, Turkey and many other tinpot regimes who have sent countless innocent people to squalid imprisonment, hard labour and death. The words 'liar' and 'lawyer' sound so very similar.

It was a genuine life lesson for Elgin sitting down in his cell contemplating how this had run full circle. He was the one who had been slighted, but took the wrong option of a threatening phone call. His advice to anyone in similar circumstances at the local police station is; don't trust the duty solicitor. It makes sense that the guy on the rota isn't going to create problems for the Old Bill. It's obvious that they want someone down there that they can work and liaise with. Isn't hindsight a wonderful thing?

    The two months he spent on remand at Leicester prison actually did him good. Apart from worrying about the charge, he de-stressed from the pressures of the business and the problems of losing staff. He had a great crew of workers carrying on who kept the ship afloat. He even learned who the main prosecution witness was going to be; Michelle Croxford - surprise, surprise. The police had contacted her after Elgin's arrest, enquiring if he had threatened anyone else. The simple answer to that could only be negatory - as he hadn't, but there was every chance she had provided them with juicy tit-bits of slips, misdemeanours, peccadilloes and various sins of the accused. This could weaken Elgin's chances of a fair hearing.
    They say hell hath no fury like a woman scorned. Well, the chickens were now all coming home to roost.

    Geoff Brundrette came to the rescue. He organised the appointment of a proper brief and she eventually got Elgin out on bail with conditions attached; there was a strict curfew between 7pm and 7am, he had to sign on at the police station every evening at 6pm, surrender his passport (ouch!), do not on any account contact witnesses and last, but not least, stay out of Derby.
    With any travel to Spain out of the question for the foreseeable future, he needed to ask Geoff for another favour. Elgin needed to clear out his pristine residence over there, so Geoff took his wife Jeanette, his two girls, Becky and Lucy, and his mother, to have a bit of a holiday at the same time. It was late December, so the house had been empty since early September, except for the Duffy family's two week stay after the Hounds' had left for Blighty. They had left the building in a right state - just like various housing tenants had done as depicted on the TV show, *Tenants from Hell*. There was rotten food in all the kitchen units, dirty bottles, half-finished pizzas in boxes, unwashed plates and bowls in stinking, stagnant water in the sink. All the waste bins were foul and overturned after rats and dogs had gone through them and strewn detritus everywhere, and all the bed linen was filthy... really filthy, like a mud wrestling team had slept there. You could only imagine the stench as well after the Spanish Autumnal sun had beat down for over three months too. Geoff was furious. There were all kinds of vermin in there, and this was after the Duffys had gone home... they were the main instigators.

Jeanette and his mum heroically cleaned up, and it was way beyond the call of duty. But this happens when you do a so-called friend a favour. They could have had no pride in themselves leaving someone else's property like a pig sty. Elgin actually journeyed up to Tim Duffys house some years later after he had moved to Aberdeen. If anything, it was far worse. It was a right shithole. So what they did in Spain was normal for them. It's a funny old world, Elgin should have suspected something when he entered the passageway and spotted mud flaps on the Hoover.

When Geoff arrived back from Spain he was like a broken record. He wouldn't shut up about how he had pulled Elgin out the mire the last two times. He knew the time of day - he was making Elgin feel like he owed him big time. Geoff's business, Stafford Caterers, was less than half a mile from the pub they all drank in, *The Telegraph*, on Wolverhampton Road which heads southwards out of Stafford. He spent most of his day in there, mostly on his own with Baz, the landlord, so he was always on the phone to Elgin and Big Col asking them to come up and keep him company. He wasn't slow at using his newly-acquired leverage with Elgin after his benevolent mercy missions allied to the ongoing curfew as well. He would be on the phone to Elgin's office every lunch time, "Come on the lad, (he called everyone that, good friends and strangers) you can't have a drink tonight, so you may as well come down now."

Elgin would reply curtly, "Fuck off Geoff, I'm dead busy. There's loads to get done."

He would then play his trump card, "Oh, I see... it's fine now that I've sorted all your problems out, but it's too much trouble for you to give me a bit of time back, blah, blah, blah... I'll get you one in, hurry up!"

This behaviour of two intelligent grown men will be read one day by a top lady psychologist and she will confirm the female species as the superior one.

All of this frivolous banter though was hiding a tragic secret: Geoff was drinking excessively to numb the pain he was experiencing every day of the week from a serious kidney condition. He was doubled up each day, so was bollocking down barrels-worth of lager and gin to desensitize the agony. It was daft really, because he was creating the proverbial vicious circle. He was a man's man though, he was like us all, we didn't go to the doctor or dentist unless the pain was unbearable. It's a male thing - we are all arrogant enough to believe we are indestructible, but we are, in reality, just mere mortals who one day will go into the ground forever. He carried on riding this mad merry go round for a couple of months until Jeanette rang Elgin, "Can you persuade this idiot to get to the doctors, he's stopped going."

Elgin went straight round. Good old Geoff says, "What you doing here, let's get down *The Graph* for one."

It took Elgin ages to get him in his car, and then down to the doctor's. He was in the waiting room while Geoff was in the consulting room. Dr Logan came out and asked Elgin to take Geoff up to Accident and Emergency at Mid-Staffordshire Hospital, there would be people expecting them at the other end.

Elgin didn't realise at the time just how serious Geoff's situation was. He was only 36 and as tough as teak, but he got a phone call two days later from Jeanette confirming it was worse than he had ever imagined. He rushed up there to find Geoff had deteriorated badly and saw that he had developed the sickening, yellowish hue of jaundice. The nurses were having murders trying to make him keep his oxygen mask on, but he was having none of it. It was the first time Elgin realised that Geoff might not be coming out this ward alive. Jeanette begged him to make Geoff wear his mask as he wouldn't listen to anyone else. Elgin was frightened as fuck for him and didn't know whether to laugh or cry when he said, "I'm off the booze for three months after this the lad."

It was so sad to see, a big man as helpless as a baby. Elgin and Big Colin stayed with him the next two days and witnessed one of the most moving sights of their lives.

When the end was near, the nurses asked him to take off his mask and kiss his two young daughters goodbye. Becky would be about twelve and Lucy would be nine or ten. Jeanette was also now expecting the boy he was always so desperate to have - a son he'd never see. It was absolutely heartbreaking to watch and cruel really, but every family in the world will experience that terrible day. The only blessing was that the man was freed from an existence of excruciating pain on earth and hopefully going on to a far better place than here.

I'd actually bumped into Geoff on the Aston Fields Industrial Estate a few weeks before he died. He was as white as a ghost and I said, "Bloody hell mate, you look like shit."

He replied, "Thanks a lot." And we both laughed. It was just banter. I'd worked with Geoff and we'd been good friends for years, but that was the last time I ever saw him. I was devastated. I must mention his older brother Stan here. I had two businesses with him: *Country Caterers* on the Newport Road and *The Sportsman Club* at Coton Fields. They weren't everyone's cup of tea in Stafford, but who of us are. Stan went young as well with cancer in his mid forties.

Neither of them saw fifty which is tragic in itself, but I was proud to be a friend to them both.

REST IN PEACE
STANLEY AND GEOFFREY BRUNDRETTE

Elgin was in bits. But they do say that bad luck comes in threes. In the space of twelve months, he'd lost both his dad and best mate and was about to stand trial on a trumped up charge. Just before the trial he met up with his barrister and asked him what his prediction was; fifty-fifty, a coin toss, levels you devils to be found guilty and, if the verdict went against him, the sentence would be a minimum of seven years. SEVEN FUCKING YEARS for a three-minute phone call, first offence. The world was going mad. Yet it was all about interpretation. In Elgin's mind he had done nothing wrong. He'd been set up and the CPS were happy and keen enough to throw away the key. But there was no way Elgin would swallow that... no fucking way.

He didn't realise at the time that ALL barristers and solicitors paint a very grim picture of what is to occur, even if they do a bad job and a defendant receives a guilty verdict, the sentence is always less than their guesstimation. That way it looks like they've been on fire in the courtroom. It's all pats on the back and you telling all your mates that you had an ace brief. Doctors and consultants do exactly the same but with a reverse strategy; "How long have I got to live doctor?"

"Six to nine months at best."

Three years later you're still walking about carefree telling everyone your doctor is a miracle worker! You know it makes sense.

This was the moment Elgin made the biggest mistake of his life. He decided a swerve to Spain was the only answer. When he got home after the meeting he told Lucy what he was planning to do. She was dead against it. Here's hindsight again. He wishes he had listened to her because it became a nightmare looking over his shoulder for many years after that. When he was finally arrested in Florida (back in chapter one) he knew the police would dig this little escapade up just to rub salt in the wounds. Yet he was relieved the long chase was finally over. He was extremely worried though about the severity of the sentence after the authorities had bent over backwards to extradite him back to England. Elgin wouldn't recommend anyone else do what he did, without first going through every possible alternative, but it was made all the worse subsequently when one of the Derby CPS lads perused his file at a later date and said a guilty verdict was most unlikely. Even if he got one, he was looking at two years maximum, but at the time Elgin thought it was the best and right thing to do for himself and family.

He'd made his bed, and now it was time to lie on it.

* * * *

CHAPTER THIRTEEN

Breaking Bad

So the die was cast: there was only one small problem - Elgin needed a passport! The kosher one had been surrendered as part of his bail conditions. At that time (1995), people could go to the post office with two forms of ID (not even of a photographic nature) and get what was called a *British Visitors Passport.* This was a twelve-month passport that was valid for travel throughout Europe and a few Commonwealth countries, but the beautiful part was that it was issued right there and then. Cowabunga! They didn't half make it easy in those days for rascals and scallywags. He just popped into the main post office with a mate's details, two photos of his good self and ten minutes later he was the proud owner of a new passport. No wonder cannabis king Howard Marks had over fifty of them, all in different names - it was easier than falling off a log! It makes you nostalgic for the last century, tales like that.

A couple of days later Elgin and Big Col were at the airport on their way to Malaga. Colin was having a two-week holiday and would keep Elgin company until Lucy and the kids arrived in a fortnight. Elgin rented a nice villa in Calahonda, just South-West of Malaga and soon started to feel at home after meeting some of the chaps 'on holiday' out there. During the first week he walked into *Sully's Bar* for a drink and he noticed what could only be described as a group of 'interesting characters' staring over at him. After a while one of them sauntered over and asked Elgin what he was doing there. Safe in the assumption that this little firm wasn't the Old Bill, he told him he was 'on his toes' from England.

The conversation went like this, verbatim: "On your toes, eh? Where are you from ?"

Elgin replied, "Stafford."

"You're from Stafford are you? Do you know Norman (Johnson)?"

"Yeah, I know Norman. I was having a drink with him a few weeks back."

The guy starts nodding slowly, "What's your name?"

"I'm Elgin. Elgin Hounds."

"Alright Elgin... I'm Bobby and with that, he went back and sat down. It suddenly occurred to Elgin that they all may be thinking he was a copper, so he whacked his drink down and mooched off sharpish.

A few days later he was walking past *Sully's* with the family looking for somewhere to eat. Lotte, his daughter, wanted to go in because they had yellow chairs and wouldn't take 'no' for an answer. He sat Lucy and the girls down and went to the bar for drinks and a menu. Up pops Bobby again out of the blue, but smiling radiantly this time, "Allo, Elgin. Look, here's my number if you need a bit of graft. You'll like it in Calahonda. It's the biggest open prison in Europe." He had called Norman and found out that Elgin was exactly who said he was and, much to Lucy's disappointment, he'd got a blinding endorsement, so he was now in with a right set of lads.

* * *

Author's alert! I was Norman Johnson's partner for the best part of a decade. His reputation as a hard man was thoroughly deserved. He commanded massive respect in Stafford, Liverpool, London and New York. We took bets on the racetracks together and we ran The Studio Club in north Stafford with his youngest daughter, Rachel. We got into some scrapes as well. The week after the twin towers came down we got arrested in Antwerp on trumped-up charges, spending five weeks in a large cell with seven Albanians. Oh, what fun we had! But, forgive me dear reader, that is another story for another time.

We lost the great man in 2013. There wasn't a dry eye up the crem. He is still sadly missed by all in Stafford, but his memory lives on. If anyone hasn't read my best seller, BLACK EYES AND BLUE BLOOD, it's a fantastic story about the only man to work with the Kray twins and the Mafia... and much, much more.

* * *

What a touch Elgin had bumping into that lot. He soon needed a proper passport in another name, but they sorted that out post haste. Lucy even 'passed her driving test' in *Sully's* - even though she could drive competently, she'd never taken her test back home. Well, £100 soon sorted that out. Not a copy either! It was a real license in her own name. If anyone is now worrying about death on the roads, she has since passed her test in

England. The Hounds' wouldn't want people thinking they weren't *bona fide* citizens.

Sully's Bar became their local. It was run by John Sullivan - a right proper geezer, helped out by his lovely wife, Sue, who knocked out the best British grub on the coast. Sully was a great guy. Elgin walked in one day and Sully said, "Give me 20mil (£100) Elgin, I've got something for you."

He knew Elgin still had his business back in England and it had been costing a fortune on the phone attempting to run it from Spain. He'd bought Elgin a magic phone card from Tony Muldoon. A phone card with special powers, you put it in the phone box, made your call, pressed a little button on the top as you withdrew it and it always recharged. Lovely jubbly! It saved Elgin a fortune, but poor old Tony got a tug a few months later - grassed, he'd been. The Spanish police weren't amused either, they kept him locked up for two years until he agreed to tell them how he'd done it. The phone company, *Telefonica,* had to change the mechanism in every single phone box in Spain. It must have cost them millions. Elgin gave great kudos to one man who had outsmarted a multi-national company with fortitude, panache and genius.

Elgin and family had been living out there for about four months and everything was hunky dory, but Elgin was starting to get keyed up and jumpy. The feds back in England had been proactive in combing the Midlands for him. How long would it be before they figured out he was sampling foreign climes? He suggested to Lucy that South Africa might just be far enough away from unwanted prying eyes, but they needed to take a comprehensive look-see to eliminate making any rash decision. This wasn't a time to be burning all their bridges. If they were going to move to an unfamiliar environment on the dark continent, they had to have assurance.

It was a long zig-zag flight; Malaga to Madrid to Frankfurt to Johannesburg to Durban. It took twenty hours to get there (twenty bloody hours, it's only seven to America, I've never wanted to go to South Africa, but if I flew from England, I'd imagine I was over half way there after crossing The Med. Just how bleeding big is Africa? Rant over, back to the story.)

They eventually got there, and what a beautiful country it was. Elgin was spellbound. He immediately went looking for opportunities which could give the family a comfortable living. It was down to him to locate an opening here by using his God-given ability to see a profit where others didn't. Things looked promising, but everything that glitters isn't always gold.

There were outside influences that they hadn't taken account of - forget about snakes, rhinos, lions and sharks, there was a far deadly species in the shadows of the city.

They booked a palatial suite in a five star hotel on the ocean front for £40 a night. Remember that next time you go to a two star bed and breakfast in Rhyl. They ate the most fantastic meals and saw the most marvellous wildlife on their travels. Elgin couldn't put his finger on it, but he had a sickening feeling about an undercurrent of danger - it was like a sixth sense. Lucy felt it too. Their fears were sickeningly realised when a guy tried to snatch the girls. Two blonde-haired cuties were worth a fortune out there. Luckily Elgin was ahead of the game and well aware what was just about to happen and averted a nightmare situation, but it could have been so different on another day. Lucy was hysterical and screaming, "Look where you've brought us to, get us out of here!" She was spot on, it didn't bear thinking about.

Back at the hotel she eventually calmed down. It had shaken everyone up badly, so they decided to fly up to Jo-burg the next day to see if it felt any safer up there. They had been at the hotel for two days when one of the coffee waitresses got talking to Lucy. She said that her uncle had been shot dead at the shopping mall last week when some lunatic opened up with an AK 47 and seemed to be killing anyone unlucky enough to come into his line of fire. So that was Africa off the agenda. Lucy promptly declared, "We're off! You stay if you want, but me and the kids are going back to Spain!"

That was an offer Elgin couldn't refuse. As beautiful as the scenery was, the local *Homo sapiens* were just too dangerous. Give him a gun and it went off the scale. He now had twenty long hours back on the plane to contemplate what might have been.

Everyone ended up back in sunny Calahonda. Sully and Bobby sorted them out with a beautiful house near where they lived. They enrolled Lotte into the private English School in Marbella and Sylvia into a nursery. The only thing Elgin now needed was a decent income. His business back home was only pootling along without him. It wasn't pulling up any trees, so he had to fall on another cash stream. Just as his funds were dwindling to dangerous depths of loose change, it fell right in his lap again. Elgin 'Lucky' Hounds was back in business.

Right on cue he had another touch. Now, in this period of his travels I call him, *Naughty Elgin*. None of us are saints and we do what we have do to survive - in his case it was to feed, clothe and shelter his family. There are periods in your life when your back is against the wall. Of course certain things are off limits, but others are a necessity to get through tough times. An old Irish guy in his nineties once told me - and I've never forgotten it - *"You're only as honest as your pocket allows you to be."*

What a wonderful statement. I personally have no qualms about getting one over a bank or financial institution, rightly or wrongly I see it as a victimless action. I also take into consideration that when the shoe is on the other foot, a struggling business or householder months behind on his mortgage are both routinely and readily thrown into the gutter with all their family when the money men don't get their thirty pieces of silver on time. I shed no tears for these usurers. It's a tough world - banks are always protected by government. With that, I rest my case.

Elgin also had the added pressure from the past - if he became potless, he'd have no alternative but to go home and be re-arrested, put in custody again and be staring at a longish sentence coming his way. So he might as well be hung for a sheep as a lamb. He knew full well judgment day was coming some time in the future as sure as eggs were eggs, but another decade or two in the sun and on the run would be jolly nice before the police came to rain on his parade. Perhaps most like minded people would concur with that sentiment.

To get money from Elgin's business in England, Lucy paid company cheques into a bank account in Calahonda. Annoyingly they took three weeks to clear. One week Lucy came storming out the front doors, the bank had only gone and let *Telefonica* take over two grand out of their account. They didn't even have a house phone either. The bank couldn't have cared less, they refused to take one iota of responsibility. The onus was on the Hounds' to take it up with the phone company. This effectively meant that they were two big ones down with very little chance of getting it back anytime soon. This was all coinciding with the family scraping the bottom of the barrel just to live day to day. Maybe it was a perverse payback from a really ratty *Telefonica* for Elgin having had one of Tony Muldoon's magic phone cards... Who knows? Stranger things have happened.

He was absolutely fuming. The bank had crapped on him from a great height (Where have we heard that one before?) The only thing to do was dispatch the old bank to history and open up another account at a new bank. Simples, really! It might just have been the best thing that they ever did.

Lucy comes out after opening a new account laughing her socks off. That worried Elgin as merriment had been in short supply over the last few days. She hops into the motor and says, "You won't believe this - but when do you think we can draw off this cheque?"

Elgin was not really in the mood, "The King of Spain's birthday?"

"NO... TOMORROW! Because it's a company cheque... and wait, there's more." She was doing Jimmy Cricket impersonations now, but Elgin was definitely perking up.

"They've only offered us a credit card as well. I'm picking it up tomorrow."

Elgin's mind immediately started racing. A bank that allows you to draw off uncleared cheques? Hmm... It took him less than a minute to formulate his master plan. He was back in amongst them again. Life is like that, many ups and downs. The darkest hour is just before the dawn, or as I like to say, "The sun will come out tomorrow, you bet your bottom dollar!"

They don't write them like that anymore.

Elgin had a duffle bag crammed full of old cheque books from companies that he'd put into liquidation. He would never throw anything away. Go around his house today; he's got a rubber band ball. Most folks' are the size of a fist - his is the size of a medicine ball. He uses it as a door stop. He won't mind me telling you this, but he's still got sheets of Green Shield Stamps and books full of Embassy cigarette vouchers in case either of them make a comeback. But if you ask me, he's just nostalgic for the good old days. (I lend him my rose-tinted glasses occasionally.)

His plan was crystal clear: bang a load of these cheques into accounts and draw off them before they bounced. He didn't want to jeopardise the assumed name he was using by opening up an account in that name, but he did have a residency card in his real name that could be used. The card had his address as being in Torrevieja so it made a lot of sense to go up to the Costa Blanca to pull off the scam, not least because that narrowed the chances of ever bumping into someone from the bank in the street. Elgin always had a philosophy: *If you are going to screw up, screw up BIG!*

He was going to take them to the cleaners. Eight trusted people were recruited for the tasks ahead. Watches were synchronised and every man knew the procedure. They were going to be opening accounts all the way up the coast. Elgin would be paying them 50% commission on all the money that went through the accounts in their names. Everyone opened the accounts on the same day, but at different branches. They then returned the next day to pick up the money and pick up the credit cards that also cloned as ATM cards. *Double bubble, no toil or trouble.* It was a dead cinch. The other lads couldn't believe how easy it was. In simplicity there was genius and there were three more weeks before the first cheque bounced. They would all meet up every morning and Elgin would issue everyone with a cheque for that day. Then he would put each card in the wall to draw money off it. This was a safety mechanism to test if the cards were going to be swallowed or not - if they all paid out that meant they could then walk into the banks without worrying if something was amiss. It was a well-oiled, military style, ongoing heist and a chance in a lifetime to fill their boots.

As those halcyon days rolled on they got braver and braver each day, that is, Elgin would incrementally raise the amounts written on the cheque. But the secret was not to be too greedy - attempting a transaction for an abnormal amount of money might alert a suspicious staff member. A person going into a bank and drawing out four or five grand a day was going to set alarm bells ringing, so Elgin started recruiting tourists. In Spain you can make a cheque out to 'Al Portador'. (Al has since become the richest man in *Espagne*. I jest; it means 'The Bearer') This meant that anyone with possession of a cheque made out to 'Al Portador' just ambles into the bank, hands it over with ID and walks out with the dough. It didn't need to go through an account.

So the lads rounded up a crowd of holiday makers and paid them 5,000 pesetas (£25 each. The Euro was still a few years away, becoming the currency in 1999). All they had to do was mooch into the bank and cash the cheque. As Dire Straits used to sing, *Money for nothin' and your chicks for free*. It caught on quickly with the British public. Arrangements were made to meet them every day at certain banks at the same time. Fuck me, they were turning up with loads of friends and family! There were grannies going in on wheelchairs, all sorts - it was better than *Supermarket Sweep*! Bob Hoskins was on TV at the time fronting an advert for *British Telecom*. His catch phrase was 'free money'. Lying bastard. You had to buy a phone to get that - the holiday mob were the only ones onto a proper buckshee winner.

They had three delightful weeks of this. There was never a hitch. They stayed with Jan and Jeff from Delboys as the money piled up, then 21 days exactly after they banked the first cheque the ATM's swallowed all the cards. They had managed an extraordinary golden run. They were even already packed and ready to go, just as anticipated. Elgin nipped round to his mother's to say bye-bye and they were off back to the Costa del Sol with two big holdalls full of wonga in the boot.

Even though this was one of the best touches in Elgin's life, he still needed to sort out an income. This massive amount of dough wouldn't last forever... well, not the way he burned through money at least!

So, what was he going to do ?

Well he couldn't sell damp course could he? There had been a drought in Spain for the last five years and a severe water shortage. Winter was fast approaching and Elgin was twiddling his thumbs in the front room, when he heard *pitter patter, pitter patter*. One drop of rain on your window pane doesn't mean to say there's a thunder storm coming of course. But on this occasion - it did! It rained for days and days... then some more. It was persisting down day and night like the monsoon season. People had never seen anything like it. Some DJ in Ibiza reckoned he'd seen Noah's Ark passing the Island, chugging across The Med... but he was probably tripping.

Elgin began to notice damp in peoples' houses. We couldn't have that could we? *Lucky* was back in the 'Juego de Humedad' - the damp game. He had a year-long plan; damp in the Winter and long-life paint in the Summer. He was going to run it mean and lean. He would do all the selling, Lucy would be ably answering the phones in the office and Geordie Al would be doing the fitting, aided and abetted by Leicester Baz, Nick the Brick, Dodgy Eyed Mike and Stafford Baz, with a few other rum coves. (That last lot sound like the crew from *Pirates of the Caribbean*!) It didn't take long to get established either as they were the only damp outfit on the coast. Other people had thought about giving it a shy, but Big Jeff, Ivan and Ant had always managed to talk them out of it. They must have been very persuasive. Although the fact that they were all about 18 stone and built of rippling muscle was surely a coincidence. Big Jeff lived a few doors down from the Hounds' while Ivan and Ant worked for him running all the security for the timeshare resorts along the coast. Amazingly, there weren't many instances of disgruntled customers or confrontations. Nice that people could get along.

There were many big properties along that coast and up in the hinterland with well-to-do residents. It wasn't uncommon to fit a large damp course for up to three million pesetas (£15,000). Some British ex-pats were real charismatic characters with the means to have whatever they wanted from life. One such person was the classically eccentric, 'Mrs B', who lived in Sotogrande, a very tidy, prestigious resort between Estepona and Gibraltar, not for your common hoi polloi.

She called Elgin in because she had damp in her ceiling. She had had numerous Spanish people in to try and solve the problem, but to no avail. As we mentioned earlier, 'the Spanish workman' didn't have the greatest reputation for hard work and diligence. There is a reason why Manuel was in

Fawlty Towers. Elgin had a feeling that the problem wasn't simply 'damp' and called over Geordie Al. Sure enough there was a hole in the roof. But Elgin also spotted the fact that she had bad rising damp all around the base walls. And the constantly leaking roof wouldn't have helped that at all. He gave her an offer she couldn't refuse; he would fix the hole in the roof for nothing, but she her walls badly needed proper damp course treatment, so she would simply pay for that element of the deal. She was over the moon - that would solve both problems at the same time. Elgin measured up the property and did all of the work. The final bill came to just under £8,000.

It wouldn't be the last time they would hear from her.

The following Summer she was on the dog and bone again. She told Lucy her house was as dry as a bone after the damp workmen left, but could she now have an estimate for the longlife paint. Elgin sent his four workmen down for a week's graft. Yet Mrs B's only interest was if Leicester Baz was 'on the job'. (As the two old dears on the Harry Enfield show would say; "*Oh, young man! He's a lovely young man!*")

The paint job then morphed into landscape gardening and then into a walk-in conservatory on the side of the house. Apart from the paint, she had a local builders merchants supplying her with all the materials, so Elgin was trying to work out each week what she owed for labour - it was seemingly never-ending. Each and every day she would request Baz to take her down the shops and they would always stop at a posh restaurant on the way back where she would always buy him lunch. He was her unofficial toy boy - but without the nookie. That daily manoeuvre suited all the other guys left at the house, because at dinner time they'd down tools and go swimming in the pool or sun bathe on the loungers until they returned. They had been there solid for eight weeks. But other work had been put on the back burner resulting in delays for other customers getting their urgent damp problems put right and, as a result, Elgin was starting to experience a cash flow problem in this two month period during which no money had changed hands.

It was time to disembark.

The lads' wages were well over 20k. It was an hour each way in fuel with wear and tear on the vans to boot. The office staff needed paying as did all the miscellaneous bills. Of course, Elgin and Lucy weren't grafting to run the company on charity either, they had personal bills like everyone else. He had a fixed price in his head of 35k and that was the amount he was going to present to Mrs B. He arrived to be greeted by the good lady herself. "Elgin, these two months are going to be costly aren't they?"

He nodded solemnly.

"Well, I have some money deposited in Gibraltar, but it probably won't cover it, so I'll have to dip into my life savings on the Isle of Man." If she was coming the old sob story, it was right on cue and perhaps devastating. He reluctantly said, "Listen, if it helps at all, I can do it for 32k."

He was then aghast to hear, "Oh Elgin! I thought you said it would be expensive! I've easily got that much in good old Gib. I'll drive down there now and get it for you."

Well, who said you couldn't con a conner. She'd played him like a fine Stradivarius. And what's more, his four workers had earned more out the marathon shift than he had. It wouldn't happen to him ever again, but you can't win them all. On the drive home, Lucy rang him and asked,
"Did you get the money?"

"Most of it."

"Why, what's happened?"

"Just get ready... we're off out for a drink. I'll tell you all about it, but I need to drown my sorrows."

In my own experiences of dealing with little old ladies, they are the hardest business executives out there. They don't cut you an inch of slack. You go in thinking it's going to be a pushover, but you come out having your pockets pinched and not realising it.

Mrs B was eccentric, but others were downright crazy - or 'loco' as the Hispanics would say. One such couple - their actual names escape Elgin - were 'Mr and Mrs X'. (We'll call them that mysterious name because they would be an enigma to the rest of the human race.) They were living in Benal Beach, an upmarket apartment block in Benalmadena. They called him round because their upstairs terrace at the front was leaking on to the downstairs terrace when it rained. They were nutters. What difference did it make if it was raining, wet was wet. Elgin explained nothing needed doing - that it was pointless, but they insisted on having the leak staunched. So Geordie Al was sent over to do some simple grouting. While he was there, Mr and Mrs X said that they had very noisy neighbours to the left of them, and that they could hear everything that happened next door. They had seen the advert about the long-life paint - and they wondered, "Did the company have any sound proof paint that would cut noise out?"

Trying not to laugh, Al said that they had a couple of tins in stock, he could come tomorrow, but they'd have to vacate the apartment for the day as the fumes were very pungent until the paint had fully dried. All he did was buy two sheets of 8 x 4 sound proofing boards, attach them to the wall then paint over them with the long-life paint. They returned and were absolutely delighted with the results! All of the noises coming from next door were muffled and Mr X said, "The guy who invented that paint must be a billionaire, it really works well!"

Al was gagging to laugh but held himself together. The loony couple would be telling all and sundry about their *new miracle paint*. You couldn't catch your breath... Beam me up, Scotty!

All the while the Hounds' were making this nice dough, they could forget about the travails from England. The family members were having the time of their lives; lovely houses, quality cars, eating in the finest restaurants and generally enjoying all that the Costa del Sol had to offer. This money was for spending! One of their favourite restaurants was the *Red Pepper* in Puerto Banus. Lucy and the girls loved it there, because they'd encourage Elgin to drink a lot for ulterior motives. After the meal, they'd leave him having more than a few brandies with Steve the owner, while they looked around the designer clothes shops. They knew that on returning he'd be that sozzled, he wouldn't put up any sort of resistance to paying for all the clobber they had picked out. One such Sunday lunch time they had Emelia and Marco (his oldest son and daughter) over on holiday with them, so it was a happy family affair with all his children. Elgin had ordered a big bottle of champagne when Sylvia, his youngest who was only three at the time, piped up, "Can I have some champagne, dad?" A nearby waiter overheard her and suggested to Elgin that he would fetch some special champagne for Sylvia. Thinking he was getting something like *Sprite* or *7 Up*, Elgin agreed and thanked him.

Twenty minutes after the 'special champagne' arrived, Emelia taps Elgin on the arm and enquires, "How often does Sylvia perform that little trick?"

Elgin swivels around to see Sylvia sitting, head right back, blankly gazing upwards, captivated by a ceiling fan which was rotating in synchrony with her little head. Elgin didn't have a technical term for the condition, but he knew the layman's answer - "She was pissed." He tore a strip off the waiter, the tosspot had only gone and given two glasses of cheap Spanish Cava to a three-year-old. Juan stood his ground protesting his innocence. He insisted that Elgin had given him the go-ahead to do it. These colourful exchanges are often called 'Lost in Translation' moments. It's more than probable the reason why the EU is currently imploding and, of course, let's not forget about our glorious maritime past when we sunk their saintly Armada. I don't think they will ever get over that debacle, not to mention the occupation of the Rock of Gibraltar for centuries. Of course the sequence of events in the restaurant was yet another triumph for Elgin. Sylvia had to be taken straight back home, so all the ladies never got the chance to bang out his credit card to submission that afternoon. He has always remembered that fine, thoughtful waiter with a fond, nostalgic reverence.

As the weeks turned to months, they acquired a beautiful villa in the rugged hills out in the country. They would sit by the swimming pool and admire the wonderful vista sweeping back down the valley to urban Malaga. Because of the secluded position they could retreat back to the residence when the madness and mayhem on the coast got too much and relax in comfort and safety. They used to joke that the police would never discover they were there.

How wrong they were and how quickly their little piece of paradise was swept from under their feet.

It all started to unravel in quite an innocent fashion. The new girl in the office took a phone call. (At this juncture we must remember that Elgin was in Spain on a false passport using an alias name) Unwittingly she asked the caller on the other end if he wanted to speak to Elgin Hounds. He said that he didn't but the mention of that name rang alarm bells at the other end.

Things were going to deteriorate very quickly as the police got involved. Elgin Hounds was the name on all the bogus cheques that the British holiday makers had changed into cash.

The merde had hit the fan.

Lucy got pulled into the police station. The *Guardia Civil* had passed the information up to the *Policia Nacional* who tried to play hardball. They wanted to know where Elgin was and they threatened her with jail and having her children taken away. Most women at this stage might have cracked with this serious level of interrogation, but Lucy was made of sterner stuff and stood her ground. After two or three hours they had to release her as they had no incriminating evidence, but it was the beginning of the end for their stay in Spain. All the bank accounts were frozen, their two pet spaniels, *Scooby* and *Scrappy* were kennelled until they could be airlifted back to England and their two husky guard dogs, *Catana* and *Bravo* were quickly re-housed. Money was going to be tight. Lucy managed to scrape together a cool grand which was matched by Elgin, they were about to do a moonlight flit to sunny Portugal in the car.

It was a sad time, but speed was of the essence.

On the way they arranged to collect some unpaid money for work they had done from a trusted customer in Manilva on the outskirts of Malaga. So, with all that done they headed for the border. They relaxed a tad after crossing into Portugal - destination: *Faro Airport*. They parked up the motor on the airport car park - permanently. (Somebody would have a nice touch selling that)

They bought one-way tickets and waited for the big bird to fly them home.

* * * *

CHAPTER FOURTEEN

Horses and Damp Courses

The tyres screeched and skidded on the wet Manchester runway. It was persisting down as usual. They say fair exchange is no robbery, but round the clock sunshine for thunder and lightning was a real bum deal and the weather reflected Elgin's finances; very gloomy with more downpours forecast. What a dire predicament to be in. Here he was with his kids who had previously gone to private schools and would have a scream up if they couldn't have lobster starters for Sunday lunch. Lucy had become used to the best of everything, and a mere two thousand quid in his pocket wasn't going to cut it, especially with nowhere to live, no motor and no job prospects. The Old Bill were certainly still on the look out for him, that was a given. He couldn't afford to drop his guard as one bad careless slip now would see everything he'd worked so hard for careening downhill to Palookaville.

It was time for Elgin to weave his undoubted magic once more. You probably all know by now that he could come up in clover. They arrived back on June 30th 1999, but just six months later he'd flipped it all on its head to such a degree that they flew first class on Christmas Day to Barbados for a three week holiday to see in the new millennium. This is a clear sign of Elgin's special talent - we all have our moments of inspiration sporadically, but to keep climbing back off the floor time and time again when all seems lost is a gift not endowed on many. It's the easiest thing in the world to give up, especially these days, but winners never quit and quitters never win.

Have a read of the biographies by various world class sportsmen, businessmen and politicians and you will be amazed how many of them achieved their success after adverse beginnings. Life has never been a cakewalk whatever one's circumstances, but strive to achieve, improve a little each day and always be positive - nobody likes a 'moaning Minnie' full of lame excuses.

When you decamp from somewhere very hastily, you tend to leave behind all your thingamajigs, doo-dahs and whatchamacallits. In other words, all of the little items that make day to day living easier - and it usually costs an arm and a leg to replenish what has gone. So who did Elgin call on first? You've got it in one! His old Stafford hombre and confidante Mr Michael O'Rourke, then the new owner and landlord of *The Jolly Jockey* public house opposite *The Reynolds Nightclub*. A man who had spent a fortune on buying the lease, new tills and many other pub necessities before completely redecorating inside and out. I owed Elgin five grand from before he went out to Spain, it was like an insurance stipend for him if things turned sour on the continent. Well, that day had arrived. As bad timing went, I wasn't that flush when he landed back on the tarmac, but I'd hit the ground running with the pub and proceeded to pay it all back within three months.

Elgin's clan had descended on Lucy's mother Edwina. Her house up the North end of town would be ideal until they found their own place. She was delighted to have them all there, because she hadn't been able to get over to Spain as often as she'd have liked to. The second person Elgin was going to visit was his brother Ivan. He had run up a huge debt with Elgin over the years and now it was payback time. He still owed him the cash his father had lobbied for before he died. When he couldn't pay it back, Elgin had given him a job at Derby. But unbeknown to him, Ivan had devised another dirty deed. He had told Michelle Croxford to put extra cash on his wages every week because he had squared it with Elgin. Now, a normal woman would just probably casually mention it in passing to the boss, "Was it ok to be doing this? - but Elgin didn't find out for ages. He went berserk with Michelle. She duly countered with, "I'm sorry I didn't inform you, but I never thought your own brother would stitch you up."

She obviously didn't know Ivan for what he was.

Not too long after the wages heist, Elgin was backed into a corner where his only get-out was to have Ivan run a bank account for him. He told Ivan this favour would go some way to ameliorating his many past indiscretions and help towards rebuilding their fractured relationship. He watched him like a hawk with binoculars for a time, slowly regaining his trust for the younger brother, then out the blue, *WHAM BANG!* Ivan merrily helped himself to a great wedge of cash in the account. He was morally corrupt and couldn't be trusted.

Fast forward again to the present with Elgin back in England short of funds. He called Ivan for some of the money he owed him. But not a chance, not even twenty nicker a week. He was very consistent in his lifelong claims of penury - money never came out of his pockets for other people, it was all for him. Three months later when Elgin was back on his feet, he decided to go and meet Ivan to tell his brother exactly what he thought of him. He also needed another passport, so if Ivan would consider helping out, he'd knock a big chunk off the 'national debt' that was still outstanding. It was years later that Elgin read the transcript of their conversation.

Ivan had only gone and taped what had been said and, at a later date, handed the tape over to the police. It's desperately sad when one brother would commit an egregious act like this. You can choose friends, but you're stuck for life with your family, good or bad. Elgin's final thoughts on the matter were that he wished he had left Ivan down that drain instead of the other lad when they were kids, wallowing around down there with the other rats.

Anyway, onwards and upwards. I had a nice bijou back room office in the pub which would serve Elgin down to the ground as he built up his damp battle battalion. It was reciprocal too, as all the workers would come in for a few jars after work to wet their whistles. I'd brought my younger brother into the pub business, but it quickly became evident he didn't want to work nights... which was about as useful to me as a chocolate fireguard. I asked Elgin, as a favour, to take him on as a manager, show him the ropes, maybe he could strike Klondike gold with tutoring from the master. They never hit the mother lode though, and things simply petered out. The damp just wasn't in his blood, although it wasn't averse at times to show a high alcohol count, but three months later just before Christmas his race was run.

I was horse racing mad at this particular time. *The Jolly Jockey* was festooned inside and out with horse racing memorabilia. All around the first floor exterior were cartoon caricatures of laughing horses and jockeys. Everyone thought they were the dog's bollocks. Everyone, that is, apart from the town council of course, who told me to take them down. I gave them 'two fingers' and refused. They had no sense of style! Listed building my arse. It's a Chinese takeaway these days with big neon signs. Don't mess with the 'yellow peril'.

The opening night was a belter. My mate, Pompey fan and horse owner Terry Pritchard, and top Wolverhampton trainer Nick Littmoden, came over to celebrate this new start-up business. I knew I was on to a big winner straight away. *The Reynolds Bar* night club directly across the road was uber-busy on Thursday, Friday and Saturday nights - they had three floors full of over a thousand, raving alcoholic, head cases, most of whom it seemed had partaken of a few cocktails at *The Jockey* earlier on those nights. *The Jolly Jockey* had a large function room with bar upstairs for parties, weddings or birthdays. It was booked months in advance on Fridays and Saturdays. On the so-called quiet nights and days we had four pool teams, three darts teams, two cribbage teams, two football teams, a dominoes team and a quiz team. It was another golden era for me, and I suddenly became amazingly irresistible to females once again. It must have been the *Kouros* aftershave driving them into a frenzy of debauched Bacchanalia. All very shallow I know, gambling, drinking and getting my leg over most nights, but I had five years of it and very happy days they were too. That said, if it had carried on for another five years, I'd be dead by now - so moderation is a life saver. If you are offered a piece of cake always take the smallest slice. You know that's best.

It was around this time that I became a bad influence on Elgin - he didn't need much persuading though. We got heavily involved in the racing industry. I had a bang average horse that I had syndicated at Wolverhampton race track called *Pippa's Pride*, trained by Angus McNae (now a top presenter on Racing TV), and a poor horse, *Rowlandson's Jewel* trained by Ken Comerford at Aylesbury. That one never won a race for me, but *Pippa's Pride* was a trier. I'd paid over two grand for him. He had won four races in the not-so-distant past, but finished second five times on the trot for me. The worst case of seconditis I'd ever come across and, as most pros will tell you, the difference between first and second costs a fortune.

Ken Comerford, a genial, little, bald-headed Irishman who looked every hour of being 50 years old, had the piss mercilessly taken out of him by our crowd when we spotted that he was actually 30 years-old in the birthday section of the *Racing Post*. He had been offered a horse by another trainer who was retiring and asked me if I wanted to buy it. I declined, but said my pal Elgin might be interested. He gave Ken two and a half grand and became the proud owner of *Trojan Hero* - a horse which was fit with some fair form behind him. Ken entered him into a six furlong race that was due to be run in ten days time at Southwell on the all-weather track. Elgin and I turned up: we always had dinner at the races in the restaurant. On the next table, dressed all in black, was Lee Westwood the millionaire Ryder Cup golfer. Lee was a Nottinghamshire boy and this was his local track. He lives in Florida these days, but he's always had a big interest in British horse racing.

Trojan Hero's race was fast approaching: we had our job jockey, Tom McLaughlin on board. I strongly opined he couldn't be out of the first three, but Elgin said, "Fuck that, we're banging it on the nose!"

That slightly perturbed me after months of watching my own horse run up a sequence of seconds, but Ken said he hadn't had to do much with the horse. In other words, he was fit and fancied and raring to go. He was second favourite of the twelve runners at odds of 7/2. After our money went on he was in to 11/4. In theory we only had the 2/1 favourite who had won his last race to beat. He got up in the last furlong, winning by a length from the favourite. We were cheering like men possessed! There's no feeling like seeing your own horse win. Elgin was hooked from that moment on, but I'd been dangling on that rod line for years.

We had booked a hospitality box for the fab pre-Christmas Wolverhampton night meeting for all Elgin's staff and workers and all my employees from *The Jockey* for meals and drinks. After the racing was finished there would be a disco. You couldn't knock it. I copped off with Elgin's office manageress who had legs up to her armpits. It was a real problem concentrating on reading the form in the Racing Post though... what was a man to do? My brother didn't fare as well - he was there with his live-in girlfriend of two years. All was bliss until someone in the ladies toilets whispered in her ear that he had been shagging Judy, *The Jolly Jockey* barmaid for the last few months. That sort of *Stop Press* information never goes down too well. They then proceeded to argue like cat and dog for ages at maximum decibels until they were warned at least three times to tone it down by the management, but to no avail. They were soon escorted off the premises by security and they were barred for life. I had to laugh - airing your dirty washing in public. I'd have loved to have been a fly on the dashboard on that drive home. They split up not long after. It was inevitable really and he got a losing double up when he and Elgin parted ways as well.

Some time after, the police approached him to make a statement against Elgin, but he wouldn't do it because he didn't know anything was amiss as he'd only worked with Elgin for three months. The police piled the pressure on him, telling him that he would join Elgin in the dock unless he helped them with their enquiries. It was utter bullshit by them of course, my brother hadn't done anything wrong, but they had managed to intimidate him - but, at that point, all he had to do was say "no comment" to every question and they would have had to have mooched off muttering under their collective breaths. Instead they drew up a cockamamie statement, put it under his nose and he signed it. Not his finest hour at all and now he had dropped Elgin right in it. But we are not all moulded from the same clay. Some of us bend in the wind and some of us break under duress. But he had folded like a Mars Bar on an electric fire element. The police use these corrupt practices to nail people they want arrested. Why let the truth get in the way of a tall story if it ends in a conviction?

That malarkey was all to come though, and in the meantime Elgin had recruited his best ever sales force; a team of all talents which had propelled him from the basement to the penthouse. His best salesman was a guy from Manchester known as 'Basher' - an absolute natural, but he came with baggage. He was in his mid-forties, looked like a bank manager, was very articulate and had an attitude of 'can do', yet allied with professionalism. He had only recently come back with his family from Florida and needed big money pronto, but he rapidly established his El Dorado in the Midlands and was earning in excess of five grand most weeks, hitting home runs for fun.

Elgin couldn't believe his luck, the bloke was nearly as talented as he was! He surely must have had a weakness or even a foible? It was perhaps all too good to be true. But Basher wasn't Superman. Early doors he had confided in Elgin that he had a strong penchant for the Colombian marching powder (cocaine) and it had been the cardinal reason for his withdrawal from The States. He'd been in trouble a few times with the authorities over there after being under the influence of drugs, and it had all reached a crisis point when he told the wife and kids to escape from the house while he phoned 911 (emergency services) and relaying to the operator that there were armed commandos in his garden. The person on the other end wasn't aware he was talking to a nutter on drugs and proceeded to send round a top SWAT team armed to the teeth. They obviously weren't over the moon when they arrived to find it was all a figment of Basher's imagination. There would be serious consequences and full reparations to pay... but not by him though, he was off. An ocean away might just be enough distance to placate the baying Feds.

Unluckily for Elgin that was the only mind-bending frailty he knew about: there was another secret lurking in the dark shadows ready to introduce itself - and this one was a doozie. A few months into his new vocation, Basher started to take his foot off the gas pedal and even go missing.

Elgin had no favourites at work: if anyone wasn't on full throttle they were hit in the pocket and he started doshing out £1,000 fines every time he wasted a hot lead. Now, that was a lot of money, so after being fined a few times and accepting it gracefully, a puzzled Elgin asked him why he was fouling up. He couldn't have been more surprised when he heard the response. Basher said every time he scored with the white stuff, he had to dip into it straight away. He would always check into a motel, making sure he had a ground floor room, change out of his three piece suit into a dress, stockings and high heels, but not before opening the room curtains a little bit, in the hope unsuspecting people would peep in and watch his slinky antics. Lucky, lucky them.

Elgin was gobsmacked. It wasn't often that he was lost for words, but what a hideous, repugnant sight it must have been to have had the gross misfortune to encounter Basher performing his kinky Danny La Rue routine. Each time he went missing after that, the girls in the office got Elgin to put his mobile on loud speaker so they could all hear what he was getting up to. However after a few months of these charades getting more perverse and perverted, it stopped being funny and was starting to become rather sickening. So, Elgin stopped listening, dished out a fine and duly gave him his next lead. Basher was the one that was disappointed the most as he seemed to get sick kicks out of sharing his grubby little netherworld with prim suburbia.

They definitely broke the mould with him, but it takes all-sorts for a great big box of liquorice.

All the salesmen were piling on the profits for the business. The Hounds' were enjoying *la dolce vita* again, lovely new house, great motors, world-wide holidays - the good times were back! I was on a roll myself also. *The Jolly Jockey* was killing all the opposition up the north end of Stafford, so you could say, à la Thin Lizzy; *the boys were back*. So that only meant one thing - off to the racetrack two or three times a week. Wolverhampton was our main local track, but we had one wonderful memorable day up in West Yorkshire. Ken Comerford, one of our three trainers, who had given Elgin his winner at Southwell, had a horse known in the racing game as a 'sleeper'. This is an animal who has shite form on the book. In his case, six duck eggs on his last six runs - but give him his conditions and distance and he would morph into a real athlete. It's criminal to confess that I have forgotten the name of that wonderful equine animal and after spending hours on the internet to no avail, his name now is as illusive as Ken Comerford himself, who has disappeared off the face of the earth. The last ever time I saw Ken he said he was off to sunny South Africa. Apparently they have a shortage there of little bald-headed Irishmen who age quickly. Forgive me, I am again digressing! Ken's horse had stamina for fun. He didn't do anything in a hurry, but he'd be still doing it when other horses had downed tools. He had to have his conditions though, very heavy going, the deeper the mud the better. (He had hooves like flippers.) All we needed to win was rain - and by God did the heavens open. And our fella was ready to rock. We will call him *Monsoon* because that was his weather.

The night before the race, it was raining cats and dogs. On the drive up to 'Ponte' Elgin had the windscreen wipers at top speed, it was bloody lashing down. We parked up and got soaked walking the 200 yards to the grandstand. The footfall was right down. I'd been on that track in the past with monstrous crowds in attendance, but the inclement weather had put a dampener on that - the hardy Yorkies obviously didn't like a drop of rain. But it started coming down like stair rods and our one and only big concern was the possibility of the race meeting being called off. *Monsoon* was running in the third race in what was the second longest flat race in the world - over two miles, five furlongs and only a hundred yards shorter than the big stayers race at Ascot, the Queen Alexandra Stakes. Pontefract's full circuit was the longest in horse racing at over two miles long. Ken reckoned that's when the horse would be warming up, to plough through the last five furlongs.

There was about a line of only perhaps twenty bookies there and they had no idea what was going to win the marathon race. There were about 15 runners with four horses at the top of the betting, each of them 8/1 joint favourites. Business was very slack until two wet wallies from Stafford went all down the line backing *Monsoon* from 16/1 into 8/1 joint favourite. One bookie said to Elgin, "Why are you backing that?"

He replied, "You'll see why in five minutes." Another said to me, "He can't win!"

I said, "Is that right?"

Monsoon was 33/1 in the morning papers, but here he was joint favourite at eights. A real springer in the market which hopefully some sharp-eyed punters in the betting shops around the country noticed him being backed heavily on track. I don't recall seeing anything in the race apart from the last two hard furlongs. Visibility was atrocious and the foul weather was affecting most of the track and seemed to be replicating the miasma of a JMW Turner oil painting. You couldn't see nowt but mist. They came into sight just over two furlongs out. I say 'they' - there was only two horses in it, neck and neck and a furlong clear of the third. "Who the fuck's that keeping up with Monsoon!" I shouted with utter disbelief. The horse was bloody phenomenal whatever he was called. It was nip and tuck all along the tough, uphill final furlong. They didn't exactly flash past the winning post together. Both horses were exhausted as it had been a real war of attrition. "Photograph, photograph!" was quickly called by the race announcer.

Tom McLaughlin wasn't sure about the outcome. The wait went on for about four minutes, but it felt like four hours. This would hurt the bookies if it went our way. I had 'dead heat' in my mind the longer it went on, which would be no disaster as we were still winning big, but to be beaten by a nose would be devastating. The tannoy announced the winner; it was *Monsoon*! You could hear the wails of grief and despair along the line of drenched, wretched, waterlogged bookmakers. We picked up a small fortune that afternoon! We had beaten the book and at least five of them took down their pitches and fucked off with half the meeting remaining. That was the only race we punted on that day as we were 'holding, folding and keeping it'. The champers came out in the owners' and trainers' bar.

It was the last time we ever saw Ken, but a happy day to remember for the rest of our lives. God bless him wherever he is. A little Gaelic diamond. I still see Tommy now and again. He's retired now, but when he was in his pomp and the money was down, he was THE jockey for your horse. A brilliant all-weather rider, who never got right to the very top of his profession: partly because he was a man who was like us. He enjoyed a tipple (or two) but people in the know and there was a lot of those, had him down as one of the great horsemen of his era. We wish him and his lovely family good health and providence.

Elgin had the bug now. He had really missed going racing in Spain and was now making up for lost time. Lucy thought he had lost the plot, but his two girls loved the idea of him owning horses even though they were bitterly disappointed on finding out the neddies were going to have to be kept at the trainers stables and not at home. He had *Trojan Hero* in the bag, and had bought a large share of *Pippa's Pride* and had purchased two other horses *Mutabari* and *Schedule B* to be stabled with the resident Wolverhampton trainer, Angus McNae. Elgin rang me one day and told me he had bought a fifth horse - an un-raced two-year-old. I said, "Fucking hell Elgin, who do you think you are, the Aga Khan?"

He laughed. It was going to be trained by octogenarian trainer, Reg Hollinshead at his Upper Longdon Stables near Rugeley. We all became great friends with Reg, the oldest trainer in the country and probably the wisest too. A man who could pull off a large gambling coup better than men half his age. We lost the ace genius in 2013, just months before his ninetieth birthday. His close family and rescued greyhounds always gave us a warm welcome when we visited and his daughter Bella, and granddaughter Stephanie, carried on his marvellous work at the racetrack, sending out plenty of winners right up to the present day.

Elgin was experiencing a wave of enormous euphoria, streams of expensive champagne and bucket loads of God-given confidence. These were great days for the family. Every Saturday morning the kids used to insist on visiting the racing stables to give the horses polo mints and carrots. The scenario was bloody expensive though as Elgin's idea of balancing the books was to heavily back his own horses when his racing connections gave him the nod to bet. This tactic, plus the winning prize money, had him way ahead of the game, but there was a traitor in the operation: greed and selfishness would send him crashing back down to earth.

Mutabari was a new horse being trained by Angus McNae on the all-weather track at Wolverhampton. This beautiful American-bred, six-year-old gelding would win seven times in his career, but the 12th of December 2000 would go down as a day of infamy for our little betting cabal.

Elgin had hired a spectators' box for his birthday party and invited about twenty friends over for meals and drinks. For Stafford people, a freebie day of betting, drinking and scoffing was heaven-sent. We could have filled three boxes, but we trimmed the numbers down to a score after some of them were demanding *BFH* (bus fare home). We were ready to rock and roll. Elgin was adamant the horse would piss in, but Angus put the dampeners on, suggesting that we, "Run him down the park", as he was wary that the favourite would beat him and we could get better odds next time he ran. I went down to the paddock - the horse looked a million dollars. I returned upstairs to the owners' and trainers' bar and suggested to Angus that *Mutabari* looked primed to run a big race. He said the horse was one week short of full fitness and would come on for the run. I reluctantly conceded as he was the expert. I'd known Angus for five years previously on the racetrack, he'd been very friendly over that period and I had no reason not to trust his equine judgement.

So myself and Elgin didn't have a bent copper coin on *Mutabari* - none of our crowd did in fact. Elgin actually backed the favourite with Gary Wiltshire; a £400 fun bet. The bookies observed our crowd backing other horses and pushed *Mutabari* out to 33/1. We returned upstairs to the bar to watch the twelve runner, seven furlong race. They're off! *Mutabari* bursts out of the stalls and gets an easy three length lead. I say to Elgin, "Ah, that's how they are going to do it... go off too fast for five furlongs, tire and come in amongst the stragglers." Well, that was my theory anyway. It's one of the oldest tricks in the book, break out like a startled cat, overreach and come in fatigued and well-beaten

They get to the final bend and *Mutabari* is still two lengths ahead and galloping. Elgin says, "For a horse that's having a pootle around, he's still seems to be firing on all cylinders."

As they go round the bend, the pack catch up and a few get up to his withers. "He's thrown the towel in Elgin, half a dozen will go past him in the straight."

What did I know? From watching many races in my time, some natural front runners get a big lead, let the chasers close in, whilst at the same time the jockey is giving his horse a breather and then off they go again. If our tiring horse wasn't trying, that wouldn't happen would it? It only fucking well did! *Mutabari* went away again and, as the pack closed in once more near the finish line, won by just over a length with a great piece of riding by Tommy McLaughlin. It was silent in the owners' and trainers' bar.

You could hear a pin drop. Elgin and myself were eyeing daggers over to Angus at the bar, who was looking decidedly sheepish as he sipped his half a lager.

Lucy and Elgin go down to the winners enclosure. *Mutabari* is lead in, Tom dismounts, grinning from ear to ear like an Irish Cheshire Cat, "Happy birthday, Elgin!" The TV cameras are on him and the crowd is milling closely around. Elgin is smiling back because everyone is watching, but hisses through his teeth, "You're fucking dead, Tommy."

He turns white and whispers in Elgin's ear that Angus told him to win. The horrible cunt (this is the first time that word has been used in the book, but I think you'd all agree it is truly merited on this occasion) had punted the horse over in Ireland that morning then persuaded us all not to back the horse on course which would have shortened the price of *Mutabari*.

A diabolical liberty had occurred.

To say Elgin was annoyed was an understatement. It soon transpired that Angus was in dire money straits, but a double-cross was a filthy act of cowardice. Elgin would have lent him money if he had asked, but he had crossed all bounds of decency, robbing and lying to people who were paying him to be up front, honest and professional. I was disgusted with what he did. You think you know someone until they kick you right in the balls. Nothing really surprises me with human beings, most of them never fail to disappoint. As for karma, Angus still hasn't got his, he works today as a well-respected front man for Racing TV. Butter wouldn't melt in his mouth, but we know what he is, he's a rat and will always be a rat. If you ever bump into Angus on your travels, mention old *Mutabari* and the day he became a vile, back-stabbing, sewer rodent.

He might even give you his own twisted version of events.

After the race, Angus had done one, he was nowhere to be seen.

He gave up his position at the racetrack a day later and skulked off into the night. Lucy hadn't had a bad afternoon though, she'd ignored the learned trainer and had punted fifty nicker each way on *Mutabari*. She'd won just over two grand. Elgin asked her for half of the money. The second word of her reply was "off." He'd had better days; he had told all and sundry not to back his horse. Mugged off wasn't the word. His gilded reputation had been ever so slightly tarnished and his love for racing would never be that strong ever again, but his company business and prolific work ethic were still steaming full speed down the railroad track. He would always have something to fall back on. Tomorrow would be just another day when the fair trade winds would blow again.

The feel good factor in *Elgin World* was again in its ascendency. He had never earned this much money before and he had another touch when he noticed one of his fitters, Marc Green, was showing potential and leadership qualities in his work. Elgin quickly promoted him up to office duties and eventually put him in charge of the whole kit and caboodle. This gave the boss plenty of free time, so on every school holiday he took all the family away - that was, except for eldest daughter Emelia, who was busy studying so she could go on long-haul holidays. Elgin always called her *Daddie's Little 'Angle'*; she had written that on a birthday card when she was younger instead of 'Angel'. They thought it was just a spelling mistake, but the next Christmas she wrote a wish list to Satan. The curse of dyslexia was alive and well. She wouldn't let it beat her though, and with determination she graduated from Manchester University with a 2:1 degree in Sales and Marketing. It was the proudest day of dad's life. She was definitely a chip off the old block.

It's a wonderful blessing to have the financial clout to do anything you want. You've probably noticed that Elgin doesn't care much for the rainy day theory - he's a spender, a lender and often goes off on a bender. A sort of complex easy come, easy go mentality, knowing he can always earn big again if things go pear-shaped. One weekend he took Lucy to Paris for her birthday and booked a massive suite at The Ritz Hotel. (Little does he know I once bought two big boxes of Ritz Crackers... *eat yer heart out baby*... and I still had change left over for some Camembert).

It was *only* two grand a night: the rich and famous were there in spades. The couple went down to the bar and, sitting just three feet away from them, was Dr Henry Kissinger. Well, you know Big H wouldn't be slumming it in *Gay Paree*. It was doubtful if Elgin and him had much in common, but these were the type of venues to which he could easily afford to turn up.

Elgin felt out of his depth for the first time in his life. He told Lucy that he felt just like Delboy in *Only Fools and Horses* when he turned up uninvited to that stately home for the shooting weekend. When his cocktail arrived with fruit adornment and an umbrella in situ she said, "You look like him now as well."

This was the 'nouveau riche' life they were now leading. If you had the money, anything was possible; getting pissed, falling over and breaking Louis XIV furniture... *au contraire, au contraire*.

And yet a change was coming. Elgin couldn't see much point in living in England anymore now that he had 'Little Marc' running the show, so he engineered a plan to get Lucy to move back abroad again. They had been together a good while now and of course the ardent fires of their courtship days were now flickering on just a few candles. Most relationships go into auto pilot with familiarity. He still wanted to be with her as he didn't want to miss his two girls growing up like he had to a certain extent with his first two, Marco and Emelia. So while they were on holiday with the kids at Easter in 2001 he suggested to Lucy they sell all the horses and buy a villa. She wasn't a horsey person so she was on it like a Bengal Tiger.

It was back to the continent.

I was really sad they were making an exodus, but the wild bunch would meet up again in the future. It was still bye-bye but not farewell. Those few years had been some of the happiest days of my life and I know Elgin looks back on those crazy times with a nostalgic fondness as well. We had some great memories with plenty of laughs, but new opportunities were appearing out the blue for us both and we just had to follow our wandering star... *With or without Lee Marvin*.

At about the same time Elgin was feeling consumed by wanderlust again. Wetherspoons had moved into a pub premises in the town centre. That spelt trouble. The company would buy huge quantities of barrels of short-dated beer and lager direct from the brewers. This meant they could sell at vastly-reduced prices, while *The Jolly Jockey* was tied into a binding contract with those well-known robbing bastards, *Enterprise Inns*. It was supposed to be a partnership, but I'd have fared better teaming up with Ebeneezer Scrooge. That first weekend saw the writing on the wall, takings were well down, as were the tills in the *Reynolds Night Club* over the road. I'd grafted hard for years to build the business up only to have the carpet pulled from under my feet.

I deftly let it be known that my lease was available for free. I'd paid

15K for it years earlier in better economic times, but what could you do? I'd had a good run and saved up a nice five-figure sum to tide me over in bonny stead. A good friend of mine and Elgin's, John McMahon, gave me a bell and came round to have a gander. Two big bedrooms upstairs with living quarters, kitchen and bathroom - it was an impressive building. I told John that weekend takings had gone south from the glory days and there was even a rumour that *The Reynolds Bar* was on borrowed time after police and council made a concerted effort to shut it down. He loved the place though, and he planned to have his eldest lad Sean run it. We agreed on a fair price for the tills and furniture and he was the proud new owner of *Access All Areas*.

John was one of us: from inauspicious days of drinking in the boozer in his teens, he became a Stafford Legend. Plenty can talk a good game, but the man who does the deeds, wins. He started off hiring out jet skis at Saredon and Trentham Gardens before finding his niche as a tour manager for acts such as PJ and Duncan (Ant & Dec), Belinda Carlisle, Craig David, Westlife, Boyzone and Girls Aloud. The day he came round, I told him, "Jesus, John! You're in tremendous nick!"

He was as fit as a butcher's dog, while I looked like... well, a landlord who had indulged in too much in alcohol and junk food for half a decade. I was only three years older, but you could tell who went down the gym every week and who never did. His star was on the rise - lean, mean, intelligent, good looking. He didn't have my comedic genius of course, but you can't have everything. Even without it, the man was a winner. I was really proud of him, and Elgin was in awe of what he had achieved.

They took over the pub in October 2001 just before the Twin Towers came down. Sean told me that they had a good first year, which heartened me greatly, but there wasn't going to be a happy ending for the McMahon family. I did contact Sean to ask if myself and Elgin could pay tribute to his dad, we both wanted to be on record to say what an absolutely marvellous guy he was. In a way my recollection was another of those strange coincidences that have popped up in my life every now and then.

I had moved to Market Drayton in Shropshire after leaving the licensing game and just to keep my hand in was working part time as a driver for Westside Taxis in Stafford.

It was Tuesday evening, Christmas Eve 2002, I was vacillating over going in to Stafford as contrary to opinion that the aforesaid night is not half as busy as most folk think it is. New Years Eve is the big one for manic madness. Westside wanted me in though and it was double bubble after midnight, so off I went. It was well early in the morning on Wednesday, Christmas Day and the last of the stragglers were safely dispatched. I had cleared at Parkside and asked the operator if I could do one as it was the right end of Stafford for me. I headed for Great Bridgeford after going under junction 14 of the M6. Half way up the road a police woman was just starting to close the road off with red and white tape. She told me there had been an accident up ahead, probably a fatality. It gave me a sick feeling in my stomach, Christmas day of all days, so I took a detour. I was a lapsed Catholic and agnostic, but said a little prayer on my way home. The next day someone told me John McMahon had been killed driving home on the same road I had been on. I was devastated. My thoughts were with John's family, wife Sharon, brother Mark and sons Sean, Paul and Adam. It's coming up to twenty-two years since that awful night - never forgotten, but hopefully the passing of time has helped partly heal a real tragedy for all of us who knew him.

 The funeral was in early January and well over a hundred mourners attended the service at St Austin's Church in Stafford. Apart from family and friends, all the ladies from Girls Aloud were there alongside Craig David. It was a poignant moment in a good way that the girls had their first number one on Christmas Day. John left as he lived - on top spot. The song stayed there at number one until after the funeral. It was fated to be so. No one knows why these sad events happen; if you have faith, it stretches it, but there are no easy answers. Elgin and I are just chuffed that we were good mates with a Staffordian who will never be forgotten.
 One of the best ever.

RIP JOHN MCMAHON

(1959-2002)

 The *Reynolds Bar* closed for good in 2004. The corrupt council and vindictive police knocked back the license in court. It was all over. The north end of Stafford never recovered - all the vibrancy, energy and night life gone and all directly from a decision from lazy, inept bureaucrats who could never hold down a real job if they were forced to. Nothing is here forever. Cherish the good times while you can. Each and every day that you wake up, you are blessed. Sometimes memories are all we have, but a golden one is worth more than any amount of money in the bank. Love and friendship is everything.

At the same time as Elgin was selling his own horses, I decided to sell *Pippa's Pride*. It had never won for me, but had that string of seconds, so I ended up getting most of my purchase price back. Alas, it never won for the new owner either and was gracefully retired about a year later. I hope that the horse was looked after and appreciated when its racing career was over, because far too many end up at the slaughterhouse and, until recently, most retired greyhounds fared even worse. It's a cruel old world out there and you'd go insane if you fretted about a lot of it.

That wasn't me done with the racing game though, far from it. In the last year of being pub landlord I had started a premium rate telephone tipping service. I had made many contacts around the country. Trainers and owners who were friends included the late, great Ed Weetman, the national haulage boss who had many horses, and big Paul Dixon, a man who had sold his business for hundreds of millions and put his son, Scott, in charge of training his 40 horses on the Southwell Racecourse. He went on to become the main man at the ROA (Racehorse Owners Association). If Paul told you red was blue, I'd believe him. Not a man to mess with, another cracking fella who owned the ace sprinter *Milk It Mick*. (I wonder if he named it after me? ...doubtful!) He ended his career running in Group 1 races in America.

I had to proof my runners through to *The Racing Post* for a month before they'd let me advertise in their paper. I sent quite a few big priced winners over and they accepted my money (they were all heart). I used to advertise only on the biggest racing day, which was Saturday. A credit card-sized advertisement would set me back £250 plus vat - not cheap, especially if your tips were shite. I did it for three months. If you sent out regular winners perhaps 100-200 people would pay the subscription. But, if you had a bad Saturday, you were back to square one. The worst day I had was receiving just sixteen calls. The pressure sending out winners was mind blowing. The day I called in to quit, the guy on the other end said, "You can be proud of yourself. In the last three months you have been the country's most profitable tipster in two of them. I have no reason to believe he was blowing smoke up my ass. I had ended up in profit and achieved one of my lifetime ambitions of being a professional tipster.

My hero in those days was legendary tipster, Peter Sandrovitch. He took out full page adverts in *The Racing Post* costing 15K. What a man! I met him in Zongalero's restaurant on the Wolverhampton racecourse and we struck up an immediate rapport and became close friends. He had 12 horses in training in those days and I was on the top table with Nick Littmoden at his wedding in Ashby de la Zouch. We fell out of touch a few years after he got married however. You know what it's like when a woman gets in amongst a crowd of blokes betting and gambling. I heard that he had moved to Guernsey. I was desperate to meet up again, then out the blue, I located him this year up on the Lancashire coast, still tipping and sending out winners. The man is a mathematical genius with all aspects of the betting game and I was dead chuffed to be connected again with the master tipster.

A few notable mentions of horses of 'Christmas Past': *Premier Bay*, my first syndicate horse trained by Peter Harris, won twice - once on his debut and once at Ascot. The wonderful filly *Trojan Girl* (no relation to Elgin's *Trojan Hero*). I was part of a syndicate put together by Terry Pritchard at Wolverhampton where she was trained by Nick Littmoden. What a little sweetheart. She really would bust a gut for you. She won six races in six months at the Wolves. We will never get another one as quick as her. She was bought for two thousand and sold for ten thousand - very happy days. More recently there was *Kaminski Kabs,* trained by Phil McEntee in Newmarket, bought jointly with Stafford taxi owner, Big Dave Kaminski. I can only apologise to Dave who wasn't the biggest horse racing fan before I got him involved... and he wasn't afterwards either. The filly was out of *Pastoral Pursuits,* the champion sprinter of Europe, but someone forgot to tell her who her dad was. In four races she never bettered fifth. In fact I can safely say that Dave himself would have beat her in a sprint. But I loved all my horses, win or lose. The most important thing was they all came back uninjured, safe and sound.

I'd been a pro tipper, now I wanted to see if I could be a pro gambler for a year. It was a couple of years since leaving the pub, and I had put ten grand aside. I didn't work elsewhere or claim off the government. I wanted to back myself against the bookies. This meant that my mortgage, food bills and all expenses would have to be paid for by betting. If the ten grand was lost, so be it, I still had other savings, but it was sink or swim. I wasn't punting in the betting shops, I was going to the Midland courses. The main ones being the all-weather tracks at Wolverhampton and Southwell. I kept a record of every bet. Wolverhampton was a goldmine for me. Each of the 19 meets

I attended were all profitable ones. To be fair, in two of those meetings I needed to get the winner of the last race to do it, but God favours the brave. Britain's most famous bookmaker, Gary Wiltshire, larger than life TV pundit would say to me and laugh, "I wish you'd bet with somebody else!"

I'd known Gary for donkeys' years and always loved his humour, especially his cockney catchphrase, "I've done my bollocks again." A year went by and I had nothing more to prove. My profit/loss record was £10,224; not a life-changing sum, but I'd proved you could beat the bookie.

Next up was to become one.

I applied for my bookmaker's license at the Stafford Courts. I was a bit apprehensive. The local bobbies knew I was a bit of a rascal, but there was no objection and it all went swimmingly. It was one of the proudest moments of my life. I had achieved the impossible treble in four years; professional tipster, professional gambler and now, professional bookmaker - an exceedingly hard trio to pull off. I opened two betting shops; one in Stoke-on-Trent about a mile from the Britannia football stadium (as it was called at the time), and one in nearby Cheadle under the name *Shire Racing*. Over the years I acquired more than 50 pitches at Midland and Northern race tracks, including No. 1 pitch at Wolverhampton and No. 3 pitch at Southwell, which I bought off Gary Wiltshire. The first time Paul Dixon saw me at his local Southwell track he said, "Ah! Poacher turned gamekeeper is it Mick?" I told him I was a jack of all trades. He laughed and pushed two hundred quid into my mitt. Thankfully his horse lost. He was far better equipped to take a beating than I was.

I won a great contract to be the bookmaker at Stoke City FC's Britannia Stadium. We had eight booths there with advertising hoardings around the pitch. It was brilliant to see your own company on the television on match day. Thankfully, defensively-minded Tony Pulis was manager at the time and goals were at a premium. The most popular bet by a mile was first goal scorer/correct score. A lucrative bet if you could pull it off, but a bookie's benefit if the game ended 0-0. I recall one such match gave us a profit of over 15K. Players used to come in the Stoke bookmakers shop - Stoke legend and lovely guy, Terry Conroy liked a punt, as did Chris Iwelumo. It's obvious what country Chris was from... yeah, you nailed it, Scotland!

That would have been an interesting tartan.

I had five wonderful years in the shops and on the many racetracks, but change was coming in the betting industry. Peter Coates, owner of Stoke

City, kept doubling my rent every year. It went from 6 grand to 24 grand in just three years. As a pragmatist, I couldn't blame him. He wanted his daughter's company, *Bet365*, in the stadium.

I'd have done the same. I was a big boy, so no problem.

Small betting shops were becoming like pubs; obsolete and unwanted. The only facility paying the rent were the roulette machines on which you could lose £100 per spin as a punter. I saw two people at different times lose over a thousand pounds in less than 15 minutes. Evil really, of which I wanted no part, if that was the only way to survive. Denise and Peter Coates sold all 50 of their shops to the giant *Coral Bookmakers*. If they were getting out, so was I. *Bet365* have gone on to become a huge player on line, making record profits. I offered my shops to several national bookmakers, but no dice. The takings weren't high enough to warrant a purchase, so I simply shut them. I got most of my outlay back with the on-course pitches, but even those in the last five years had seen their value plummet. Now *Betfair* and the internet have changed the game forever. There is now no place for the small man.

The last word on betting here. Hopefully you have found it entertaining, because it's supposed to be a leisure sport. In the last five years I have teamed up with my old pal, 23 stone of geniality, the great Gary Wiltshire, star of *Sky Greyhounds* and *BBC 1 Royal Ascot*. We have stood together on racecourses taking bets at Wolverhampton and Uttoxeter using his license, and have other enterprises in the pipeline. I feel privileged to have been asked to have written his second biography entitled, A*ngels, Tears and Sinners*. It was published about two years ago and it's still selling very well. If you like a rollercoaster ride, funny, but often with melancholy moments, it's worth giving it a whirl.

One very last word: Elgin and myself still like a bet, some things never change.

Elgin and Lucy booked a flight to Cyprus after Lucy's mum agreed to look after the kids for a week. It was the longest they'd ever been away without them. They booked a charming suite at *The Annabel,* which was then the best hotel in Paphos. Elgin's first night there reminded him why he didn't drink whisky. He's what you call a 'happy drunk' - but if he hits the scotch he turns into a raging monster. While Lucy was powdering her nose upstairs getting ready, he decided to go down to the cocktail bar for a quick slurp. It was another upmarket place. There was a black guy, it could have been Dooley Wilson playing a grand piano, plates of canapés were being handed round by waiters to professional looking middle-aged couples in their best evening dress sipping martinis and Camparis.

Being on his own and feeling like a fish out of water, Elgin mooched over to the bar for a sit-down and chinwag with the barman. It was a whisky-tasting evening. There was fancy malt from all over the world and it was all free. What could possibly go wrong later on? The barman offered him a scotch he'd never heard of, he thought, "Well, one won't hurt."

He was spot on as per usual. Lucy was taking forever to come downstairs and in that time he'd knocked back six whiskies from six different countries. (It would be unfair just to favour Scotland.)

She finally arrives and wants to go into the restaurant, but Elgin now has the taste for it. He wants another. "Barman, can I try that little number from Surinam? Make it a double will you?" He downs that and Lucy manages to point him in the direction of the restaurant. If anything, it's even more civilised than the bar area - white-jacketed waiters serenely carrying top quality food in on silver salvers, a young lady playing the harp on stage - it's definitely a cut above The Red Lion back home.

It kicked off before they were escorted to their table. He was well-pissed at this stage on a drink with which he had some 'history'. Through his drunken haze, he notices that Lucy isn't wearing any of her expensive jewellery, so not very discreetly he hisses, "Where's your fucking Tom?" ('Tom Foolery' - rhyming slang for jewellery). Poor old Lucy is trying to explain that she's left it in the safe, but Elgin in his alcohol-induced state is having none of it. They get to their table but he is now accusing her of losing the gems and he is getting louder with it. A 'Hooray Henry' on the next table gives Elgin the dirtiest look ever. Elgin leans over quite menacingly and enquires, "What the fuck are you looking at pal?"

Unsurprisingly he doesn't get a reply back. The poor fella is sitting there with his elegant wife in beautiful surroundings having a wonderful meal, with a 17-stone, intoxicated fucking English lunatic looming over him.

It wasn't a mystery why the service to Elgin and Lucy's table speeded up rapidly after that. You could hear the audible sighs of relief throughout the room when they had finished their meal and retired upstairs. It would have probably been a jolly night for someone like Oliver Reed, but Elgin was ashamed in the morning, he didn't go down for breakfast and, in fact, never touched scotch again.

We've all done it though - had nights when we felt that we could take the world on. It was cider and Stella Artois (snakebite) with me and that's a good enough reason why I've hardly touched a drop for the last thirty years.

Two days after 'Whisky Galore', they went off in search of a holiday home. Lucy had the inspired idea of buying some land and building a villa to their own specifications. Elgin was hardly in a position of strength if he wanted to knock it back either after letting the side down imbibing too much looney juice previously. They found a stunningly beautiful spot just outside the urbanity of Paphos and immediately went back to put down a hefty deposit.

Thunderbirds were go!

To a lot of people on the outside looking in, it might seem that Elgin and Lucy had the perfect lifestyle; a lovely house back home, Lucy had the new 7 series BMW, Elgin had a new S Type Jaguar, they had more money than they could spend and two beautiful daughters being brought up and experiencing a lot of the best things money could buy. However, they had started to argue all the time. They simply weren't getting on. It's fair to say neither of them were happy. They had fallen out of love a while ago and the kids were the glue keeping them together. It's a really strange phenomenon - watch ABBA after they had just won the Eurovision Song Contest with *Waterloo*, the joy and energy is amazing. They wouldn't even be rich at that stage, but they knew they were going on an exciting journey just like a lot of newly-weds. Now watch them almost 50 years later, all billionaires and as miserable as sin.

Well, married life can be like that. It ain't about the money, if you're not enjoying living with someone then you have to go your separate ways. It's not unusual to throw the towel in - and both Elgin and Lucy were blameless - but they were probably one gargantuan argument away from a permanent schism.

As they say, it takes two to tango.

* * * *

CHAPTER FIFTEEN

You Can Go Your Own Way

After they had bought the plot of land in Cyprus it gave Elgin *carte blanche* to go over every two or three weeks to supervise and keep his beady eye on the construction company carrying out the building logistics. Normally when the cat was away, the merry mice would play, but that wasn't going to happen on his watch. They had chosen a Paphos-based group called *Leptos* - the Cypriot *Barrett Homes* of their day - to build the residence. The liaison officer was a right good hombre named Nick Salatas and together they would formulate all the plans. They were often in harmonious agreement which gave them plenty of time to go out golfing everyday. It's a tough old life clunking that golf trolley around sometimes.

The more Elgin saw of Cyprus, the more he loved it. He would go back home and tell all the Stafford lads about it. On all the follow up trips he always had company with him: on most of the flights would be his pal, Andy Potts ('Potter') - five foot five inches of maniacal, mad, hysterical, hilarious human being. Potter was an interesting character to say the least. God had fated that he and I lived only six streets apart on the Parkside Estate of Stafford. In our late teens we both drank in the infamous *Sheridan* Public House (boxing booth) in town and we would walk home together after spending all our money on beer. They used to say of Laurel and Hardy that one was an idiot and the other one was a total idiot. Well, that could have applied to us I guess. As I was six foot five, we looked a fine pair of chumps, but we became inseparable. He was incredibly funny and together we were dynamite. If it was a lads' night out, everyone wanted the Parkside deadly duo on it.

We would get bored walking the three mile trek home from the pub, so now and then we'd do something ridiculous. For example, one night I told Potter that the manager at the Stafford Rangers Social Club, Brian Bradbury, hated my guts for being a football hooligan and had barred me from having a drink on match days. Potter wasn't having that and suggested breaking into the club. Now, that seemed like an excellent idea with eight pints of lager in my system, but what relevance it would have on the guy who just worked there was completely lost in the genius of the plan. I never paid to get into the ground on match days - there was a toilet wall on the far end of the ground that was child's play to scramble over. You just had to be careful jumping down the other side on unsuspecting blokes having a piss. A wrong manoeuvre could become unhygienic for both parties, especially as the guy relieving himself was generally looking down, zip open, admiring his skill at propelling leaves and matches along the urinal and not exactly prepared for a large body coming out the sky and landing on him.

Anyhow, without digressing further, the toilets were empty; not a mystery really at midnight. In complete darkness we sneaked across the football pitch to the club house which, in those days, was inside the ground. It was just a glorified Nissen hut which the German Luftwaffe wouldn't have wasted a bomb on. We easily got inside through a window, but the bar had metal shutters round it. We looked at each other like the pair of plums we were: we'd accomplished the mission but for no reward. Just to compound our luck there were flash lights and walkie talkies approaching outside.

Those were days, dear reader, when you called the police and they would be round in ten minutes. Potter came up with a brilliant escape plan: *Let's hide under a table.* I still had faith in my criminal mastermind accomplice and, like the bloody fool I was, went down among the chairs.

Six months later we both got probation at the magistrates court. We weren't Public Enemies Number One yet, but although chastised we hadn't learnt our lesson, not by a bloody long chalk. We were just going to have to find out the hard and painful way.

A few months later the *Sheridan Pub* was running a coach trip to Morecambe for a Stafford Rangers away league game. In those days that was our home town team although everyone supported a big club as well; Manchester United, Liverpool, Everton, Stoke, Villa, Wolves, Chelsea and Spurs were among the usual suspects, but if a big non-league match came up or a trip to the seaside, you could always guarantee a full coach of fifty mental, headbanging, knuckle-dragging alcoholics. Potter wasn't really a footy man, his main interest after beer and money was women. He'd mount anything with a pulse or wearing a skirt... well, apart from a Scotsman that is. These days he'd even draw the line at Eddie Izzard. Quite right too. He wasn't too choosy either once his beer goggles went into action. I'd been with a few 'munters', but I wouldn't have touched some of his with a ten foot long hop-pole.

By popular demand he was coming on the Morecambe miracle trip. What could go wrong? There weren't a lot of role models going that day, it made a lot of media headlines - but for all the wrong reasons. We'd got an awful long way up the M6 with no problems, until the driver decided to pull into (Forton) Lancaster Services. We were only ten miles from Morecambe, and people were already rat-arsed. They had all been drinking in the *Sheridan* early doors and had brought enough cans and bottles of booze on board to sink the Bismarck. I knew it was going to kick off when our lot were bringing out armfuls of chocolate and pies from the gift shop without paying at the till. I nipped into the toilets. Potter said, "Hey Mick! Watch this!" and proceeded to rip the towel rail off the wall exposing all the plaster. If that was a challenge, I wasn't coming second and kicked out at a pedestal sink smashing it to pieces. Other people weren't going to miss out and in five minutes there were broken ceramics and torrents of water shooting everywhere. That's what copious amounts of alcohol does to teenagers. Thank God I stopped drinking at 30. It's a curse.

We arrived on the outskirts of Morecambe 15 minutes later to be hailed down by four police cars. All the booze was confiscated and the whole coach - apart from the driver - were put in the cells for three hours then told matter-of-factly to 'fuck off back to Stafford and not come back'. They obviously hadn't taken it well. The escapade made the BBC six o'clock news that evening and was in half a dozen national papers and on all the local front pages. Stafford Rangers issued a statement saying they didn't want to be associated with supporters like us. Well, we wouldn't want to be associated with them these days either.

Not long after the football debacle. I got a job at *Southern and Evans,* a builders merchants yard who were about to be taken over by *Magnet* down by the River Sow besides Sid Taylor's scrap yard (A book could be written on that man, but hey-ho). Ironically, I had gone from smashing up bathroom fittings to selling them. Was there no end to my talents? But it was bloody hard work and it was me doing all the moving and lifting. The manager, a useless fat pillock named Eddy Dyer, had just been pensioned off by the RAF. His work ethic was to sit in his office drinking coffee all day watching me sweating my bollocks off. I gave him an ultimatum, get another pair of hands in or I would be giving it all a swerve. The thought of any manual work had scared him shitless and he was on to head office, pronto. Good news - he reported back that a third person was permissible. He said that *an advert in the paper might do the trick*. I said *save your money*... I knew someone who would be ideal to fill the vacancy. There could only be one man to call up, Potter.

We had been pushing our luck over the past few years; we were both approaching our 20th year. Of course at that age you imagine you are invincible and bomb-proof, but we were about to get our comeuppance. Judgement day was just around the corner. We had free rein at the warehouse - Dyer would arrive everyday at nine, go home to wifey for dinner at twelve and leave bang on five o'clock to go home. There were no cameras or security in those days - and was twenty pounds a week ever going to satisfy two ambitious men about town? Doubtful wasn't it?

Potter and I both had sets of keys and every builder that came in wanted discounted stock. If we had been straight shooters they'd have eventually corrupted us, but we needed no encouragement to bolster our pittance of a wage so, they came in early, they came in at dinner time and they came in after hours. What was not to like? It soon became a pound for us a pound for *Southern and Evans*. We weren't greedy, we always shared our booty equally with our good, but frugal employers, for without them we would be living on gruel and water. One Saturday I even won a thousand pounds at *Corals* bookmakers on two big-priced winners. A trainer called Mason had given me the tips at the races. It was a time of milk and honey; we were kings of the world, but that all stopped when *Magnet Kitchens* bought out the previous owners and somebody with a warped sense of humour decided to do a complete audit of the Stafford Branch. Oops! That couldn't have painted a very pretty picture could it?

We heard nothing for a month then, out the blue, four Stafford CID officers came down. I was requested to go in one office with two of them and Potter went into another office with the other pair. A lot of builders, plumbers and joiners stopped trading there after we told them *Magnet* were going through the sales paperwork with a fine-toothed comb. They couldn't give a shit about us two, they just didn't want their names mentioned at any cost. Most were offering us big money if we took the whole rap. It had all come on top. Of course there was *good cop, bad cop* in attendance, one saying, *You'll get two or three years* and the other saying, *With collaboration you might get probation*. I knew the truth was somewhere between those two stools. I had a wise legal head even when I was young and stupid, and there was no way I was grassing any workman to the police. I had to grin and bear it.

It was May 1975 and a red hot Summer was looming. Location: Stafford Magistrates Court. We had both pleaded guilty. The top CID man

Detective Sergeant Brian Tunney told the bench that we had been very uncooperative and had declined to give out any builders names. Thanks very much for that, but we weren't rats. We each copped a six month sentence at the detention centre at Werrington, in the sunny hills of Stoke-on-Trent. With good behaviour we'd be out in August a lot fitter and lighter than before we went in. Most inmates there between 16 and 20 years of age were on three month tariffs, so we were like the *Mr Bigs* of crime, but we hadn't been mugging grannies or pinching pushbikes. In fact I felt sorry for a lot of them because many were from broken homes and were poorly educated. They would perhaps go on to endure a life of 'crime through circumstance'. The discipline officer at Werrington was a red-faced cove who didn't like to waste time: *Mr Flynn* took an immediate dislike to the pair of us. We were sitting in the library one day and he came over and sat down with us. Even though it was four decades ago I remember it like it was yesterday. I was reading *Tin Tin and The Black Island* - not exactly Dostoyevsky, but we've all got to start somewhere. "You two will be back in again and again. You're no good."

Potter pipes up, "We're innocent, Mr Flynn! We were set up!"

Flynn laughs and says, "Nonsense lad, if you can't do the time don't do the crime." This is one of the oldest sayings in British penal history. I decide to take the piss and start banging on the table with the base of my fist pretending to laugh hysterically, "Stop it, Mr Flynn, you're cracking me up!" Of course, Flynny thinks he's a natural comedian now and starts to warm to me from thereon.

He continues to detest Potter, but because I laugh at his lame jokes I'm in his good books. He had about half a dozen favourites in his upper echelon of inmates. He would march them around the prison doing little tasks for him and they would get extra pudding, or the odd *Mars Bar*. I never rose to those heights, but it genuinely made me laugh when he'd march his minions back to the parade ground and shout out very loudly, "ATTENTION, FLYNN'S FLYING FUCKPIGS!"

I actually had a secret regard for the grumpy old sod. But, he's probably gone now, but I remember him fondly.

Another screw Potter and I liked was the Werrington head cook, Mr Lawes. He was a funny guy, but had a psychopathic side as well. He wasn't slow to wallop an unfortunate if he incurred his wrath. As he was a Stafford man, we both had a 'get out of jail card' - not literally, but you know what I mean. He grabbed hold of this Brummie one day, "Kelly, you're a gungy bugger!" (for reasons unknown to medical science, all the inmates soon came out with very bad rashes and spots which had the collective noun of "gungy" to encompass it all). The luckless Kelly then had his head lowered and Lawes got to work with a Brillo Pad attacking the offending area on the back of Kelly's neck with gusto. There was blood and pus all over the place, but two weeks later all the rash had disappeared. I congratulated Mr Lawes on his miracle cure and he replied, "Lad, sometimes it's best to be cruel to be kind."

Wise words indeed.

A last word on the great man; he used to catch my *Bee Line* taxis years later and he would always request me if I was available. He would fall out the *The Greyhound Inn* opposite Stafford Prison, crawl over to the car and then I'd help him in and take him home to his ever-understanding wife on Bertelin Road. He would always ask me in and pour me a big tumbler of neat whisky - and he would never take no for an answer! Then he would reminisce for half an hour about Werrington, "Great days lad, great days."

I would counter with, "I'm not sure about that, Mr Lawes." But you know, they were in a way. In some ways, I'm glad I had that experience. Eventually he would fall asleep and his wife would phone *Bee Line* for another cab because I'd be pissed as well. It was only two miles home and then I would pick up the stranded taxi the next day. He was a good old soul to me and I was visibly shaken when he passed away. He must have been feared and hated by some, but he found a kindred spirit in myself. It did help that we were both as mad as hatters of course, but old Potter was never on his whisky rota... *unlucky!*

Two months into the sentence about halfway with all our remission still intact, Potter and I were called into one of the offices. We sat there puzzled and bemused. Potter suggested that they might be letting us go home early. That theory went tits-up when a large figure ambled into the room. It was our old pal from the CID, Brian Tunney. "Hello lads, how yer doing?"
He got a grunt and a few mumbles back.

"Lads, we've got a few loose ends to tie up and it will go in your favour if you can help us nail these tradesmen."

He starts writing, but has this nervous tic or twitch like John Cleese put on in Monty Python, after every sentence he half looks up to the ceiling. I'm creasing not to laugh, but could have died when Potter said, "What you twitching for?"

He seems whimsical because he still needs our help. "Are you going to help then lads?"

We both said in unison, "You can fuck off."

He didn't take that quite so well and then he vowed to screw us royally on the outside. This, of course, never happened. There was no upside for us serving our sentence to help him and he obviously took us for a pair of mugs, which we weren't. It's a small town Stafford, and years later he comes out of a big house in Rowley Park to find me sitting in the taxi he's ordered. I think, "Fuck me, that's all I need." But he's as nice as pie and even congratulates me on getting my act together. I'll never know if he meant it, but he gave me a nice tip, so all was well. He knew I wasn't a rogue and maybe he was just a good egg doing his job. I'm not a vindictive man so he can have a pass as well.

After we got out in August - the hottest Summer since 1947 - we were like Greek Gods, slim and tanned. Both of us would never look that good ever again. The following year was the famous *Summer of '76*; the hottest for 350 years. It never rained. Denis Howell was made Minister for Drought. Britain was hotter than Honolulu and Rio. So the next time these global warming zealots like *Al Gore the big fat bore*, and *Greta don't wear no sweater Thunberg* claim we're doomed, tell them to read up on the Summers of the Seventies. It never came hotter than those.

We never got a bent penny off any of the trades folk, lying bastards, but one received karma from my best mate, Mark Wood, who fell out of *The Wagon* pub one night along with my good self to encounter a fantastic, crimson *E-Type Jaguar* parked outside. He wasn't a bad disco dancer back in that day and proceeded to clamber onto that long, long bonnet and give out his personal version of the *Stafford Stomp*... in Cuban Heels as well. After he had dented every inch he jumped down, well pleased with his work, I said *we had better fuck off*. He had no idea whose car it was, but I knew. It was Fred Brown's, a builder who had made many thousands from me. If he had given me a few quid for keeping *schtum* his car wouldn't have looked like a banger racer. What a pity.

So that was a small segment on Potter's salad years. He was now older - most definitely, and a tad wiser? Double-doubtful, debatably, but still very funny, indisputably. Elgin would never be bored having him in tow as he would liven up the island no end, but could the natives take it? *They didn't like it up 'em Captain Mainwaring!* Potter used to come prepared for 'Brass Rubbing Weekends'. If you are imagining him with large sheets of paper folded under his arm and blacking balls of hard wax in his pockets, ambling from church to church then you are sadly mistaken. He hadn't morphed into an arty-farty, culture vulture in the long months following his emancipation out of Werrington, no, his brasses were those very naughty whores in the brothels of Cyprus that seemed to be on every other street corner in Paphos.

This was like heaven to Potter. You couldn't keep him out of them. It was pointless Elgin asking him if he wanted to play a round of golf because all he wanted to do was play a round with the Eastern European floozies. Elgin wouldn't have gone a hundred miles close to any of them, especially as a good percentage had the clap... *or worse.* You could bring home Sevastopol Syphilis, Georgia Gonorrhea or the new kid in town Cluj Chlamydia. As you well know *the wages of sin is death* - notwithstanding that the hours are good, but it's not a great social stance scratching your itchy gonads 24/7, but Potter was a sultry old dog, he'd been down and dirty before: he only came up for air like the sperm whales in the Atlantic.

They both stayed at *The Annabel*. Elgin had been royally pardoned for his whisky go-go night. His vast spending prowess had trumped all of his alcoholic misadventures, but Potter had put the beleaguered management on high alert again as he was parading half-naked Russian hotties around all areas of the hotel. The lads who worked long hours in the hotel for peanuts thought it was bloody fantastic, but the Big Cheese there had seen enough. He collared Elgin one morning, "Mr Hounds, we value your custom, but we are only going to accept your reservations when you are accompanied by your wife."

Potter couldn't have cared less, the soppy bleeder had only gone and fallen in love with Marina - a six-foot tall, blonde Moldovan goddess on the game. Who says romance was on the wane? Certainly not on The Med.

Elgin had Marina sussed out in ten minutes. She was top totty. Why would she want Potter though? He was no Clark Gable. A lad back in Stafford had once described him when he laughed as looking like a Chinese Fart because he squinted his eyes. Now this was a great disservice to the mini sex machine as I had noticed that another great actor Robert De Nero did exactly the same when he heard something funny. Potter could have had another career as his stunt man because they were identical when they really laughed, the only trouble was De Nero rarely broke into a smile. Every film in which he laughs, it's Potter that I see on the screen. It's ruined many a good fucking film for me. The only movie where it wouldn't have worked in was dismal apocalyptic mess, *The Deer Hunter*. People should get paid to watch that shite, everyone in it was a misery. I went around for a whole month after seeing it in a rum state of apathetic depression. If there's anyone you really hate at work or in the pub that hasn't seen it, give it a five star recommendation. Let them bastards suffer like I did.

Back to *Love Story: the Cypriot version*. Elgin knew the SP - whatever little money Potter had, she wanted it. Even his humour was lost on her. English wasn't her strong suit, she was very limited, but had some of the basics down pat, "Get me drink", "I need money" and "You buy me dress", were some of her catch phrases. What did Potter care? The boy was in love! The top of his head only came up to her shoulders. He was living in a world where her pert boobs were at his eye level for hours on end. It was tough going. The Eastern European brasses only got a three month visa and their one and only pursuit was to amass as much wonga in that short time as possible. If they managed to snare a Western European guy and marry him, it was classed as winning the lottery. Potter was very close to committing to Marina, but for some reason she never hit the jackpot and returned to Moldova.

Potter didn't learnt his lesson though; the day after she went home he quickly copped off with another one. This one was slightly more respectable and she worked as a waitress in a local restaurant. Gabriela was a raven-headed, smouldering beauty from Bucharest in Romania but, if anything, she was a much worse gold digger than Marina. Elgin was sad to see that he was falling for all this shit, but as he was a grown man he decided not to get involved at anytime.

It was costing Potter mega bucks in the pocket too. Every week Gabriela's mother back in Bucharest was having a mishap - she was more accident-prone than Frank Spencer and was racking up the medical bills to boot. The tales of woe were getting more far-fetched as well; stuff like she'd fallen down the stairs in a bungalow and getting cancer of the big toe by stubbing out cigarette butts. Elgin was having his own relationship problems like other people in a lot of marriages, so he didn't need to hear about Potter's trials and tribulations. But, as they say; *WOMEN - you can't live without them... and they can't piddle standing up*. Profound words for any young guy seriously thinking of setting up home for the first time with his girlfriend.

As Potter has dropped this chapter into the deepest well of debauchery, we might as well finish his shift with an amusing account or an actual event. Sharo Diba, an Iranian Kurd, was the floor manager at *The Reynolds Night Club*. Having a lot of excess cash and a bushy black moustache meant he garnered a lot of attention from the Stafford teenies... girls only, that is - job's a good 'un. He was a good mate and a really nice bloke, but even in this upstanding, dignified county town, an unprotected activity can come back to bite you. He walked into the pox clinic one morning, went straight up to the desk and proclaimed, "Excuse me lady, my willy is weeping." The young receptionist never batted an eyelid.

"That's all well and good, but that's a bit too much information. I just need your name and address, and then you can tell the doctor in a while what you've been getting up to."

Absolute classic and it still makes me laugh, but the moral must always be, wear a prophylactic. If you don't know what one is, look it up in the dictionary, it might help you to remember that there's eight billion of us mooching about on Planet Earth. The old girl might just enjoy a break.

Back to our star player. Elgin had a truly remarkable escape back in Stafford between his jaunts to Cyprus. The Old Bill raided a catering facility he owned. 'Lucky' had luckily left just five minutes before they pounced. They were definitely closing in, the noose was tightening again, but this was an ideal opportunity to persuade Lucy to move out to Cyprus. He went home, packed his cases and was in Cyprus the very next day. His nonchalance to the impending peril of being nabbed on home turf was becoming problematic, so his strategy of putting many miles and a lot of salt water between him and the pesky plod was by far the best solution going.

With any appearance in England coming under the *persona non grata* status, it made sense to open another business office in Cyprus and, with his Midas Touch, it was soon all purring along like a big fat Bagpuss tucking into a pound of smoked salmon washed down by a churn of full cream milk. The year was fast coming to an end. Elgin's birthday was in December and a lot of the lads demanded a drink up, so he hired a nightclub for the evening. It was for a reasonable knock as it was the off season. The owner asked Elgin how many bouncers he required to keep out the gatecrashers. He told him straight faced, "None mate. When you see our crew turn up you'll understand that a few undesirables coming in aren't going to be any source of concern whatsoever."

The morning before the piss-up was, as always, a time-honoured Hounds family tradition. He liked to play a round of golf before hitting the booze in the evening. Four of our sporting studs went off to the prestigious *Aphrodite Hills Golf Club*. Cheap it was not; for £150 a head you could hit the ball into bunkers and the rough to your heart's content. The state of play was favourites, Nick Salatas and Elgin Hudon verses the underdogs, salesmen Basher and Marco Hounds (Elgin's one and only son). They were on the fourth hole when Elgin got a call on his mobile. He had a sixth sense that it would be bad and wreck both the day out and the game. He wasn't wrong. It was Alison Trickett, a manageress of an office back in England. The police and trading standards had burst in and told the workers that the business was dodgy and if they didn't leave they MAY be arrested in the future. All bullshit, but enough to put the frighteners on people. The copper in charge snatched the phone off Alison and said sarcastically, "Oops, I hope we haven't ruined your birthday, Mr Hounds."

Elgin countered with, "Your lot could never do that. I'm playing on the most expensive golf course in the country, the sun is blazing overhead, I bet you're freezing your bollocks off over there... and tonight I've hired a night club, drinking champagne until the cows come home. What are you doing, staying in watching Coronation Street? Do you really think any of you sad wankers could spoil my big day?"

An abject silence was the response on the other end. The copper had driven his ball into a bunker the size of the Sahara Desert.

Alison got the phone back and put it on loudspeaker. All the staff were singing *Happy Birthday* to Elgin. Apparently the copper's face turned beetroot red, but he was still thinking on his feet. "Put that phone down now or I'll arrest all of you for obstruction."

That would have been a proud day for British justice in crown court number one - "Your honour, these ten people have been charged with singing *Happy Birthday* in an obstructive way. This hasn't come before a judge since the days of Oliver Cromwell."

Case dismissed.

Back at the golf game, Elgin hits a right duffer into some deep rough on the approach to the fifth hole and for the next few holes he's still playing shockingly. Basher realised that the phone call has disturbed Elgin and announced, "This will make you laugh Elgin."

He proceeds to his golf bag, pulls something out, then goes behind some bushes before reappearing in the tallest, black, patent stilettos in the world. He's parading around in 12 inch high heels on a finely manicured green on a world class golf course. It was absolutely hilarious. He said he kept all his transvestite gear in his golf bag, as it was the only place that his wife, Mandy, didn't look. They were meeting a few more of the lads in the pub after the golf, so Elgin offered him fifty quid to walk in the premises with them on. Basher said *make it a ton*, and Elgin accepted the challenge. But Basher had to wear them in the night club as well. He was, of course, well up for that as it gave him an excuse to parade in public and get paid for it. The looks Elgin got when he introduced Basher to some of the local lads who didn't know him from Adam were unbelievable, "Here is our top salesman, boys!" If they didn't think the English were mad before this, then they were quickly converted.

The two girls were soon safely ensconced in a private school on the island. It made three when his son Marco came over to join them in the same educational establishment after fucking about in his old English school. He had everything he'd ever dreamt of; family, sun, sea, money and more assets than The Sultan of Brunei (OK, a slight exaggeration there...).
So, why was he unhappy? He knew the reason. It was going to be a wrench to move out, but he was one big argument from walking away. It came over something trivial as most bust-ups do, but it quickly escalated into Krakatoa. Elgin thought it was just him and Lucy in the room, but he turned round to see little Sylvia watching from the doorway, looking terrified.
He knew that was it. He couldn't put the kids through it any more.

He left, choked up, right there and then.

* * * *

CHAPTER SIXTEEN

Bouncebackability

Well we have nearly come full circle or as I like to call it, entering the final furlong three lengths clear. Elgin was a gay bachelor again. But less of the gay, the man was 100% macho male and as virile as a stallion at his first stud encounter. He wouldn't be lonely for long. He made Harry Styles look like a wilting wallflower, especially as he went out drinking with all the Cyprus office staff as a tight knit group. The adage, *work hard, drink hard* was the policy of champions.

Kelly Rourke, the daughter of one of his mates back in Stafford (unrelated to myself - she's lacking an 'O' and an apostrophe, but it's never held her back), had suggested bringing her friend over to help with a vacant office position. Bella Smyth was an intelligent, attractive blonde. She'd do. It wasn't just a case of *we'll let you know*, it was more *when can you start?* Of course, she came on the group outings and Elgin found himself being attracted to her bubbly humour and kindly manner. That there were two whole decades between them was irrelevant on an island cram full of Latinos, where front page news was a Spanish matador being gored in the goolies and then carried a hundred yards overhead by the bull just for good measure. These people had different priorities. Tittle-tattle wasn't a talking point whilst Pepe was in intensive care with one cahoona the size of a beach ball, these people had class. So they slowly became boyfriend and girlfriend, travelled the world, got married and eventually got arrested in Florida.

We have well documented the trials and tribulations in the early chapters, but if you think that's the end of the saga, you'd be dead wrong. By Jiminy you would! We'd just be revving up nicely for the big encore, so stay well strapped in.

When the couple arrived back in Blighty, they were quickly separated: Elgin was placed on remand in the old Victorian HM Prison Manchester, built in 1868, universally known as Strangeways. The frontage is a particularly beautiful design by genius Gothic Revival architect Alfred Waterhouse. Elgin was relieved to note that the last execution in the prison was in 1964. You never knew at the time if your paperwork ever got mixed up with a serial killer's - stranger things have happened. *The Rochdale Cowboy,* comedian Mike Harding, had a big hit in 1975 with 'The Strangeways Hotel'. That was the same year Potter and I got six months each at The Werrington Motel. It was all happening for sure. Of course, in 1990 the cons went berserk and rioted - after listening to The Drifters' big hit 'Up On The Roof' - and took things rather too literally. Well, Elgin was in good company; Joey Barton, David Dickinson, Harold Shipman and Ian Brown had all previously served time there. *If it was good enough for the lead singer of the Stone Roses...*

Anyway, he would just have to keep his head down. It wasn't going to be a barrel of laughs, but he knew the 'scores on the doors' and, as they say in the turnkey trade, "Do your bird, lad." Good, sound advice and every day served on remand God willing, would come off your future sentencing.

He was actually there on remand for about a year. It's a well-known fact that the police, if they have a grudge against someone who may or may not be giving them a hard time on the outside, push for 'no bail' on weak cases, so they can nick a year or two off a suspected felon. He may well get a *not guilty* on court day, but he has been incarcerated all of the specific time that the case has taken to come to trial. No one said the world was fair, but my advice is always, *don't get caught!* No, I mean, do not hang around in those shady circles that come to the attention of the Old Bill. Believe me, a nice quiet life is much better than a restricted one. It took me thirty years to fathom that out. It coincided with kicking alcohol on the head as well.

That said, this particular moral imperative didn't apply to Elgin here: they had him by the short and curlies. He was bang to rights quite frankly. His only option was to put in a contrite guilty plea as straight away that gets one a reduced sentence as opposed to a flippant long shot not guilty plea. Elgin didn't agree with some of the charges brought against him, but he wasn't holding a strong hand for clemency. So, all he could do was stand before the court mandarins, hope for more than a modicum of impartiality and take his medicine like a man.

I visited Elgin a couple of times. Those old red brick prisons aren't Butlin's, but being on remand was a softer regime than most of those huge, famously grim, overcrowded prisons where some of the screws are more evil than the inmates. On visiting day you would be guided over to some portacabins up a modern ramp. The one thing I remember clearly was having my balls sniffed by the drug-detecting Alsatian. I wasn't getting out much at the time so this was like a day trip for me - a sort of magical mystery tour with razor wire and clanging metal doors. What I discussed with Elgin, I have sadly not much recollection. My lapsing brain is definitely wired up differently than most. As per usual, I owed Elgin more than a few bob and he needed some post haste. I do recall saying, "Why do you keep getting arrested at bloody inconvenient times for my old bank balance?" But such was life. Is there ever an opportune moment to pay back more than you can afford? I just hope the Inland Revenue aren't reading this.

Once he had gone through his induction week, he was sailing pretty. You fear things that you don't know about, but as you find your feet, the Tetris pieces start to fall into place and life becomes a cakewalk, and you wonder why you fretted in the first instance. So much so at Strangeways, when the authorities stuck him and a gypsy guy named Silas Smith on a troublesome wing, they were asked to stop any bullying if they saw it going on. Elgin was in good nick and Smith was broad and ripped with solid muscle. Needless to say, bullying didn't see the light of day again. Quite right too. The last thing you want after being incarcerated is some meat head making your life unbearable. It isn't always the screws with wicked intent.

Elgin and Silas became good friends, he partook in bare-knuckle boxing bouts. There's a terrific punch up with him and another Romany guy on You Tube. It hurts just watching it as two hard nuts knock seven barrels of shite out of each other. Thank God I'm a pacifist these days as I'd have hoisted the white flag long before the ref had finished his pre-fight instructions!
A quick word here for 'The King of the Gypsies', Bartley Gorman, a great charismatic Staffordshire man who lived in Uttoxeter. Both myself and Elgin made sure we were on best behaviour if he was ever around. He had a punch like a kick from a mule. What a character.

Another interesting guy Elgin befriended was Simon Flynn, a real nice fella. He had been sentenced to a heavy stretch, but had served most of it and was now going through the last knockings at Kirkham Open Prison, equidistant between Preston and Blackpool. The trouble was he was knocking something else at the same time, namely one of the female admin team there. That earned him recall to Strangeways. He hadn't had a lot of luck; his wife had died of terminal cancer in her early thirties, that alone could have tipped you over, but he was a pragmatist and soldiered on. Now, here is another of the many, some would even say *Twilight Zone* coincidences that abound in most chapters of this book - although you could just say it's a small world, but not if you have a flat tyre. Several years earlier, Elgin was in Portugal, in Casper's Bar (Villamoura, to be precise) and in burst half a dozen heavy feds, guns drawn. Elgin's vocal reaction was, "Fucking Nora, it's all come on top," only for the police to sashay past him and handcuff the bloke on the next table. After chatting to Simon, recalling each other's exploits, it later emerged that the arrested guy in Casper's Bar was Simon's co-defendant in his court case. All the dates and location matched, strange forces at work.

It wasn't just tediously mundane waiting for your slot before the beak though. You could happily contemplate, in times of airy optimism, in every hour of every day (and also at night) the comforting idea of a suspended sentence. And, in much darker times, of him putting on his black cap for a death sentence.

Moments of joviality were few and far between, but on one such day, Messieurs Hounds and Smith got eight likely lads to go down to the yard with rolled up towels under their arms and stand to attention in two rows of four. Ten minutes later the discipline officer comes upon our gallant octet and demands, "Why are you lot standing there with towels, like spare pricks at a wedding?"

"We're waiting to go to the local swimming baths sir."

"Get fucking back to your wing you soppy twats... who put you up to this, Hounds and Smith?"

"Yes sir!" came the response, in unison. This officer was a man who seldom smiled, but now he was having a good chuckle to himself. They say laughter makes the world go around, and this was a rare super sunbeam in a long, drab year.

Then the wait was finally over. It was March 2008 - venue: Manchester Crown Court. It was only a whistle and spit from the prison. Pointless wasting petrol in those austere times as the financial crisis had really hit home. It was the worst downturn since the Wall Street Crash of 1929. The judge was a merry old soul - *not*. It seemed like he had invested all his life savings in Lehman Brothers. They were the first huge financial institute to go bankrupt and it went downhill from there. Elgin, his son, his wife and four staff members all pleaded guilty, the police and trading standards gave statements that painted a very bleak picture. They were all in the spiders web and the tarantula was *hungry*. Elgin was cast as the mastermind. Thanks a bunch... that will add time on, no problem. He was expecting a big one as he'd been a right pain up the ass to the various legals and authorities and, of course, they all had bloody long memories. He bitterly regretted his decision to scarper years earlier, but that ship had long sailed in the distance. Here he was at the mercy of the man in the peruke. "Elgin Hounds, I sentence you to EIGHT AND A HALF YEARS." Cowabunga! Even his brief hadn't seen that coming. But what could you do? All the others got much reduced sentences. It seemed as though Elgin had their share in spades.

It wasn't much fun being a mastermind, but the leader of the pack always cops plenty. They hung the body of Mussolini upside down from a metal girder in 1945. It's never nice facing the music, but he was relieved once and for all that it was all over. He'd done a few hard and dangerous months in the USA, a year in Strangeways nick and because it wasn't a violent offence he wouldn't be in a decrepit dangerous prison. With good behaviour it wouldn't be anything like serving 20,000 Years in Sing Sing (Film). Look on the bright side.

So it was back to Strangeways Prison for an uneventful fortnight. Elgin could have been heading out to any category C nick they fancied. Orkney was nice at that time of year by all accounts. He wisely fathomed he wouldn't get preferential treatment after the runaround he had given the authorities, but was quite pleasantly surprised to discover he was going to be undertaking the shortish journey to Buckley Hall in Rochdale. Things were perking up. Buckley Hall was a forward-thinking, liberal prison of just over 400 run-of-the-mill attendees. It featured modern facilities and modern sanitation. There were football pitches, table tennis, table football and pool tables and even a gym for sport and recreation. It had a video and book library and, of course, a television in each of the cells. Educational courses and various workshops were also available. It was that cushty, the first time I visited Elgin, I joked to a warden, "Is it possible to get weekend membership here?" Unsmilingly he replied, "That could easily be arranged." I let that little quip die a slow death.

Thankfully, the darkest hour had been the one just before the light of dawn. Elgin was still locked up, but the two years he would stay in Rochdale couldn't be construed as hard labour. He was doing himself proud and, in fact, he had to admit that events could have ended up being much worse. Halfway through his term I finished my first book. *Black Eyes And Blue Blood*. I had managed to get a book deal with the well-known publishers, Mainstream of Edinburgh - and this was only on my second phone call on my first day of hawking it about. I was very proud of that. All achieved without a literary agent as well. It would be nearly impossible now. If you think that the great J. K. Rowling of Harry Potter fame was knocked back by more than a hundred publishers over a seven-year period before her first book came to print.

Alas today, she is a multi-billionaire and I still have an overdraft, but it shows what can be achieved with determination. She is a great example of that. I brought Elgin a copy of the book. I'm all heart you know. I added a little dedication inside: *Tempus Fugit*. This is Latin for 'time flies'. It was to show he'd be out in two shakes of a lamb's tail. Never forget that once you were gallivanting around the infants school playground, five minutes later you're bent over with a walking stick collecting your pension. I kid you not. Time, and not cash, is the most important aspect of your life. Don't fritter it away on the sofa or lying in bed. Memories are worth more than money. There are no pockets in a shroud.

Sorry, we were getting a touch maudlin there, and this is a happy book. But I'm damn sure he wouldn't mind that, as, despite the irony of his serving *Eight Big Ones*, he is as free as a bird today.

Anyhow one last word on the book. *Black Eyes And Blue Blood* sold out it's 10,000 print copies and is now in re-print with Penguin Random House publishers. There are two videos relating to it on You Tube and it has made a renaissance on Amazon and gone up to number 21,000 out of three and a half million books. There were rumours of another Ernest Hemingway in Staffordshire, so when I become a millionaire, if you come around asking to borrow money, you can sod off! Just putting that out there before it happens.

Footnote alert: when Elgin left Buckley Hall to go to an open prison, the rotten buggers made him give the book to the library. Now, this was either to corrupt the cons or to make them see the errors of their ways. The jury is still out on that one, but the book still sits on the shelves of the prison library.

It was on a visit to see Elgin that he told me about one of the inmates who had befriended him. Faisal Madani was an Iranian conman with an incredible life story. Elgin reckoned his experiences needed to go down in print.

After Elgin had finished his sentence I met him in swanky Bramhall, a very affluent posh suburban area of Stockport. Well on the level of nearby Wilmslow and Alderley Edge, the footballer/stockbroker area of Cheshire. He actually lived in a bungalow with Wes Brown, the Manchester United

England defender on one side, and a high court judge on the other. We immediately hit it off, and I agreed to write his story. But the book took me six years to finish as the daft bugger kept moving house or getting arrested. It became my favourite book. It is my *magnum opus* and I do have a dream of it becoming a film before I pop my clogs. Sir Alex Ferguson and a lot of United players have read it. It is hilarious and stranger than fiction.

Mike Summerbee visited Faisal at Buckley Hall one day and gave the whole prison a lift. A little snippet from LIFE IN THE FAZ LANE was Faisal going on hunger strike over something trivial. Little did the authorities know that the local takeaway was being phoned every night and with just a skeleton staff on duty, it was child's play picking the meal up after it was lobbed over the fence. When he came off hunger strike and was weighed he was 3lb heavier than when he started. The prison chaplain decreed that a blessed miracle had taken place in their midst and it had the prison staff scratching their heads, in amazement. Strange days indeed.

Elgin's two years in Rochdale had come and gone, whilst not *la dolce vita*, he couldn't really complain. His treatment had been more than fair and the penal system can be proud of the humane and educational regime they have there. An old style Borstal Breakout was never on the cards. It was a *thumbs up* to all people on both sides of the fence; a rare instance of good British enterprise.

Next port of call on Elgin's final leg was the open prison, Kirklevington Grange in Yarm, Stockton on Tees. That was a bit too far - even for me - I get a nosebleed going higher than Yorkshire. But one person who did go and had been visiting Elgin in his last months of Buckley Hall was young wifey, Bella. He had come to a painful decision. He had to set the little bird free, as it wouldn't be fair on her having to wait for him to come out now for a life so ordinary. They had shared times so fantastic, that anything from thereon would be a massive anti-climax. Her parents had blamed him for her incarceration and quite right they were too. It would be best all round if they went their separate ways. Sometimes you just have to bite the bullet and let common sense prevail. And so, with heavy hearts, they parted.

After a few months induction at the Category D establishment he started working outside five days a week at a car hire firm. He got Saturdays off between 7 am and 7 pm. He'd go to a leisure centre in Middlesbrough most of the time, where there was a gym and swimming pool. The car hire company were over the moon with his work acumen and application and gave him an old Audi banger to get around in. He started to get home leave as well to see his kids, three days one month, five days the next, then three and five again, and so on. He was finally returning to normality. He enjoyed his work and he enjoyed the responsibility of his time away from Yarm.

After a year and a half he was a free man. It had been a long haul, but he had come out unscathed, maybe a bit wiser and maybe more aware of his own mortality. The experience had no doubt changed him for the better. He wouldn't be pushing the envelope that far ever again as he now realised that with age comes wisdom.

In 2011 he moved to 3 Grub Street, High Offley, a remote residence in the Staffordshire countryside near Eccleshall. He then quickly procured a sales job repping for Niagara, the well-regarded Welsh therapy company which sold apparatus to combat rheumatism and arthritis. He was a normal bloke again doing what most do - making an honest living and not setting himself unreasonably high targets.

One uneventful day he was back in Stafford chatting to ex-wife Katrina in Exeter Street, when a young lady called Sienna came out of Katrina's sister's house opposite to them. He had taken her out for a few months in the early 1990's. Here was a single man again living alone, so he asked Katrina to knock the door and get Sienna's mobile number off her sister Florence. He got home and belled her. They started going out again and six months later he moved into Sienna's house. I was renting a few of my own properties out, so Elgin enquired if I wanted to rent Grub Street. Well, as a man who likes his grub, it was a no-brainer! I was getting racked off with Stafford as per usual so a change was as good as a rest. A country boy was I - the quietness was to die for - preferably with no 19-year-old brain-dead dickheads thraping their Subarus at 80 mph. The street had four or five houses in a terrace. I wasn't great with neighbours, but number three was the end house for some strange reason, so in reality I could only fall out with one neighbour. Which didn't happen because he or she must have been a recluse. They were like the giant speckled skylark, they were never spotted. I had a free rein as king of the shires.

Now there are men, myself included, who over the years have found it much more than difficult to take on a new partner's children from a previous relationship. For one thing, some of the kids find it hard to accept a new guy in their life and can sometimes rebel when he tells them what to do. Most of us have been there. No matter how hard you try, you will never live up to their real dad. This is not always par for the course mind you and Elgin is brilliant at adapting and conforming to new family values. He took on a stepson aged 19, an ex-soldier of the Mercian Regiment. That could have easily morphed into an alpha male square off. Add another stepson aged eight - his own offspring - and, well, it takes a special man to do that. Elgin gets on with them like a house on fire and he regularly takes the youngest one everywhere, especially to the Wolves. (Cruel swine!)

A few years ago he took on Sienna's nephew as well, treating him like his own son. They are a close-knit family and do everything together including holidays abroad. Sienna started a new business a few years ago, and she was that successful that she moved into one of the units in the Paul Reynolds Centre where the old skinflint has two rows of businesses on each side of his large indoor car park. He's well into his seventies now, but he is a legend in my eyes - a fabulous Stafford success story from humble beginnings. Yes, he has long pockets, but you don't get rich giving it away. If you ever read this Paul, buy me a drink eh? It's been over 40 years since the last one. Only joking mate! Congratulations on being on top for so long. We've had many laughs there's nowt wrong with a man with a great sense of humour like you. Best wishes to you and Lynn.

Elgin has got a fine woman in Sienna. She reminds me of Karren Brady actually. And I wouldn't cross her and I know that if Elgin ever steps out of line she will cut his balls off. I'm not kidding either... Next time you see him he could be singing karaoke in falsetto like Barry Gibb. But I can see the love and regard they have for each other, so a big up for raising their lovely family in the very best way of being decent people with a lot of decorum. It ain't easy to do.

Another nemesis of Elgin's when he was out of reach from the long arm of the law was Matt Allwright and also his swarthy Portuguese sidekick Dan Penteado. (Now, that's just too dangerously close to the word 'paedo' in my opinion) On the TV shows *Rogue Traders* and *Watchdog*, the two leather-clad bikers had been on his case over a period of several years and over exaggerated, lied and stuck the knife in when he was jailed. We know Elgin was no innocent, but those programmes can say whatever they like, misrepresent and muddy the waters, because the accused has no counter-claim or comeback, especially if you are thousands of miles away.

But karma is a sweet.

In June 2012, big Dan was nailed for claiming council tax and housing benefits of £24,000 and not declaring it whilst earning £56,000 for the BBC. He was spotted by a local councillor on the magic box as he was unashamedly posing as a crusader for justice and righteousness. You tend to lose the moral high ground when you have been caught with your hand in the cookie jar. He even failed to appear in court as well. But he was found guilty of eight offences of dishonesty and jailed for 12 weeks. Not exactly a lifer, but all the BBC would say on the matter was the evasive and banal, "Dan will not be returning to Watchdog"

What a surprise!

But high standards have slipped over the years on this once fine corporation. There was a time in the not-so-distant past when the world would listen to their daily news programmes knowing every bulletin was researched and true. Sadly that's not the case anymore, they are now a left wing, Britain-hating, elitist, woke rabble. RIP 'AUNTIE' - the glory days are gone. Do not threaten our pensioners. No one likes a bully, so let's scrap the licence fee and make them pay their own way.

But wait... Let's not get too political now - that will add another 200 pages to this ripping yarn! The heart couldn't take it either. Now, where were we? Oh yes... Elgin and Sienna. I said to him one day, "Isn't it about time you made an honest woman out of Sienna? You don't want her to slip away, you have a great partnership."

He replied, "Funny you should say that, we're getting married next Summer in Spain and I want you there to witness it."

That knocked me right out my socks. I ummed and arred, but I knew I wouldn't be able to make it. If it had been in England, I'd have been first name on the guest invitation list. Phobias are haphazard and come out of nowhere, even a spacious elevator up to the top of some high rise flats was akin to stairway to heaven in a cold sweat for me. Flying was for the birds, bats and bees. We just don't belong up there. So yes, I admit - as I've got older I've started to develop an irrational fear of flying. I've flown about thirty times in my life, and even been up in a helicopter, but the bottle has gone. I perversely look in the papers each day hoping to find a headline about an airliner dropping out the sky like a stone or smashing head first into the side of a mountain, so I could bring it up in conversation, but it rarely happens and there are many thousands of flights every day. My bloody dad, Sidney, was a paratrooper and did over 90 jumps. I'm sure we couldn't have been related as me and the milkman had a canny resemblance, but I'd done my bit up there, flying many hours. Look at the Wright Brothers, Orville and Wilbur, they only flew 850 feet in 1903 and they were known as pioneer aviators. It's not fair, I've done loads more than them! But I wasn't going up in the big bird again. People pay Elon Musk and Branson millions to go up in their rocket ships, but are they insane. Not for me, boy. So I had a chronic fear of flying, a lapsed passport and an aversion to going out to Spain in the hot season. I could have managed the heat sorted out the passport, but couldn't conquer the height.

I wasn't that bothered about falling through the air, it was meeting Mother Earth at the bottom whilst travelling at Warp Factor Seven that slightly perturbed me.

I know Elgin was desperate to get me there and I'd have given anything to attend, but more importantly his new wife and family *would be*. There would be packs of little Hounds' dogs intermingling with other generations. He was marrying a super lady. He was so lucky. Over the years all I'd had was psycho babes, bimbos and airheads. There had been two that were really special, but I wasn't the marrying type. So you could say that Elgin has had my share of weddings. If you put a gun to my head and said you have to marry someone, I'd have wed Michelle Phillips in her prime - the singer with *The Mammas and Pappas*. She wouldn't have looked twice at me, but what a Goddess of beauty she was and I wouldn't have been climbing over her to get on Mama Cass on honeymoon either. (Michelle was obviously a better singer.)

They got married on the beach at Altea on the Costa Blanca on May 25th 2022. I can't tell you too much about it because I wasn't there was I? But Elgin said it was one of the best days of his life and I believe him! Although he did tell me that he was really chuffed one Saturday when Wolves beat Chelsea... Clearly this was a one-off game that has totally vanished from my memory bank of great sporting upsets - for some strange reason.

Sienna actually had one last surprise for him. When the words, "If anyone has any objections speak now" were uttered, 'It Should Have Been Me', the Tamla Motown song by Yvonne Fair struck up and a fit looking female appearing from nowhere to come and sit on Elgin's lap. The whole crowd were laughing hysterically and Elgin looked like he was really enjoying it until he noticed that the ravishing beauty had a darker six o'clock shadow than he had! It was a geezer; a drag queen in fact, but it was first blood to Sienna.

They had a great time out there, got pissed of course but now have those memories for life so it's an opportune time to wish the happy couple well. They came back to Stafford and carried on as before, a happy family at work rest and play. We should frame them in these hard and austere times. Laughter is at a premium these days.

We know that **Working Class Millionaires** is a fun, but true account of two old Staffordshire rascals. We are now both semi-retired. I have retreated to the glory and splendour of North Shropshire, working now and then with a real good mate Steve Bulldog from Walsall and his wonderful wife Valerie. Decent people are still out there and Elgin and Sienna are enjoying life to the full with close family in their new house in the county town.
If we have made you laugh, we have done our jobs of bringing a little ray of sunshine into your lives.
But, if we haven't, get stuffed... *ha ha!*

We did our very best and you can't ever ask for more than that.
So, it's *ciao* for now. May all your days be long, loving and glorious.

God bless every last one of you and remember this: if you have peace in your life, you have more than most of the planet. Add good health and you will find that money is inconsequential. But if you have more than a few paper pals in the bank, you have the golden treble and you are next to immortal.

*   *   *   *

*   *   *

*   *

*

The End

BONUS SECTION

Elgin and Micky's
10 Golden Rules of Selling

1. **Build a rapport with the buyer.** It's the most crucial phase of building a foundation of trust. Money is never mentioned during this period.

2. **Know your product.** One must understand every facet of what you are selling. The very best salesmen recognise their commodity, device or service like the back of their hand.

3. **Always give the customers more than what they were expecting.** Go above and beyond and run that extra mile.

4. **Listen to what your buyer is telling you.** This is more important than a perfect sales pitch. Without realising it, you could both be at cross purposes. Use your ears and eyes to sail through any stormy waters.

5. **Explain every advantage and benefit.** Quietly hammer home the reasons a customer's life will be better for the purchase.

6. **Have a great product.** Sellers can subconsciously lose enthusiasm and interest if they feel their item is secondary to others on the market. Knowing you have the optimum product brings out the best in most salesmen.

7. **When money crops up never start from too high a position.** This is disingenuous and can spoil an ongoing deal. People aren't fools and rapid price drops from a fictional opening gambit fools nobody.

8. **Have an answer to every negative or critical response from a buyer.** All roadblocks can be cleared with genuine solutions, be it financial or misunderstandings about the effectiveness of the product.

9. **'Always be closing' is the maxim of every top salesman.** You can have the greatest sales pitch in the world, but if you can't close the deal, then it's all hot air. If the customer doesn't sign on the dotted line, it's *hasta la vista*.

10. **The all time classic line from the film The Wolf of Wall Street; "Sell me this pen."** Most people can't do it, the pen is actually a euphemism for anything a salesman is selling. It's used sometimes in job interviews for sales reps looking to be taken on. People tend to concentrate on the object too much and not what the purchase can do for the buyer. Sales are made on the seller's ability to create a supply and demand scenario.

* * * *

Printed in Great Britain
by Amazon